Tourism and Water

TOURISM ESSENTIALS

Series Editors: Chris Cooper (*Oxford Brookes University, UK*), C. Michael Hall (*University of Canterbury, New Zealand*) and Dallen J. Timothy (*Arizona State University, USA*)

Tourism Essentials is a dynamic new book series of short accessible volumes focusing on a specific area of tourism studies. It aims to present cutting-edge research on significant and emerging topics in tourism, providing a concise overview of the field as well as examining the key issues and future research possibilities. This series aims to create a new generation of tourism authors by encouraging young researchers as well as more established academics. The books will provide insight into the latest perspectives in tourism studies and will be an essential resource for postgraduate students and researchers.

Full details of all the books in this series and of all our other publications can be found on http://www.channelviewpublications.com, or by writing to Channel View Publications, St Nicholas House, 31–34 High Street, Bristol BS1 2AW, UK.

TOURISM ESSENTIALS: 2

Tourism and Water

Stefan Gössling, C. Michael Hall and Daniel Scott

CHANNEL VIEW PUBLICATIONS
Bristol • Buffalo • Toronto

Library of Congress Cataloging in Publication Data
Gössling, Stefan.
Tourism and Water/Stefan Gössling, C. Michael Hall and Daniel Scott.
Tourism Essentials: 2
Includes bibliographical references and index.
1. Tourism—Environmental aspects. 2. Environmental management. 3. Water supply—
Management. 4. Water resources development—Management. I. Hall, Colin Michael,
1961- II. Scott, Daniel, 1969- III. Title.
G156.5.E58G674 2015
910.68'2–dc23 2014044907

British Library Cataloguing in Publication Data
A catalogue entry for this book is available from the British Library.

ISBN-13: 978-1-84541-499-3 (hbk)
ISBN-13: 978-1-84541-498-6 (pbk)

Channel View Publications
UK: St Nicholas House, 31–34 High Street, Bristol BS1 2AW, UK.
USA: UTP, 2250 Military Road, Tonawanda, NY 14150, USA.
Canada: UTP, 5201 Dufferin Street, North York, Ontario M3H 5T8, Canada.

Typeset by Techset Composition India (P) Ltd., Bangalore and Chennai, India.
Printed and bound in Great Britain by Short Run Press Ltd.

Contents

Boxed Examples and Case Studies

Figures

Tables

Plates

Acronyms

ACC	anthropogenic climate change
AR	accessible runoff
EMS	environmental management system
ET	evapotranspiration
FAO	United Nations Food and Agricultural Organisation
gpm	gallons per minute
HARF	human appropriation of renewable freshwater
IPCC	Inter-governmental Panel on Climate Change
MFE	Ministry for the Environment
NZCA	New Zealand Conservation Authority
OECD	Organisation of Economic Cooperation and Development
PCE	Parliamentary Commissioner for the Environment
RFWSland	renewable freshwater supply on land
UNEP	United Nations Environment Programme
UNWTO	United Nations World Tourism Organisation
WEF	World Economic Forum
WHO	World Health Organisation
WTA	withdrawal to availability

Preface

Open any travel marketing brochure or website and water is an integral element of most of the holidays offered and destination images. This is obvious where the sea, lakes or streams form part of the scenic beauty of a landscape or where the pools, spas and fountains promote luxurious hotel environments.

While water is the foundational resource for a wide range of tourist activities, from beach visits and swimming, to boating and fishing, to diving and snorkelling or just 'cooling down' at water theme parks, the diverse functions of water embedded in a holiday product are often less obvious, as are the full water requirements and costs involved to make available this resource. Freshwater is needed to fill pools, irrigate gardens and golf courses, do the laundry, and a wide range of hygienic purposes (showers, flush toilets, washing hands and generally keeping resorts and destinations clean). These more visible aspects of water use have been studied in increasing detail over the last 30 years. However, perhaps some of the most significant aspects of water use in tourism are 'hidden' from many consumers. For example, only recently has it become clear that tourism's potentially most significant share of water use is embedded in fuel and food production. These insights call for new approaches to water management in tourism.

The expanding global tourism sector depends on the availability of vast quantities of natural resources, including food, water, energy and land. The provision of such resources is a growing challenge and often increased costs, which in some areas interfere with the livelihoods of local populations in less developed regions of the world. Over the last 50 years, global water use has tripled and an estimated two billion people already live in water-stressed areas. Growing populations and climate change are expected to exacerbate this situation, adversely impacting development in many developing nations and leading to increased competition between water users of which tourism is only one. Water security has therefore entered the lexicon of strategic business and public planning as well, with multinational corporations increasingly assessing water availability and costs in longer range infrastructure and production investments.

It is within these evolving developments that this book is positioned, providing a systematic guide to the current state of knowledge on the interrelationships between tourism and water. The book's specific focus is on water management, including conservation and efficient use, as well as technology to conserve freshwater. In making a clear case for greater awareness and enhanced water management in the tourism sector, it is hoped that the book will contribute to the wise and sustainable use of this critical resource that is at the heart of our civilisations.

We are indebted to a number of people who have supported the research efforts for this book. In particular, this includes Swantje Lehners, Sustainability Management at Thomas Cook Touristik GmbH, as well as Melitta Karth-Strache, SENTIDO Hotels & Resorts, who made it possible for us to conduct the research in Rhodes, Greece in 2013 and 2014. In addition, we would like to note our deep thanks to Ann-Christin Andersson for helping with the tables and Jody Cowper for her great assistance in checking the references, as well as the support of all at Channel View.

This research has been the basis for many of the insights shared in this book. In Greece, the help of Nikos Portokallas, Mina Splakounia-Zahariou and Yannis Rizonakis have been invaluable in providing data and access, and testing new ideas. We are also thankful to Futouris, the sustainable tourism initiative in Germany, Austria and Switzerland. Anja Renner initiated and encouraged the far-reaching water project with Thomas Cook, and this has been supported by Inga Meese, Andreas Koch, Alexandra Beital and Annette Höher. In Israel, thanks are due to Noam Shoval and Yael Ram, and in Mauritius to Robin Nunkoo. Many other people who have over the years helped to develop the field, and who have shared their insights and ideas, need to be mentioned at this point. Specifically, this includes Mathias Gössling, Dietrich Brockhagen, Wolfgang Strasdas, Thomas Vodde, Edgar Kreilkamp, Jens Hulvershorn, Harald Zeiss, Ines Carstensen and Bruce Mitchell. The support of the Canada Research Chair program is also gratefully acknowledged.

On a personal front we would like to thank our partners and families for their love, support and patience: Meike and Linnea; Jody, Cooper and JC; and Tonia, Danika and Isabel.

1 Water for Life: A Global Overview

Water has many meanings for human beings. First and foremost, we need water for life. The World Health Organization (WHO, 2011) suggests that a minimum of 7.5–15 L per person per day are necessary for survival, with 2.5–3.0 L for drinking and food, 2–6 L for basic hygiene practices, and 3–6 L for basic cooking needs. This estimate of required water is for basic human needs, and not a reflection of water 'wants' for a much wider range of other purposes (Lundqvist & Gleick, 1997). Importantly, it is also only a measure of direct water use and water actually contained in food and beverages consumed (for proper hydration and bodily functions), but does not reflect the much greater water footprint of food produced elsewhere or the energy required to provide this amount of freshwater.

Throughout human history, water access and increasingly sophisticated water management practices have been a hallmark of civilisation and often one of its greatest challenges. Sedlak (2014) describes how around 700 BCE the residents of Erbil in modern northern Iraq dug tunnels to channel groundwater into the city over distances of 20 km. Similar techniques of water collection and storage were developed by cities in Greece at around the same time and independently by cultures from Chile to China. The Romans built the first water systems that would not only supply water but also provide drainage and waste water management and, by 300 BCE, when local groundwater sources were exhausted, Rome's water system was expanded to include aqueducts and pipeline systems. Such systems were built throughout the Roman world with, in some cases, their water engineering legacies lasting to the present day. As noted by Schwarz *et al.* (1990), the uses of water have continued to diversify in modern industrial and knowledge-based economies:

Over the past three centuries, the major transforming activities of humankind – population growth and urbanization, agricultural development and the expansion of arable land, industrial development and the rise of the modern world economy, and the production and consumption of energy (i.e., fossil fuels and hydroelectricity) – have directly and indirectly affected water quality and availability, which, in turn, have had a profound effect on human health. (Schwarz *et al.*, 1990: 254)

With its critical life-sustaining properties, it should therefore be no surprise that water has tremendous symbolic meaning in many cultures. Water is intrinsic to spiritual beliefs worldwide, with many early cultures having water deities and mythical water creatures and spirits as part of their folklore. For Christians, and other Abrahamic religions, partial or full immersion in water is a rite of purification (Collins, 1995). The *Qur'an* refers to the origin of life in water:

Have those who disbelieved not considered that the heavens and the earth were a joined entity, and We separated them and made from water every living thing? Then will they not believe? (Qur'an, 2014: verse 21:30)

This reminds us of human evolution from its origins in single cell structures involving carbon and water (e.g. Alberts *et al.*, 2007). Similarly, the holy books of the Hindus (the *Vedas*) explain that the inhabitants of the earth emerged from the primordial sea.

Over centuries, the sea has remained a place of mystery and exploration. The Oceanic peoples of the Pacific (Melanesian, Polynesian and Micronesian) are highly mobile voyaging peoples for whom connecting and colonising new territories have been the norm for thousands of years. The Pacific Ocean necessitated ocean-going canoe technology in order to be able to voyage across it. This was developed within the last 10,000 years (Howe, 2007), although Australia and New Guinea were settled by modern humans 50,000 years ago. In terms of human migration, the Pacific Islands were the most difficult to reach and so are some of the most recently settled parts of the world. Nevertheless, this is an important historical and cultural context as, in contrast to Westerners who view the Pacific as a vast ocean, sprinkled with a few islands, Pacific peoples see the region as a readily accessed 'sea of islands' (Hau'ofa, 1997).

In the modern era, Thor Heyerdahl (1979) demonstrated that the oceans would not divide but connect the continents, representing routes of settlement and trade in new areas. The art of navigation at sea was developed by the Phoenicians approximately 4000 years ago (2000 BCE). In the Mediterranean Sea and the western Indian Ocean, trade systems have existed for more than

2500 years. European seafarers with superior ship construction began to explore and exploit the world's oceans from the 15th century onwards. Cartographers of this time have depicted seas as full of wild and dangerous creatures. Later on, however, the sea also became part of the Romantic image of humanity in balance with nature, referring to a paradise on Earth (Jean-Jacques Rousseau), and closely related to the discovery of the South Seas by James Cook (first Pacific voyage 1768–1771; Fagan, 1998). What reached Europe were narratives of peace, hospitality, abundant food and free love:

> The Tahitians in all their innocent simplicity seemed to have achieved a happiness in this world that had escaped European civilizations for centuries. Many preferred to believe that the search for paradise on Earth was over; indeed, the myth of the paradisal South Seas persists to this day. (Fagan, 1998: 146)

While blue water, sandy beaches and sunshine remain the foundation for the most important form of contemporary tourism (Bramwell, 2004), our perception of the oceans remains one of mystery, in large part due to the fact that most humans will never enter oceans below a depth of 20 m, equivalent to a scuba open water diver. As a result, our understandings of the ocean are dominated by documentaries, movies and animations, from Cousteau's *Silent World* (1956) to Steven Spielberg's *Jaws* (1974) and Disney's *Finding Nemo* (2003), itself part of a campaign to attract international tourists to Queensland (Beeton, 2005). The deep sea remains the last frontier in exploration, recently inspiring film director James Cameron to turn his own journey into the Mariana Trench (10,908 m) into a movie (*Deepsea Challenge*). The mysteries of an alien environment containing colourful fishes and coral reef environments, and the prospect of clear, warm waters have piqued the interest of a growing number of divers and snorkelers in tropical destinations (Garrod & Gössling, 2007). For instance, the Professional Association of Diving Instructors (PADI), the world's largest dive organisation, estimates that since 1967 some 22 million divers have been certified by PADI alone, growing in excess of 900,000 per year (PADI, 2014). Yet it is the coastal zones that remain, for most tourists, the link between land and sea, and beach environments continue to be the most popular destinations (Hall & Page, 2014). Southern and Mediterranean countries in Europe, for instance, received more than 200 million tourist arrivals in 2013, and the Caribbean more than 20 million (UNWTO, 2014).

Entirely different is our perception of inland water bodies or 'lacustrine systems' (Hall & Härkönen, 2006). Used for a wide range of recreational activities, lakes and streams also form important elements of urban, mountain and other landscapes visited by tourists. Specifically, boating and fishing have been identified as recreational activities of great economic relevance (Hall & Härkönen, 2006; Jones *et al.*, 2006), although the scenic value of lakes for destinations continues to remain insufficiently understood. Rivers are equally important for tourism, supporting renowned scenic tours in destinations as diverse as the Nile River–Luxor (Egypt), the Yangtze–Three Gorges Dam (China), the Danube (Germany, Austria, Hungary) and the Mekong (Vietnam) and popular activities such as boating, kayaking or canoeing and fishing (Prideaux & Cooper, 2009). In many countries, public pools are visited by millions of visitors every day in the hot summer season (2hm & Associates, 2012; see Plate 1.1).

Many forms of tourism are also indirectly dependent on water availability and quality. The growing global golf tourism market is dependent in most destinations on significant turf grass irrigation. Similarly, an increasing number of skiing and winter sports tourism destinations utilise substantial volumes of water for snowmaking to ensure a quality snow product and to expand the tourism season. Agritourism depends on water for crop production, and wildlife tourism depends on water availability for the

Plate 1.1 A hot summer's day in a public pool in Freiburg, Germany. In central Europe, where private pools are not as common as in North America, thousands of public pools attract hundreds of thousands of visitors each day in summer. In Germany alone, there are almost 7500 public pools, probably visited by several million visitors on a hot summer's day

species observed. Both water availability and water quality changes can have negative consequences for tourism. Notable recent examples of the enormous ecological and financial cost associated with the restoration of ecosystems suffering from low water quality or falling water levels include the Everglades and Great Lakes in North America, both World Nature Heritage Sites (Shlozberg *et al.*, 2014; UNESCO, 2009), as well as the Aral and Dead Seas.

Where water quality is affected by contaminants (biological and/or chemical), or has unwanted thermal or other physical properties, the environment may be perceived by tourists as being of diminished quality. In some areas, poor water quality is already seen as the main barrier to developing tourism (Schernewski *et al.*, 2001). Where water pollution involves nitrogen and phosphorous discharge, this can result in algal blooms, which have been increasing globally since the 1970s (Anderson, 2009) and have triggered highly visible media stories that can affect destination perception and reputation (Plate 1.2). For example, prior to hosting the Beijing Summer Olympics the beaches of the coastal resort of Qingdao in China were blanketed by

Plate 1.2 Water quality is an essential aspect of a holiday. This sign warns of poor water quality in the Baltic Sea close to Malmö, Sweden during an algal bloom event in the summer of 2006. Swimmers are warned (in Swedish): 'Algal blooms can occur (blue-green algae can be toxic). Avoid bathing where concentrations of algae occur, or where the water is muddy because of algae. Shower carefully after bathing. Be specifically attentive of children', indicating that local authorities are overwhelmed by the event, relying on ad hoc crisis management

bright green algae. Algae are a health risk, but also affect aesthetics because of visual, haptic and olfactory impacts (Nilsson & Gössling, 2013).

Text Box 1.1 The Qingdao Olympic green tide

In mid-June of 2008 extensive patches of floating algae appeared in the coastal waters off Qingdao, China, where the Olympic sailing competitions were to be held in August of that year. By 27 June, the patches occupied about 30%, or 15 km^2, of the 50 km^2 region designated for the Olympic sailing (Hu & He, 2008), with the complete algal bloom covering about 600 km^2. At its peak offshore, the bloom covered 1200 km^2 and affected 40,000 km^2 and constituted the largest green tide ever reported. In order to ensure that the Olympic sailing venue could be used, more than 230,000 person days were required to remove over 1 million tonnes of algae from the beach and coastline. Wang *et al.* (2009) estimated the total cost for the clean-up at about 593 million Chinese Yuan (CNY; US$87.3 million). The cause of the green tide was due to the rapid expansion of seaweed (*Porphyra yezoensis*) aquaculture on the coastline over 180 km away from Qingdao, and oceanographic conditions which favoured rapid growth of the bloom and contributed to the transport of the bloom north into the Yellow Sea and then onshore northwest to Qingdao (Liu *et al.*, 2009).

While algal blooms appear to be the most widespread problem visually affecting perceptions of water quality, rising populations of jellyfish can also prevent bathing and swimming activities (Gershwin *et al.*, 2010). Beach and water quality are now of such importance that the Blue Flag, a voluntary eco-label that signifies high-quality environments, has been awarded to more than 4000 beaches and marinas in 48 countries (Blue Flag, 2014).

Text Box 1.2 New Zealand river water quality: Not so clean and green?

New Zealand tourism and agriculture is promoted internationally in terms of being 'clean and green' and '100% pure' (Hall, 2010). But these brand values, which are integral to tourism promotion and self-perception in New Zealand, are increasingly being brought into question, especially as a result of significant declines in lake, river and even coastal water quality.

Water quality in New Zealand is of increasing public concern and is significant for Maori (New Zealand's indigenous people) cultural and amenity values, biodiversity, recreation and economic benefits, especially agricultural production and hydro-electricity (PCE, 2012). Their aesthetic and amenity qualities are also significant for tourism and New Zealand's 'clean, green' image internationally (MFE, 2007). Although by international standards the quality of New Zealand rivers is generally good, long-term trends highlight the fact that water quality is deteriorating, largely attributable to intensified agriculture, land use and development (Ballantine & Davies-Colley, 2010). Many lakes and rivers are affected by pollution, particularly in low-elevation catchment areas marked by increasing and intensified agriculture and urban development where the net effect is increased amounts of pathogens, sediments and nutrients (Ballantine & Davies-Colley, 2010; MFE, 2007; Plate 1.3).

Plate 1.3 Warning sign for toxins and algal bloom at Lake Forsyth, New Zealand

(Continued)

Text Box 1.2 New Zealand river water quality: Not so clean and green? (*Continued*)

Pollutants include heavy metals, toxic chemicals and pesticides. However, pathogens, sediments and nutrients currently have the most detrimental effects on water quality (PCE, 2012). Pathogens are invisible disease-causing microbes from human sewage and animal manure, while sediments and nutrients are pollutants by virtue of being washed into the water (PCE, 2012). Erosion from land, while a natural process, is often accelerated by intensified agriculture and urban development. Excessive nutrients in river water, particularly phosphorus (from soil erosion and animal effluent) and nitrogen (from animal effluent), can also cause extreme aquatic plant growth, algal blooms, oxygen depletion and habitat destruction (MFE, 2007; PCE, 2012).

The main sources of pathogens are from ineffectively treated human sewage discharge from treatment plants (MFE, 2007; PCE, 2012) and untreated sewage from urban paved surfaces, overflows, 'broken sewer pipes, and poorly located and maintained septic tank systems' (PCE, 2012: 22). Although there are agreements, such as the Dairying and Clean Streams Accord (a voluntary approach for sustainable dairy farming with a focus on protecting freshwater environments; MAF, 2011), substantial diffuse agricultural pollution continues to be linked to deteriorating water quality (PCE, 2012). Critics of the Clean Streams Accord argue that a voluntary approach fails to meet principle targets, lacks appropriate measures, independent auditing and accountability and amounts to greenwashing (Deans & Hackwell, 2008).

Fluctuating and reduced flows (from damming for electricity generation and increased water abstraction for irrigation) make rivers more vulnerable to pollutants as there is less capacity to mobilise sediment (PCE, 2012). Low water flows (from sediment build-up, abstraction and reduced shade from intensified agricultural and urban development) also have a significant warming effect on water, which threatens aquatic biodiversity. Between 1989 and 2007 the national trend for water temperature was a slight increase 'approaching "significance" at the 5% level' (Ballantine & Davies-Colley, 2010: iv). Total nitrogen and total phosphorus trends increased overall, with a strong correlation between these variables and the percentage of the catchment area in agricultural pasture (MFE, 2013). Visual clarity improved on a national scale, but rivers in catchments with significant pastoral agriculture generally were of poorer clarity (MFE, 2013). Measurements for *E. coli* (which indicate the presence of disease-causing pathogens) highlight that, while rivers in urban areas show the highest levels of bacteria, rivers in agricultural areas also show high levels (MFE, 2007), with 'the worst pastoral sites that are monitored' having 'significantly higher levels of bacteria than the worst urban sites that are monitored' (MFE, 2007: 287). While there are improvements in some rivers most likely due to reductions in point-source pollution, diffuse pollution means the overall pattern is that the water quality in many rivers continues to deteriorate (Ballantine & Davies-Colley, 2010; PCE, 2012).

Intensive dairy farming is mostly blamed for river pollution. Some regional water quality agreements that allow dairy farmers to emit more nitrogen from their land than other farmers have even been described as a form of 'apartheid' (Brooker, 2014). However, there are numerous industrial uses linked to river pollution, including agriculture, forestry, urban development, electricity generation, sewage treatment and tourism (MFE, 2007; PCE, 2012). While the largest source of nitrogen pollution in rivers is attributable to livestock effluent, this can come from any animals with access to waterways, not just dairy cows (PCE, 2012). Livestock can also cause significant damage to riparian habitats along river edges through plant damage and bank destruction, which threatens natural cover and shade for aquatic life and can increase water temperatures. Nonetheless, the number of dairy cows nationally almost doubled between 2000 and 2010 and while dairy cows are not the sole contributor to water quality impairment, the intensification of dairy farming and the inappropriate land management of dairy farms continue to cause significant river pollution (Monaghan *et al.*, 2007).

Approximately 75 wastewater treatment plants in New Zealand 'discharge treated sewage into rivers and streams' (MFE, 2007: 70), and smaller plants with limited treatment capability leave behind 'much of the nitrogen and phosphorus' (PCE, 2012: 32). Wastewater discharged by dairy factories, freezing works and pulp and paper plants is also a significant point source of phosphorus. Nonetheless, 'the largest source of phosphorus pollution in rivers is the sediment from ongoing erosion – a legacy of forest clearance and topdressing' (PCE, 2012: 70). Irrigation and hydro-electricity dams also 'change a river's natural flow and cause increased sediment, higher water temperatures, and reduced oxygen concentrations. Algae and other nuisance plants may proliferate downstream from dams because the high flows that regularly flush the river system have been reduced' (MFE, 2007: 267).

(Continued)

Text Box 1.2 New Zealand river water quality: Not so clean and green? (*Continued*)

Tourism and recreation activities can have significant detrimental effects on water quality (Hall & Stoffels, 2006). Camping and tramping in catchments can create pollution, especially from sewage, accelerated soil erosion and runoff. Recreational boating and fishing can cause damage to banks and fauna from boat propellers, increased turbidity, discharge of motor fuel and oil and the introduction of exotic species (Hall & Härkönen, 2006). Peri-urban development, such as housing subdivisions and second home developments, negatively impact river water quality with increased erosion and increases in waste- and storm-water, which can overload pre-existing infrastructure (PCE, 2001; Sleeman, 2009). While much is known about the impacts of pollution in the rivers of New Zealand from industry and business activities, the full effects of current land use and development may not be seen for decades, as time lags in groundwater systems mean that current monitoring and reporting reflects the effects of land use and farming practices in the 1960s and 1970s for some catchments, rather than current issues associated with the growth of intense dairy farming, peri-urbanisation and amenity migration.

Human Appropriation of Global Freshwater

While the biological, social, cultural and economic importance of water for humans is indisputable, growing evidence suggests that humanity's water use patterns are unsustainable (Gleick & Palaniappan, 2010; Hoekstra *et al.*, 2012; Ridoutt & Pfister, 2010a, 2010b). Srinivasan *et al.* (2012) suggested that water-related human wellbeing could be grouped into six 'syndromes': groundwater depletion, ecological destruction, drought-driven conflicts, unmet subsistence needs, resource capture by elite, and water reallocation to nature. All these syndromes could be explained by a limited set of causal factors that fall into four categories: demand changes, supply changes, governance systems and infrastructure/technology. Three characteristics were identified that gave cause for overall concern for water and human wellbeing and which underlie much of this book's attention to the need to better understand the relationship between water and tourism:

(1)   unsustainability – a decline in the water stock or ecosystem function that could result in a long-term steep decline in future human wellbeing;

(2) vulnerability – high variability in water resource availability combined with inadequate coping capacity, leading to temporary drops in human wellbeing;
(3) chronic scarcity – persistent inadequate access and hence low conditions of human wellbeing (Srinivasan *et al.*, 2012).

Whereas over 70% of the Earth's surface is covered with water, only an estimated 2.5% of the global water volume is freshwater (Shiklomanov, 1993). As shown in Table 1.1, most freshwater is bound in groundwater and ice caps. Comparably little, an estimated 100,000 km³, is concentrated in large lakes, including Lake Baikal (Russia), the Great Lakes in North America, and the lakes in eastern Africa. Only 1700 km³ are contained in rivers.

Table 1.1 Water reservoirs and fluxes

	Estimated values (km³)	Range of values in literature (km³)
Reservoirs		
Ocean	1,350,000,000	$1.32–1.37 \times 10^9$
Atmosphere	13,000	10,500–14,000
Land		
Rivers	1,700	1,020–2,120
Freshwater lakes	100,000	30,000–150,000
Inland seas, saline	105,000	85,400–125,000
Soil moisture	70,000	16,500–150,000
Groundwater	8,200,000	$7–330 \times 10^6$
Ice caps/glaciers	27,500,000	$16.5–29.2 \times 10^6$
Biota	1,100	1,000–50,000
Flux		
Evaporation	496,000	446,000–557,000
Ocean	425,000	383,000–505,000
Land	71,000	63,000–73,000
Precipitation	496,000	446,000–577,000
Ocean	385,000	320,000–458,000
Land	111,000	99,000–119,000
Runoff to oceans	39,700	33,500–47,000
Streams	27,000	27,000–45,000
Ground feed	12,000	0–12,000
Glacial ice	2,500	1,700–4,500

Source: Speidel and Agnew (1982).

The understanding of the extent of global water resources available for human use and the implications of growing human appropriation of renewable freshwater (HARF) has been well recognised since the 1990s. As outlined by Postel *et al.* (1996), less than 1% of world's freshwater held in lakes, rivers, groundwater, atmosphere and biomass is available for human use. This quantity of water is referred to as the renewable freshwater supply on land ($RFWS_{land}$) and is estimated at 110,300 km^3/year). Figure 1.1 shows that $RFWS_{land}$ includes precipitation on land (from evaporation at sea), and evapotranspiration (ET) over land that represents runoff to the sea. ET is defined as the water taken up by plants and released back into the atmosphere (transpiration), as well as water that vaporises from land surfaces including plants (evaporation). ET on land accounts for the largest share of RFWSland (69,600 km^3 per year). Of this, 18,300 km^3 per year are appropriated by humans in the form of agriculture and other uses of biomass. An estimated

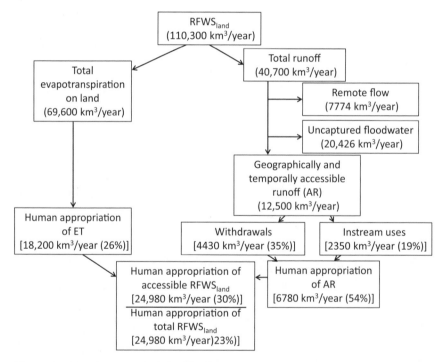

Figure 1.1 Human appropriation of freshwater resources

Notes: $RFWS_{land}$, terrestrial renewable freshwater supply; P_{land}, precipitation on land; ET_{land}, evapotranspiration from land; AR, accessible runoff.

Source: Postel *et al.* (1996).

40,700 km³ per year are runoff, i.e. part of the hydrological cycle that is directly relevant for human beings, and only 12,500 km³ per year, representing geographically and temporally accessible runoff (AR), can be abstracted and made available for human use. Postel *et al.* (1996) estimate that current human use equals 6780 km³ per year of AR (54% of total AR), plus 18,200 km³ per year of ET (26% of total ET), for a total of 30% of the accessible RFWS$_{land}$. Considering these estimates are now over 25 years old and global population has increased from 5.3 billion in 1990 to over 7 billion in 2012, the proportion of the world's freshwater resources appropriated by humans has since undoubtedly increased.

Importantly, the distribution of AR does not correspond with the distribution of the world population. For instance, while Asia is home to 60% of the world's population, it contains only 36% of global runoff. Consequently, an estimated 1.4–2.1 billion people already live in water-stressed areas in northern Africa, the Mediterranean, the Middle East, the Near East, southern Asia, southern China, Australia, the USA, Mexico, northeastern Brazil and the west coast of South America (Arnell, 2004; Vörösmarty *et al.*, 2000).

In the future, multiple stressors are expected to exacerbate water security challenges in many regions of the world. The share of global freshwater resources appropriated by humans is expected to increase with a growing population. Even if per capita water demand in 2025 remained the same as it was in Postel *et al.*'s (1996) estimate for human appropriation of global freshwater resources in 1990, with an increased global population, human appropriation of water use would increase to 70% of estimated AR by 2025 (or 9830 km³ per year). However, per capita water demand is not expected to remain constant, nor decline as some contend it needs to (Hejazi *et al.*, 2013). Instead, Vörösmarty *et al.* (2000) have shown that growing demand is likely, contributing to even greater water security challenges in the future.

Vörösmarty *et al.* (2000) suggest that developing countries in particular will see a large increase in water demand, and that the number of people living in severely water-stressed regions is likely to increase significantly from an estimated 450 million in 1995. However, even where water is abundant, the challenge will be to provide water of adequate quality standards. As global wetlands continue to deteriorate and are lost to development and sea-level rise (both through inundation and saltwater intrusion), the capacity of ecosystems to purify water will be adversely impacted (UN Water, 2014). Furthermore, 'much of the world's population growth over the next few decades will occur in urban areas, which are projected to double in size to near 5 billion between 1995–2025 and face major challenges in coping with

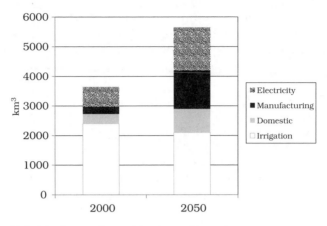

Figure 1.2 Global freshwater demand (2000–2050)
Source: Adapted from OECD (2012b).

increased water pollution and incidence of waterborne disease' (Vörösmarty *et al.*, 2000: 287).

UN Water (2014) suggest that global water demand, measured as withdrawals from AR, will increase by 55% by 2050, as a result of consumer demand and increasing standards of living or, more specifically, growing demand for manufactured goods and food, thermal electricity generation and domestic uses (Figure 1.2). As a result of increased water demand over the coming decades, UN Water (2014) estimate that as much as 40% of the global population may live in areas of severe water stress by 2050, as aquifers are overexploited and groundwater supplies decline. Hejazi *et al.* (2013) similarly show that by 2050 most continents and countries, with the exception of Australia and New Zealand, Canada, the area comprising the former Soviet Union and Latin America, will face increased levels of water scarcity. Notably, parts of Australia already face water problems during drought periods, indicating that water scarcity may nevertheless be a regional problem even within these relatively water-secure countries.

The disconcerting future of water security is further complicated by ongoing global environmental change. By the 2050s, climate change is also expected to have a notable impact on regional precipitation patterns in some areas of the world, aggravating water security challenges caused by increased water demand. Further into the future, under a +4°C global warming scenario that appears to be the most likely climate change pathway given current trends in greenhouse gas emissions (IPCC, 2013), up to 3.2 billion people could face water stress by 2100 (Parry *et al.*, 2009a, 2009b).

Text Box 1.3 Concepts of water scarcity

Water scarcity and its implications have recently also been echoed by various UN organisations, including UN Water, an inter-agency coordinating body covering all freshwater- and sanitation-related issues. Water scarcity is a result of growing demand for water, and related to and potentially exacerbated by climate and ecosystem change. It is defined as 'an excess of water demand over available supply' (UN Water, 2014: 6), and absolute water scarcity is established at a threshold of less than 500 m^3 per person per year (Falkenmark & Widstrand, 1992). The latter approach is a water-crowding indicator which is often expressed as people per unit water or water availability per capita.

The UN indicator is a withdrawal to availability (WTA) indicator and is the most widely used indicator of water scarcity. Whereas the Falkenmark indicator focuses on natural water endowment, the WTA indicator focuses on how countries are using that endowment. Therefore, 'a country with apparently ample water resources per person by the Falkenmark indicator may be considered stressed by the WTA indicator if it is using a great deal of water per person, either because it is wasteful or because it is exporting water-intensive products' (Anisfeld, 2010: 78–79). The latter indicator is a focus for this book because of the extent to which water is embodied in food used in tourism and hospitality. The WTA also has several weaknesses:

- Data quality: it relies on the adequacy of data collection which may be a problem in many countries.
- Timing: it does not take into account the different relationships between annual and dry season water availability and its implications for water supply.
- Appropriateness of water use: the indicator provides no indication of the appropriateness of the levels of water withdrawals.

A further issue with analysing water scarcity is the importance of understanding the implication of scale of analysis and where analytical boundaries are drawn in relation to watersheds. A sampling frame of water scarcity based on government boundaries may give quite different understandings from one based on watersheds. Another dimension of water scarcity is the concept of economic water scarcity that refers to a situation in which economic rather than physical constraints, such as

(Continued)

Text Box 1.3 Concepts of water scarcity (*Continued*)

lack of water infrastructure, result in a lack of water availability to individual users (Anisfeld, 2010). Two other significant concepts used in relation to water scarcity are groundwater overdraft, which refers to a situation in which groundwater is used a greater rate than the rate at which it is recharged, and drought, which is not defined in terms of low water availability (aridity) but as negative deviation from normal water availability. Four types of drought are usually recognised:

- Meteorological drought: a deficiency in precipitation relative to normal conditions.
- Agricultural drought: low soil moisture leading to negative impacts on crop growth; this may also occur as the result of anthropogenic impacts on the soil's capacity to hold moisture, i.e. poor agricultural practices.
- Hydrological drought: a decrease in surface water flows and groundwater levels as a result of meteorological drought.
- Socioeconomic drought: the socio-economic impacts associated with meteorological, agricultural and/or hydrological droughts.

The Complexities of Water Use Measurements

Considerable differences exist in water use and water availability between and within countries. For example, the average per capita water withdrawal is 225 L per day in Chad and 4315 L per day in the USA (data for 2005; FAO, 2014), indicating huge differences in water use. However, this does not necessarily mean that these values correspond to the amount of water actually consumed, as there is a substantial international and inter-regional trade in 'embodied water' that is not captured in such measures of direct per capita water use. The idea that considerable amounts of water are 'embodied' in goods, particularly agricultural produce, was first captured in Allan's (1998) concept of 'virtual water', which was developed in the context of water scarcity in the Middle East. This concept was subsequently developed into the more comprehensive water footprint concept (Hoekstra & Hung, 2002), in order to capture the full implications of human consumption on freshwater, and to subsequently compare the water embodied in consumption in a country as compared to the water embodied in production.

Various examples illustrate the differences in restrictive versus comprehensive water use measurements. Chapagain and Orr (2008) suggest that, although a can of soft drink contains only 0.33 L of liquid, the sugar contained in the beverage may have consumed 200 L of water in order to grow. Meat will require up to three orders of magnitude more water for production than its own weight (Hoekstra & Chapagain, 2008). This has considerable implications for countries' water consumption. Hoekstra and Chapagain (2008) point out, for instance, that Jordan uses about 1 billion m^3 of its domestic water supplies, compared to 5–7 billion m^3 of virtual water contained in goods imported from outside the country. Studies of the trade in embodied water have revealed the vast scale of water traded between countries in the form of goods and the water dependency of some countries (Dalin *et al.*, 2012; Lenzen *et al.*, 2013; Yang *et al.*, 2003, 2007; Table 1.2). This is also true for tourism (Gössling, 2005), which causes considerable shifts in water use between countries and within regions; this is discussed in detail in Chapter 2.

The consumption-based national water footprint concept is a central metric in this book and measures the amount of freshwater residents of a country use directly as well as the water used to produce imported goods, and excludes water embodied in goods produced in the country, but exported to other countries. The water footprint also consists of three water 'types', i.e. blue, green and grey water. Green water stands for the precipitation on land that becomes soil moisture in the unsaturated soil zone that plants then use to grow (Falkenmark & Rockström, 1993). Blue water refers to surface and groundwater, i.e. water in its conventional sense found in rivers, lakes and aquifers and used for irrigation. Finally, grey water is defined as the amount of water that is required to dilute pollutants from food production (such as fertilisers and pesticides) to such an extent that water quality remains above given quality standards (cf. Water Footprint Network, 2013).

Figure 1.3 shows how a national water footprint measures the total volume of water used for all goods and services consumed in this country (Hoekstra & Chapagain, 2008). The footprint distinguishes green, blue and grey water used domestically for agricultural, industrial and domestic purposes, but excluding exports. As shown in Figure 1.3, this country primarily exports agricultural produce, containing a large share of green water. To calculate the national total, imports have to be added, although potentially subtracting re-exports. For instance, this could be the case for strawberries imported to produce yoghurt, which is then exported for consumption in another country.

Table 1.2 Select examples of virtual water flows

Country	Gross virtual-water flows (10⁶ m³/year)								Net virtual-water import (10⁶ m³/year)			
	Related to trade in crop products		Related to trade in livestock products		Related to trade in industrial products		Total		Related to trade in crop products	Related to trade in livestock products	Related to trade in industrial products	Total
	Export	Import	Export	Import	Export	Import	Export	Import				
Sweden	2,034	4,747	808	1,203	1,639	4,316	4,481	10,256	2,703	395	2,678	5,776
Switzerland-Liechtenstein	1,163	6,172	401	752	1,555	5,208	3,119	12,132	5,008	351	3,654	9,013
Syria	4,025	3,131	512	143	126	213	4,664	3,488	−894	−368	87	−1,176
Taiwan	329	11,708	3,559	3,535	0	0	3,888	15,243	11,380	−24	0	11,355
Tajikistan	1,014	0	36	0	0	0	1,049	0	−1,014	−36	0	−1,049
Tanzania	3,173	970	52	11	2	85	3,227	1,066	−2,203	−41	83	−2,161
Thailand	38,429	9,761	2,856	1,761	1,655	3,596	42,940	15,117	−28,668	−1,096	1,941	−27,823
Togo	1,920	400	2	8	7	34	1,929	443	−1,519	6	27	−1,486
Tokelau Islands	2	1	0	1	0	0	2	2	−1	1	0	0
Trinidad and Tobago	350	493	15	169	81	193	446	854	143	153	112	409
Tunisia	11,013	3,502	78	211	72	524	11,162	4,237	−7,510	133	452	−6,925
Turkey	11,069	14,069	337	1,206	1,902	2,941	13,308	18,216	3,000	869	1,040	4,908
Turkmenistan	1,071	165	27	43	72	92	1,170	301	−906	16	21	−869
Tuvalu	0	1	0	1	0	0	0	2	1	1	0	2
Uganda	4,432	1,201	77	3	1	88	4,511	1,293	−3,231	−74	87	−3,218
UK	8,773	33,742	3,786	10,163	5,113	20,321	17,672	64,226	24,968	6,378	15,208	46,554

Source: Hoekstra and Chapagain (2008).

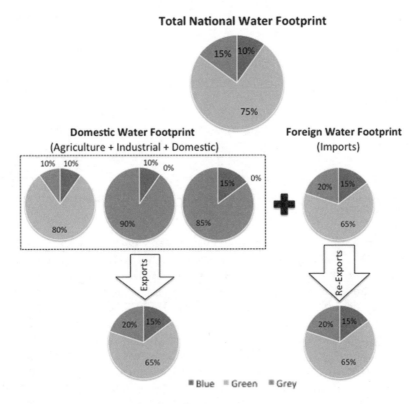

Figure 1.3 Determining the composition of a national water footprint
Source: Adapted from Chenoweth *et al.* (2014).

Water Use by Subsector

Because of the dominance of agricultural water use in many countries, total human water use can be divided into agricultural and non-agricultural uses (Hejazi *et al.*, 2013). Agricultural uses include rain-fed or irrigated agriculture as well as livestock breeding and, as shown in Table 1.3, is the major sector consuming freshwater, accounting for 70% of global freshwater withdrawals, followed by industry (19%) and domestic uses (11%) (FAO, 2014). Non-agricultural water uses include primary and secondary energy production, manufacturing and domestic uses. A fourth type of water use, evaporation from artificial lakes or reservoirs associated with dams, will be considered in the future by the FAO (2014).

Table 1.3 Global freshwater use by sector

Sector	Global water withdrawals	Global water consumption
Municipal	13.0%	5.4%
Electricity generation	14.0%	6.3%
Primary energy	0.5%	0.5%
Manufacturing	5.6%	2.2%
Agriculture	66.0%	84.0%
Livestock	0.5%	1.4%

Source: Figures regarding distribution of global water consumption and withdrawals by sector in 2005 from Hejazi *et al.* (2013).

An important distinction in analysing water use is also whether it is consumptive, representing the sum of water input less the water that is recycled or reused (US Department of Energy, 2012: 3). Water use for irrigation is particularly problematic, because 90% of this is consumptive, i.e. the water is lost for downstream use due to ET (FAO, 2012). Consequently, even though the agriculture sector is estimated to withdraw 66% of global freshwater, it consumes 84% of global freshwater (Table 1.3). UN Water (2014) reports that energy production is the second most water consuming human activity, requiring an estimated 15% of the world's water withdrawals, mostly for cooling in thermal power plants that account for 80% of global electricity production. Electricity production is currently less consumptive, with only 11% of the water used being lost for downstream use, but this might change in the future when power plants use more advanced cooling systems, or when larger quantities of biofuel are used. As discussed in further detail in the following sections, fossil fuel production is far more consumptive of water than electricity production.

Taken together, agriculture and energy production thus account for 80% of overall water withdrawals and 91% of freshwater consumption (Table 1.3). The remaining share of global freshwater consumption is being used for various manufacturing and production processes, as well as domestic uses that include household consumption, municipalities, commercial establishments and public services. As food and energy production have such dominating importance for global freshwater use, these sectors are examined in more detail below. Considering the dominant global water use by these sectors, it should perhaps come as no surprise that they have primary roles in water use by the tourism sector as well (Gössling & Hall, 2013). This is nonetheless a relatively new understanding of water use in tourism and hospitality, and past discussions of water use by the sector have almost entirely focused on domestic water use at tourism facilities such as hotels and resorts (e.g. Deng & Burnett, 2002; Stipanuk & Robson, 1995; Tourism Concern, 2012).

Food production

Food consumption is highly unequally distributed between countries, with an estimated 870 million undernourished people worldwide (FAO, 2013). While the food requirements of these people are not met, there is also an increasing part of the world's population that has changed its dietary preferences towards higher order foods, involving more energy- and water-intensive production of beef, poultry and pork (Smith *et al.*, 2009b). Consequently, globally growing demand for meat will demand greater use of irrigation, fertiliser and fodder production, all of which are energy intense and will increase water use in comparison to plant-based diets. Consequently, agriculture not only accounts for 70% of all freshwater withdrawals, but food production and supply chains also account for 30% of total global energy consumption (FAO, 2011b), which increase the total water use of this sector through the embodied water in the energy they consume. In the future, with expectations that the world's population will grow to 9.3 billion by 2050 (UNDESA, 2012), global food production will have to increase by 60% to meet the demand of additional people even if diets (and the embodied energy and water) remain the same as they are today (Alexandratos & Bruinsma, 2012).

With regard to freshwater embodied in food consumption, UNESCO (2009) suggest that, depending on local climate, crop varieties and agricultural practices, 400–2000 L of water are needed to produce 1 kg of wheat, and 1000–20,000 L of water are required to produce 1 kg of meat. Considering daily food (caloric) requirements, human diets require 2000–5000 L of water per person per day, based on an estimate of 1 L of water per kcal. As Figure 1.4 illustrates, the total water required by a human diet is greatly influenced by the type of food and beverage consumed. As a global average, the production of 1 kg of food may require between 74 L (beer) to 17,196 L (chocolate) of water (Figure 1.4). This refers to all water used for production. However, as discussed previously, an important distinction needs to be made between the green, blue and grey water components of the food-related water footprint. Depending on the foodstuff and its origin and composition, the amount of green/blue/grey water contained in 1 kg of foodstuff can vary widely (Figure 1.4), both in absolute (litres of water needed) and relative (percentage of green/blue/grey water) terms (see also Chenoweth *et al.*, 2014).

While the components of the total water footprint of different foodstuffs are useful in order to assess the total water demand of food production, and

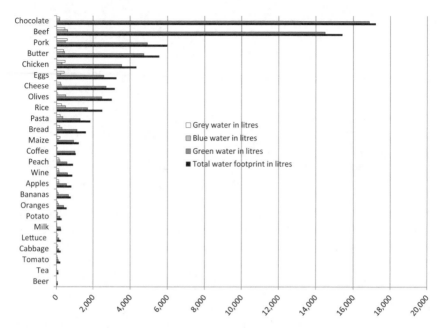

Figure 1.4 Total water embodied in 1 kg of produce, approximate values
Source: Based on Mekonnen and Hoekstra (2011a, 2011b).

hence the water needed to maintain the tourism system's vital and often luxurious food and beverage component, several concerns have been raised with regard to the use of green water. For instance, Ridoutt and Pfister (2010a) have argued that green water consumption does not contribute to water scarcity, as this water cannot be used for purposes other than agriculture. It may also be argued that blue water use in tourism has far greater implications than green water use. In Figure 1.4, both total water footprints as well as green and blue water shares are depicted, showing that food production has far smaller blue components. Yet total water is needed in order for these foodstuffs to be produced, and the question arising out of blue water component calculation is whether it would have been more favourable to produce these locally or to import, as food production in dry climates is more water intense than in humid climates (Chenoweth *et al.*, 2013). Consequently, importing food for tourism may in some cases save water use at the global scale, although this also depends on the amount and type of energy used to transport food, and the subsequent implications for water consumption.

Figure 1.4 also illustrates that the share of blue water contained in different foodstuffs is relatively small, varying between 1% (chocolate) and 30%

(tomato) on global average. In comparison, green water accounts for 56% (lettuce) to 98% (chocolate), and grey water for 1% (chocolate) to 32% (lettuce) of total water requirements. These values represent global averages and can differ markedly between countries (Chenoweth *et al.*, 2014). There is a consensus, however, that diets consisting primarily of meats and dairy products result in considerably larger water footprints because animals are fed with processed food, such as pellets, which are often imported over vast distances. Moreover, animals require large amounts of water (Vanham *et al.*, 2013a, 2013b). As shown in Figure 1.4, the average water footprint of tomatoes is thus only a fraction of the footprint of meat. Significantly, the above values represent direct water use for production, to which energy for production, processing, distribution, retail, preparation and cooking need to be added. Globally, an estimated 95 EJ/year of energy are needed in the food sector (FAO, 2011b).

These trade-offs in green/blue/grey water associated with food consumption reveal the complexities of measuring and understanding the impact of water use and transfers associated with the tourism sector, both at the destination scale as well as the global system scale.

Energy

Interrelationships of energy use and water consumption have become increasingly clear in recent years, as water provision and treatment consumes energy, while energy production in itself also requires water (Figure 1.5). Energy production now accounts for a large share of the consumptive and non-consumptive use of water in most countries, ranging between 10% and 20% in developing countries (including industry, and reaching up to 50% in developed countries, where less is used for agriculture and more for power plant cooling; UN Water, 2014).

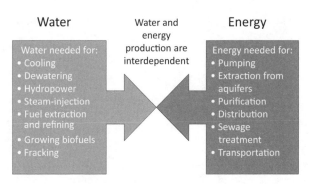

Figure 1.5 The interrelationships between water and energy

Energy is needed to pump, distribute and treat water, with relative energy intensities of water provision depending on elevation change (pumping), distance, pipe diameter and friction, as well as the source of the water and its quality and the treatment type. Pumping is generally energy intense because of water's high density. Drinking water requires extensive treatment to exclude any potential health issues, and used water needs to be treated again to make it safe to be returned to the environment (Table 1.4). Depending on the process, treatment can be less (ultraviolet: $0.01–0.04$ kWh/m^3) or more (reverse osmosis: $1.5–3.5$ kWh/m^3) energy intense. Note that water for agriculture is usually untreated, requiring only energy for pumping. Surface water is generally less energy intense and easy to distribute, but may require intensive treatment. Vice versa, groundwater usually requires little treatment, but more energy for pumping. Seawater desalination is the most energy intense form of water provision. Globally, an estimated 16,000 desalination plants produce a total of 70 million m^3 of freshwater per day, for which an estimated 0.4% of global electricity consumption (75.2 TWh/year) is required (IRENA, 2012). Desalination thus remains expensive and energy intense.

Energy production in itself is also water intense, irrespective of the form of energy, i.e. including electricity, fossil fuels and biofuels. With regard to electricity, an estimated 90% of global power generation is water intensive (UN Water, 2014). Hydropower uses water directly, as do all forms of thermal power generation, including nuclear, coal, natural gas, petroleum, solar or biomass, i.e. where heat is used to generate electricity. For instance, in Europe thermal power generation is responsible for 43% of total freshwater withdrawals (Rübbelke & Vögele, 2011). Depending on electricity generation and cooling technology, water consumption per MWh can involve between 1 and 10,000 L of water, with somewhat lower values of consumptive use in the case of combined-cycle gas turbines, fossil steam and nuclear power generation. Wind and

Table 1.4 Amount of energy required to provide 1 m^3 of safe drinking water

Water body	Amount of energy (kWh/m^3)
Lake or river	0.37
Groundwater	0.48
Wastewater treatment	0.62–0.87
Wastewater reuse	1.0–2.5
Seawater	2.58–8.5

Notes: The figures do not incorporate critical elements such as the distance water is transported nor the level of efficiency, which will vary greatly between locations.
Source: WBSCD (2009).

solar PV currently require the least amounts of water. Global electricity demand is expected to grow by 70% up to 2035, mostly in China and India, and coal is expected to remain the major fuel used for electricity generation through to 2035 (UN Water, 2014). This will have concomitant repercussions for water use over the multi-decadal lifespan of these new facilities.

Water is also used to produce fossil fuels and biofuels, demanding considerable though greatly varying quantities of water. For instance, per tonne of oil equivalent (toe), water volumes of between 1 and 1,000,000 L of water may be used, with conventional gas and gas-to-liquids potentially being the least water intense. Coal is water intense because seams need to be dewatered, and this water is not subsequently available for other uses. Unconventional fuels, such as refined oil from oil sands, are more water intense than conventional fuels, and biofuels are the most water-intense fuels because large amounts of water are required for biomass growth. Figure 1.6 shows that most water use for energy production is consumptive, and greater for biofuels.

Considerable amounts of water are needed for the production of gasoline and oil, which are the most relevant energy sources in tourism (particularly

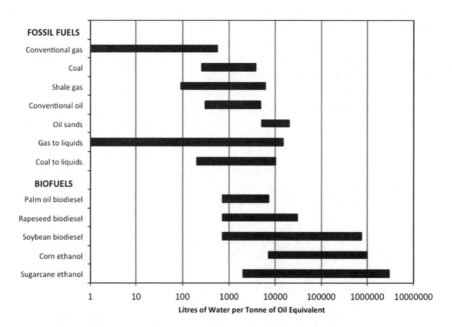

Figure 1.6 Water consumption and fuel production
Source: Adapted from IEA (2012); logarithmic scale.

for transport) in addition to electricity. For instance, the Worldwatch Institute (2004) suggested that the production of 1 L of gasoline requires 18 L of water, while Energies Nouvelles (2011) reported 1 L of oil requires 3–5 L of water. Beal *et al.* (2012) and Sanders and Webber (2012) report slightly higher values for extraction through refining of petroleum-based fuels, i.e. 7–15 L of water per litre of fuel. Where oil production is mature, water use increases, as more water is needed to produce fluid (known as the water–oil ratio), which can be as high as 14 L of water per litre of fuel (Energies Nouvelles, 2011). The share of water that is consumptive in oil production is lower, however, ranging from 2.1 to 5.4 L of water per litre of crude oil (USA production) to 1.4–4.6 L/L (Saudi Arabian production), to 2.6–6.2 L/L (Canadian oil sands) (US Department of Energy, 2012). Furthermore, water sources can involve freshwater, saline water, desalinated water or steam to change the viscosity of heavy oils and oil sands (UN Water, 2014), i.e. potentially requiring further energy inputs for production. Overall, oil production may require 1.4–6.2 L of consumptive water use, or 3–18 L of overall water use per litre of fuel.

Even renewable energy production requires water, and biofuels in particular are very water intense. Traditional biomass (woodfuels, agricultural by-products and dung) currently represents 9.6% of global final energy consumption, modern biomass (solid wastes and residues from agriculture and forestry) 3.7%, and biofuels 0.8% (Banerjee *et al.*, 2013), but their contribution to global final energy consumption is expected to grow rapidly over the next several decades. Biofuel production has increased rapidly since 2000, in part due to rising oil prices and energy security concerns. However, there are also massive subsidies provided for biofuel expansion, which can have considerable consequences for water demand, as biofuels can be two orders of magnitude more water intense than conventional fuels (Figure 1.5). As shown in Table 1.5, major biofuel crops may require between 750 and 10,000 L of water per litre of fuel. The implications of trends in the use of fuel types (e.g. biofuel development and utilisation for aircraft, electrification of ground transport, solar power installation at resorts) for tourism sector water use are discussed further in Chapters 2 and 3.

Text Box 1.4 The cost of water

The price of water and how water economics are conceived and understood by government clearly has an extremely important role to play in influencing how organisations, businesses and individuals use and conserve water resources. The situation has been well described by Anisfeld (2010: 2476–2477):

Some people believe that water should be free. After all, it falls from the skies as a gift from the hydrological cycle and flows downhill to us without cost. If natural waters belong to the public, how can water utilities get away with charging us for what was ours to begin with?

Upon reflection, though, most people realize that what is being delivered from their taps is not the same as what falls from the sky. The water company must extract the water, treat it, and deliver it all, all of which costs money. Moreover, the water company must construct and maintain an extensive system of infrastructure – pumping station, treatment facilities, miles and miles of pipes, thousands of water meters – which also costs money.

From an economic perspective, the ideal price of water would equal the marginal cost of water delivery (including the supply costs) and the value of the raw water, usually expressed as the opportunity cost, which is the value of the water when used for other purposes. However, the problem with this expression is that water is different from many other natural resources:

- Water is clearly essential to life.
- Water delivery is a natural monopoly.
- Water has uses, such as ecological values, that are extremely hard to value, i.e. the price of the extinction of a species because it is denied water because it is being used by humans for other purposes.
- Water is, generally, publicly owned.

As Anisfeld (2010: 248) asks: 'How do we charge customers the marginal cost of water – including the value of the raw water – without essentially giving away the raw water to the utility?'

Water Futures

A shortage of water resources could spell increased conflicts in the future. Population growth will make the problem worse. So will climate change. As the global economy grows, so will its thirst. Many more conflicts lie just over the horizon. (Ban Ki-moon, UN Secretary-General, 24 January 2008)

Table 1.5 Indicative yields and water requirements for biofuel crops

Crop	Fuel product	Annual obtainable yield (L/ha)	Energy yield (GJ/ha)	Potential crop evapotranspiration (in mm, indicative)	Evapotranspiration (L/L fuel)	Irrigated or rainfed production	Rainfed conditions		Water resource implications under irrigated conditions (assuming an irrigation efficiency of 50%)
							Actual rainfed crop evapotranspiration (in mm, indicative)	Irrigation water used (in mm, indicative)	Irrigation water used (in L/L fuel, indicative)
Sugar cane	Ethanol (from sugar)	6,000	120	1,400	2,000	Irrigated/rainfed	1,100	600	1,000
Sugar beet	Ethanol (from sugar)	7,000	140	650	786	Irrigated/rainfed	450	400	571
Cassava	Ethanol (from starch)	4,000	80	1,000	2,250	Rainfed	900	–	–
Maize	Ethanol (from starch)	3,500	70	550	1,360	Irrigated/rainfed	400	300	857
Winter wheat	Ethanol (from starch)	2,000	40	300	1,500	Rainfed	300	–	–
Palm oil	Bio-diesel	6,000	193	1,500	2,360	Rainfed	1,300	–	–
Rapeseed/mustard	Bio-diesel	1,200	42	500	3,330	Rainfed	400	–	–
Soybean	Bio-diesel	450	14	500	10,000	Rainfed	400	–	–

Note: 1 GJ/h = 277.8 kW.

Source: UN Water (2014).

As this chapter has emphasised, a growing number of scientific and government assessments have raised concerns that the world's water demand will grow significantly over the next decades due to world population and economic growth leading to an expansion of agriculture as a result of a growing demand for food and an associated demand for energy, housing and infrastructure (UN Water, 2014). Ultimately, this is caused by population growth, as well as more energy-intense lifestyles. As outlined, global food consumption is expected to increase by 60% until 2050 (Alexandratos & Bruinsma, 2012), and with regard to energy, UN Water (2014) conclude that, even though there are policies promoting renewables, this will not be enough to change the reliance on fossil fuels, which are expected to continue to dominate energy supply. Only in some OECD countries, where energy demand is not expected to rise significantly, will there be a reduction in the use of oil, coal, and in some cases nuclear power (IEA, 2012). These trends, as well as the growing consumption of manufactured goods, will increase pressure on already stressed water resources in several regions. For instance, Gleeson *et al.* (2012) report that an estimated 20% of the world's aquifers are currently over-exploited, and the global rate of groundwater abstraction is increasing by 1–2% per year (WWAP, 2012). Groundwater supplies are thus diminishing, while energy-intense forms of freshwater production involving desalination are growing (UN Water, 2014). As shown in the world map depicted in Figure 1.7, this will lead to growing

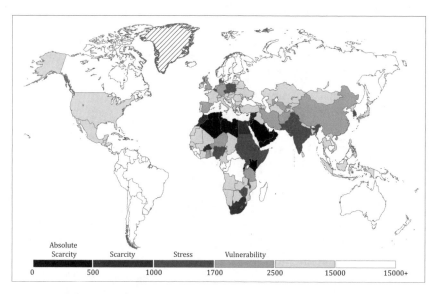

Figure 1.7 Total renewable water resources, 2012 (m³ per capita per year)

stress in already water-scarce regions. For example, India is already considered to be a water-stressed country, while China is 'vulnerable'. Together, these two countries account for more than one-third of the world's population and are among the regions where international and domestic tourism are expected to grow the most through to 2030 (UNWTO, 2012).

Water security is increasingly influencing strategic business decisions, including the siting of production facilities, supply chain sourcing and other long-range investments (Carbon Disclosure Project, 2012; Ceres, 2009; Ernst & Young, 2012; JPMorgan, 2008; Lloyd's, 2010; WWF, 2014). While there is a clear trend to further understand the water risks for business and to identify strategies to maintain business in markets that are projected to increasingly suffer from water scarcity, there is limited evidence that the tourism sector is considering future trends in water security and costs. When combined with growing pressure from sustainable and ethical travel organisations and consumer movements that lobby government for stricter water use regulations of domestic tourism companies operating in foreign countries (including a 'beyond the resort walls' community-based perspective), trends in water use measurement, efficiency and future water scarcity remain emerging strategic blind spots for tourism investment and development.

Further reading

Useful general overviews of global water issues include:

Anisfeld, S.G. (2010) *Water Resources*. Washington, DC: Island Press.

Tourism Concern (2012) *Water Equity in Tourism: A Human Right, a Global Responsibility*. London: Tourism Concern. See http://www.ircwash.org/resources/water-equity-tourism-human-right-global-responsibility.

UN Water (2010) *Climate Change Adaptation: The Pivotal Role of Water*. New York: United Nations. See http://www.ircwash.org/resources/water-equity-tourism-human-right-global-responsibility

UN Water (2014) *Water and Energy. The United Nations World Water Development Report 2014*. New York: United Nations. See http://unesdoc.unesco.org/images/0022/002257/225741E.pdf.

On water footprints see:

Hoekstra, A.Y., Chapagain, A.K., Aldaya, M.M. and Mekonnen, M.M. (2011) *The Water Footprint Assessment Manual: Setting the Global Standard*. London: Earthscan.

Hoekstra, A.Y., Mekonnen, M.M., Chapagain, A.K., Mathews, R.E. and Richter, B.D. (2012) Global monthly water scarcity: Blue water footprints versus blue water availability. *PLoS One* 7 (2), e32688.

Ridoutt, B.G. and Pfister, S. (2010b) Reducing humanity's water footprint. *Environmental Science and Technology* 44 (16), 6019–6021.

2 Interrelationships of Tourism With Water

With global freshwater availability coming under increasing pressure (WWAP, 2012; see Chapter 1), water consumption in tourism has received growing attention from organisations such as the United Nations World Tourism Organization (UNWTO, 2013b), the United Nations Environment Programme (UNEP, 2011) and the Organisation of Economic Cooperation and Development (OECD, 2013). These organisations have also put forward various calls to reduce water consumption in tourism which, however, is only feasible on the basis of sound, evidence-based understanding of water use patterns.

Water use has been studied from a wide range of perspectives, all of which have delivered important insights for water management. The most prominent focus of water studies in tourism has been the direct and indirect consumption of freshwater in destinations and hotels, usually from an applied management perspective, i.e. to measure, understand and more effectively use freshwater. Where this focus has dominated, results have usually included measurements of water use per guest or guest night (e.g. Bohdanowicz & Martinac, 2007; Essex et al., 2004; Gössling et al., 2012). A few studies have also explored the role of tourism in shifting water between countries (Cazcarro et al., 2014), and a related research area has considered the sustainability implications of water use, including water scarcity and competing uses between tourism and other economic sectors or local populations (e.g. Cole, 2012, 2013; Gössling, 2001; Hadjikakou et al., 2013a; Page et al., 2014; Tourism Concern, 2012).

Sewage and wastewater have received some attention as an outcome of water consumption. Where sewage is not treated, or is inadequately treated, there is a possibility of nutrients and pollutants being released into aquifers and coastal waters, potentially leading to the eutrophication of waterways. Wastewater can also contain fertilisers and herbicides, which may for instance be used in hotel gardens or golf courses (Gössling, 2001; Shaalan,

2005). Finally, as a result of these interrelationships, water management has received increasing attention as a tool to reduce water demand (Gössling *et al.*, 2012; OECD, 2013; UNEP, 2011). The following sections consequently examine in more detail three important aspects of the sustainability of global tourism-related water use: (1) spatial and temporal aspects of water use; (2) changes in water quality; and (3) competing water uses.

Spatial and Seasonal Concentrations in Water Use

Although people also consume water at home, there is strong evidence that tourism increases overall per capita water consumption, shifts water consumption between continents and regions, and concentrates water consumption in time, often the dry season (Gössling *et al.*, 2012). Estimates of tourism's water consumption are provided in Chapter 3. There are no general estimates as to how much water tourists consume directly, either generalised by nationality or by type of hotel or activity. Hence, only global assumptions of average per-day water use, including in-room consumption, pools and irrigation, can be made. This water use is possibly in excess of 350 L per day. Domestic at-home consumption varies considerably, and in many parts of the world, average water availability per day is below 10 L per day (UNDP, 2006; see Table 2.1). Only in a few countries in the world, for instance Mexico, Japan, Italy, Australia or the United States is average daily domestic water consumption higher than for an average tourist; as a global average, the FAO assumes that domestic water consumption is 161 L per capita per day (FAO, 2011b). However, it is likely that a share of this high water demand is for the irrigation of gardens or pool fillings at home, and that this water consumption will continue even when people are on holiday.

The world's major tourism flows involve six regions: North America, the Caribbean, Northern and Southern Europe, North East Asia and South East Asia (UNWTO, 2013b). Data for these flows for 2002, which represent 86% of all 715 million international arrivals, is shown in Figure 2.1. In this year, 58% of all international tourist arrivals occurred within Europe, 16% in North East and South East Asia, and 12% in North America. Within the regions, 350 million international arrivals in Europe are generated in Europe itself, 92 million in the Americas, and 88 million in the Asia Pacific region. Intercontinental and major regional flows thus include Northern Europe to the Mediterranean (116 million), North America to Europe (23 million), Europe to North America (15 million), North East Asia to South East Asia (10 million), North East Asia to North America (8 million) and North America to the Caribbean (8 million). These flows have shifted a little over

Table 2.1 Average water use per person

Country	Average water use per person per day (L)	Freshwater withdrawal per capita per year (m³/year)
USA	575	1583
Australia	493	1152
Italy	386	789.8
Japan	374	714.3
Mexico	366	700.4
Spain	320	698.7
Norway	301	622.4
France	287	512.1
Austria	250	454.4
Denmark	210	118.4
Germany	193	391.4
Brazil	187	306.0
Peru	173	787.6
Philippines	164	859.9
UK	149	213.2
India	135	613.0
China	86	409.9
Bangladesh	46	238.3
Kenya	46	72.96
Ghana	36	48.82
Nigeria	36	89.21
Burkina Faso	27	54.99
Niger	27	70.53
Angola	15	40.27
Cambodia	15	159.8
Ethiopia	15	80.5
Haiti	15	134.3
Rwanda	15	17.25
Uganda	15	12.31
Mozambique	4	46.05

Source: Per person per day (1998–2002), UNDP (2006); freshwater withdrawal (domestic, industrial and agricultural combined) per capita (most recent available figure, CIA (2014).

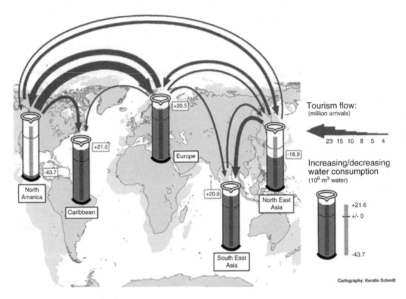

Figure 2.1 Shifts in water use between regions
Source: Gössling (2005).

the last decade, particularly in Asia and the Middle East, but nevertheless provide an indication of shifts in water flows due to tourism (Gössling, 2005). As the figure indicates, tourism may cause shifts in water consumption from water-rich to water-poor areas at large continental and regional scales, i.e. from Northern to Southern Europe, from Europe and North America to the Caribbean, and from inland areas to coastal zones (e.g. Eurostat, 2009). However, given the limited understanding of actual water consumption in the destination and reductions at home, the figure is only illustrative of the potential magnitude and geography of the redistribution of water use because of tourism.

The overall impact of tourism becomes even more complicated considering water embodied in fuel and food. No research has to date been carried out on the implications of these on global water availability, and the potential increase in water scarcity in some production areas that are already facing water stress. Tourism and hospitality are, however, in large part dependent on economics of scale, and food is often likely to be sourced from world markets where the focus is on mass production, and where little consideration is given to the environment (Gössling & Hall, 2013). This will result in water imports embodied in food for some countries, and exports for others. For example, Hadjikakou *et al.* (2013a) have shown how in five different holiday scenarios, food water footprints for specific diets result in net imports in water or, depending on perspective, 'savings' of water that are not needed for local production.

Production chains and purchasing behaviour in global tourism may therefore potentially work to the detriment of more efficient or appropriate water use depending on what the broader goals of water policies are (assuming they exist in the first place). How significant this can be for national tourism economies has, for instance, been shown by Cazcarro et al. (2014), who presented an assessment of the net water footprint of tourism in Spain. By including the water embodied in goods and products consumed by tourism in this country and adding imported water, but subtracting water exports, Cazcarro et al. concluded that the Spanish tourism system requires 6.9 km^3 of freshwater annually. This example shows how tourism, on national and global scales, is both reliant on virtual water embodied in inputs of goods from other sectors (Briassoulis, 1991), while also representing considerable shifts in water consumption between regions.

One of the hallmarks of tourism is that it is not only concentrated in space, but it is also concentrated in time (Hall, 2005). The effects of seasonal tourist demand may mean that for many destinations peak demand may often occur in dry seasons, when rainfall is reduced or even non-existent, when it is hotter, and water availability is restricted (e.g. Eurostat, 2009; Gössling, 2001; WWF, 2004). Information on concentration in time is scattered, but statistics have presented for some areas of the Mediterranean, showing that the ratio of local residents to tourists can change by an order of magnitude over the year, with tourists outweighing the number of locals by more than six to one (e.g. Eurostat, 2009). For example, in the Balearic Islands (Spain), water consumption during the peak tourism month in 1999 (July) was equivalent to 20 per cent of that by the entire local population in the entire year (De Stefano, 2004). In French tourist regions, concomitantly higher water use values in July and August up to 260% higher than on annual average have been reported (IFEN, 2000). Such statistics also do not usually incorporate the demands at some destinations of large numbers of day-trippers. Where precipitation occurs mostly in winter, as in the Mediterranean, this can imply inverse relationships between water availability and water use (Essex et al., 2004; Gikas & Tchobanoglous, 2009; Kent et al., 2002).

In a study of the tourist and second home destination of Akaroa in New Zealand, Cullen et al. (2003) found that the tourism sector's share of water use during August 1999 to December 2002 was 14.7% on average, but showed substantial variation ranging from 5% to 41% of a month's actual water use. The tourism sector's water demand during summer could be as high as 60% of the total peak water demand in Akaroa.

This relationship between rainfall and tourist arrivals has been statistically shown in Zanzibar, Tanzania (Gössling, 2001), but can be shown for many destinations, such as Greece (Figure 2.2). As Figure 2.2 illustrates, arrivals are highest in July and August, when rainfall is at a low, increasing pressure on aquifers (Gössling, 2001). Where water demand is high during the dry season, as for instance in Cyprus, mixed solutions are usually implemented, such as storage of winter precipitation in dams and reservoirs, or transfers from more humid parts of the island. However, this may, as in the case of Cyprus, go along with unsustainable developments such as greater focus on desalination and overexploitation of coastal aquifers (Koundouri & Birol, 2011). Unsustainable water supplies can lead to greater energy use (desalination) or cause saltwater intrusion in coastal freshwater aquifers (groundwater overexploitation; Gössling, 2001). Peak tourism seasonal demand is thus of particular interest for water management and infrastructure costs, as peaks can only be handled through investments in infrastructure that will remain underused during the rest of the year (De Stefano, 2004).

The interrelationships between water availability and water use during dry seasons are relatively well understood, although there are also implications for relative water use levels as well as 'fixed' versus 'flexible' water

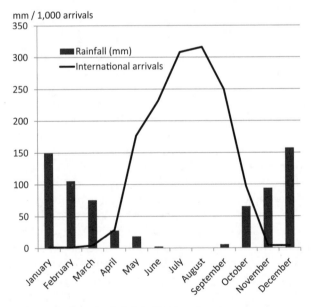

Figure 2.2 Tourist arrivals and rainfall in Rhodes, Greece
Source: Based on Europetravel (2010) and Hellenic National Meteorological Service (2014).

consumption (Gössling *et al.*, 2012). Tourism infrastructure requires specific amounts of water to be operational, a situation that has also been characterised as 'water lock-in' (Gössling, 2015). For instance, once a pool is built, it has to be filled with water, both for initial fillings and subsequent 'topping up' to replace evaporated water. Similarly, once specific resources such as golf courses and gardens are established as part of the tourism product, then they will also require specific amounts of water, often provided via reticulation during dry periods, in order to be maintained to a particular standard. This direct water use cannot be reduced below a certain minimum level, as it is needed to offer a tourism product that lives up to the quality expectations of the guests. Fixed water use is thus problematic from a water management perspective, as it affects direct water consumption rates over a season, and results in relationships of relatively higher per capita per-day water use during the low season as well as for establishments even if they have low occupancy rates (Figure 2.3; see also Antakayali *et al.*, 2008).

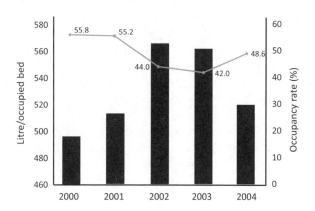

Figure 2.3 Interrelationships of water consumption and occupancy rates in Tunisia
Source: Eurostat (2009).

Text Box 2.1 The water demands of the golf courses of the Algarve

Golf is an important component of the attractiveness of the Algarve region of southern Portugal for tourism and amenity migration. The climate is characterised by mild winters with slight rainfall and hot and

(Continued)

Text Box 2.1 The water demands of the golf courses
of the Algarve (*Continued*)

dry summers. The region has an annual average temperature of 14°C
and annual precipitation that rarely exceeds 500 mm year^{-1}. Since
most of the rainfall falls in the winter, irrigation is needed during the
remaining months of the year in order to meet the water demands of
golf courses to maintain their greens and fairways. In order to do this,
Algarve's 40 courses are being irrigated with approximately 18 million
m^3 of water a year. Nearly all of the sprinkler water for the golf courses
is taken from boreholes.

Gago Pedras *et al.* (2014) examined three decades of meteorological
data and the long time-series of images taken by the US Landsat space-
craft to identify changes in the state of vegetation and chart changes in
water management practices on the courses. They found that, although
the consumption of water had increased five-fold since 1980, the practices of golf courses had become less wasteful. More efficient usage is
occurring because: grass technologies are being used that require less
water; the soils are being managed so that they hold more water; the
agro-climatic parameters are being more frequently monitored; and
water is being taken from a wider variety of sources. 'Deficit irrigation
strategies' are also being implemented, meaning that there is an accep-
tance of a reduction in quality during the driest times of year when
green-keepers and players recognise that overly lush greens and fairways
would be inappropriate. According to Gago Pedras, 'I think players who
understand the issues and the need to conserve water will accept playing
on courses that are a little yellow' (Amos, 2014).

Competing Water Uses

Tourism is usually considered as a labour-intensive industry that requires
limited skills, and thus is often favoured, particularly in poorer countries, as
an economic development opportunity (Zapata *et al.*, 2011). As such, tourism
is often supported by tax breaks, but there are also reported cases where the
sector has been favoured over others in terms of the allocation of resources,
including land and water (Hall, 2008). Such favoured allocation may be com-
pounded by other aspects of resource use, such as the fact that tourism will
usually have a higher purchasing power than other economic sectors. In
terms of water intensity, competition between tourism and other sectors is

most likely in coastal areas in developing countries or rural areas, where tourism may compete directly with agriculture or domestic consumption (e.g. Rico-Amoros *et al.*, 2013). For instance, in the case of Spain, the value added to water by tourism has been reported to be up to 60 times higher than in agriculture (Auernheimer & González, 2002, quoted in Downward & Taylor, 2007). With its considerably higher purchasing power, tourism can consequently outcompete agriculture, although this may also involve other sectors such as hydro-electricity production. Eurostat (2009: 9), for instance, noted that during the Mediterranean summer high season, use conflicts exist between 'agriculture, hydro-electricity production and household consumption', and hotels have sometimes been given priority in water provisions.

Equity issues in water resource allocation are also becoming increasingly recognised. For instance, average per capita uses of freshwater in Zanzibar, Tanzania were found to be 15 times higher for tourists (685 L per tourist per day) than for local residents (48 L per capita per day) (Gössling, 2001). In Cyprus, average consumption by tourists was estimated at 465 L per day, whereas local residents consumed 222 L per capita per day (Iacovides, 2011). On aggregated levels, similar relationships have been reported for Lanzarote, Spain, where tourists consume four times more water than residents

Plate 2.1 Biankini, Dead Sea Beach, West Bank. In recent years the water levels of the Dead Sea have been dropping at the rate of 1 m a year as a result of upstream water abstraction. This has meant that some tourism infrastructure that was at one time beside the sea is now some distance from it

(Medeazza, 2004), as well as in Indonesia, where villagers in the island of Bali were found to walk up to 3 km to collect water, whereas the island's golf courses were found to use around 3 million L of water per day (Tourism Concern, 2012; see also Cole, 2012, 2013). Similar concerns have been raised on several Caribbean islands regarding the development of golf tourism or water provisioning of cruise ships in water-stressed basins that have very limited storage capacity for local residents.

Water use conflicts between countries can be even more serious. Tensions about water are known to have existed in the Middle East for a long time, making countries including Israel, Jordan, the Palestinian Authority, Egypt and parts of Lebanon and Syria particularly vulnerable to conflict over water security issues (Hall *et al.*, 2004; Lipchin *et al.*, 2007). Particularly in Israel and Palestine, water is scarce, and surface water pumped from the Sea of Galilee and the drying up of the Jordan River and the Dead Sea have caused tensions with Jordan, which also depends on water from these sources (Eurostat, 2009).

Water Quality

Tourism depends on water of high quality, ideally of drinking water quality, to meet the expectations of tourists with regard to water safety. However, tourism also affects water quality as a result of wastewater and sewage discharge, which may contain nutrients as well as other pollutants such as chlorinated pool water or chemicals used to dissolve fats and oils during cleaning as well as in kitchens (Kuss *et al.*, 1990; Lazarova *et al.*, 2003). The impact of these substances on ecosystems will depend on various factors, such as their relative concentration, ocean currents dissolving these, and the background concentrations in the environment into which these are released. Nutrient discharge, for instance, is particularly critical in the tropics, where coastal waters are typically poor in nutrients (D'Elia & Wiebe, 1990). Where discharges of nutrients increase, this will usually result in biomass growth, especially growth in macroalgae, which can affect ecosystems and tourist perceptions negatively (e.g. Englebert *et al.*, 2008; Tomascik & Sander, 1986). For example, in an *ex post* survey of tourists in southern Sweden and their perceptions of algal blooms that occurred in the previous year, Nilsson and Gössling (2013) found that less than 1% perceived blooms as entirely unproblematic. Two percent of travellers were reported to have shortened their stay by returning home, 4% shortened their holiday in an affected area by moving to another one, and 10% changed activities. Most importantly 11% of respondents reported that experiences with algae had impacted them to such a degree that they would chose a different destination in the future.

As outlined above, marine algae growth is closely related to water quality. Yet, in the Mediterranean, the most important tourist region in the world, only 80% of all wastewater from both residents and tourists is collected in sewage networks, the remainder being discharged directly or indirectly (Scoullos, 2003). Compounding this, only half of all sewage networks appear to be connected to actual wastewater treatment facilities, with untreated sewage being discharged into the sea. In 2001 it was estimated that more than half of the largest coastal cities in the Mediterranean (>100,000 inhabitants) had no sewage treatment systems (UNEP, 2001), and only 10% possess a primary treatment system, 38% a secondary system and only 4% a tertiary treatment system (Hall, 2006). Furthermore, inappropriate siting of tourism facilities and infrastructure on foreshores, dune systems and wetlands can also exacerbate the impact of wastewater. UNEP (2001: 14) observed that mass tourism exacerbates issues of urbanisation impacts, 'leading to habitat loss for many wildlife species', and estimated that there has been a reduction in the wetland area of approximately 3 million ha by 93% since Roman times,

Plate 2.2 A water-efficient urinal at a bush-bar in Zanzibar, Tanzania. Unlike this home-designed appliance, modern urinals do not need water for flushing at all, and are odour free. A remaining problem in the case of the bush-bar and coastal areas worldwide is that wastewater is not treated, and is discharged into the ocean or seeps into the ground. Tourism can generate comparably large volumes of sewage where it is concentrated, but where background nutrient concentrations are low, as in the tropics, even small amounts can affect coastal environments

of which 1 million ha has been lost since 1950 (Hall, 2006). Such losses are significant, as wetlands can act as natural filters for wastewater as well as having many other environmental and economic benefits.

Tourism can contribute to comparably large amounts of sewage and wastewater, and is an activity usually concentrated in comparably small areas. As an example, the Hong Kong hotel sector was estimated to have generated more than 12 million m^3 of sewage in 2003 (Chan, 2005a). Discharge of wastewater into the sea is specifically problematic in the tropics, where oligotrophic waters are poor in nutrients, and where sewage can severely affect background concentrations of nutrients, leading to algae growth. However, in some cases, tourism can also contribute to improvements in water quality, for instance when sewage treatment systems are built that incorporate the wastewater generated by local communities, or when treatment systems are built in order to meet tourist expectations of higher water quality.

National levels of water use and their characteristics

In early assessments of water use in tourism focusing on direct water use, it was postulated that tourism is, on a global scale, a less significant factor in water use, contributing to an estimated 1 km^3 of freshwater use (Gössling, 2002). In light of more recent research, this conclusion has to be revised, as indirect water use is far more significant than direct water use. For instance, Cazcarro et al. (2014) calculated the net water footprint of tourism in Spain, i.e. including the water embodied in all goods consumed by tourism in this country, and excluding water exports. They conclude that the Spanish tourism system alone consumes 6.9 km^3 of freshwater annually, indicating a substantial underestimate of water demand in tourism if considering only direct freshwater use. Even other previously published results should be reconsidered in light of this. For instance, only one example of a destination appears to exist in the literature where tourism accounts for a significant share of direct water use. Saito (2013) calculated direct water consumption in Big Island (Hawaii) as 44.7% of total water consumption on the island. In all other countries, the share of direct water use appears to be considerably lower. In Cyprus two independent studies have estimated the proportion of tourism-related domestic water consumption as ranging between 15.2% (Gössling et al., 2012) and 16.9% (Iacovides, 2011). For most other countries, the share of direct water use appears to be considerably lower. Gössling et al. (2012) found that among the 55 countries they analysed, the share of domestic water use from the combination of domestic and international tourism ranged from 40% in Mauritius to less than 1% in Canada, Ukraine and Romania. Nonetheless, tourism accounted for a not insignificant amount greater than 5% of domestic water use in 22 of the countries. The proportion of domestic water used by tourism is shown in Table 2.2 for the top 10 international destination countries (by arrivals in 2013) and a sample of islands and semi-arid destination countries. The share of domestic water use by tourism was substantive in several island and semi-arid nations (Mauritius, Cyprus, Malta, Barbados), but others (e.g. Cape Verde, Mexico, Egypt) were less than in Spain and France (Table 2.2).

Table 2.2 also illustrates the differential economic value generated by tourism sector water use in these selected countries. A number of countries

Table 2.2 Tourism sector water use in major destination countries

	Domestic tourism share of domestic water use[a]	International tourism share of domestic water use[a]	Total tourism share of domestic water use[a]	Tourism % GDP in 2010[b]
Top 10 international destinations (by arrivals)				
France	6%	4%	10%	3.6%
USA	2%	<1%	2%	1.3%
Spain	6%	6%	12%	5.2%
China	3%	<1%	4%	1.7%
Italy	4%	2%	6%	3.2%
Turkey	3%	1%	4%	3.6%
Germany	4%	1%	5%	3.5%
UK	4%	2%	6%	3.5%
Russia	1%	<1%	1%	2.4%
Thailand	5%	1%	6%	9.5%
Major SIDS and semi-arid region destinations				
Mauritius	20%	20%	40%	16.8%
Cyprus	2%	17%	19%	15.2%
Malta	2%	12%	14%	17.9%
Barbados	3%	10%	13%	26.0%
Greece	4%	5%	9%	5.9%
Cape Verde	3%	3%	6%	26.3%
Israel	5%	1%	6%	3.4%
Morocco	2%	1%	3%	8.7%
Egypt	2%	<1%	2%	4.6%
Mexico	1%	1%	2%	1.7%

Source: [a]Adapted from Gössling *et al.* (2012). [b]World Economic Travel and Tourism Competitiveness Index (2013) *Data Analyser* (http://www.weforum.org/issues/travel-and-tourism-competitiveness/ttci-platform).

have a less than a 1:1 ratio between the proportion of national GDP generated by tourism and the proportion of domestic water use consumed by tourism (Mexico 1.7:2; Mauritius 16.8:40), whereas others are able to generate ratios of greater than 2:1 (Egypt 4.6:2; Barbados 26:13). This type of economic comparison will become increasingly important in the future (see Chapter 5) and deserves greater study to determine why these differences exist and how countries at the lower end of the water efficiency to tourism economic activity ratio can be improved.

Even though tourism's share in direct water consumption has been calculated at less than 5% of domestic water use, the inclusion of embodied or indirect water use is likely to substantially increase this share, particularly in water and tourism hotspots, such as small islands in the Caribbean and countries in the Mediterranean (Clarke & King, 2004; Gössling et al., 2012; Hadjikakou, 2014). Water management thus not only needs to take into account direct and indirect flows of water (see Chapter 3), but it also needs to consider grey, blue and grey water flows, and whether these water flows are consumptive. Figure 2.4 illustrates this for a hypothetical destination, where part of the produce consumed in tourism – for instance local foodstuffs – is grown with local water, involving both rainfall and surface water for irrigation. A share of this water will evaporate or transpire and be lost to the local water cycle. Another share is embedded in the produce; this will be eaten and then return to the water cycle as grey water, which again can be treated and partially be reused, or be discharged as sewage (black water). A considerably larger proportion of

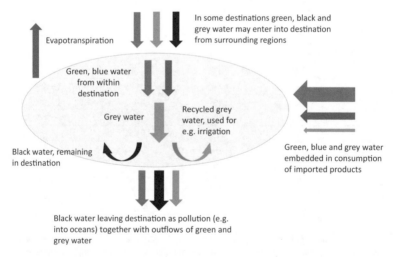

Figure 2.4 Water flow in a destination: Blue, green, grey and black water flows

the water used in the tourist destination will, however, be imported, with a small fraction entering the destination's water cycle as grey water.

Conclusions

Even though water use is anticipated to become more efficient in the future, overall consumption will increase significantly in both absolute and relative terms. For instance, Vörösmarty et al. (2000) suggested that global water use (AR) will be 4700 km^2 per year by 2025, to which tourism would by then contribute almost 4% (175 km^3; cf. Gössling & Peeters, 2014). However, this excludes a considerable share of water use (cf. Cazcarro et al., 2014), where water is partially abstracted in areas that are already facing water stress. Water issues are also set to become even more demanding given the implications of greater urbanisation and climate change (see Chapter 5). Given this context there is greater imperative for the tourism industry to become more efficient in their water use and limit production of wastewater. In order to understand better how this might be done, the next chapter looks to better understand and measure the impact of tourism on water consumption and wastewater.

Further reading

Useful regional studies on tourism and water use include:

Cazcarro, I., Hoekstra, A.Y. and Sánchez Chóliz, J. (2014) The water footprint of tourism in Spain. *Tourism Management* 40, 90–101.
Gössling, S. (2001) The consequences of tourism for sustainable water use on a tropical island: Zanzibar, Tanzania. *Journal of Environmental Management* 61 (2), 179–191.
Hadjikakou, M., Chenoweth, J. and Miller, G. (2013a) Estimating the direct and indirect water use of tourism in the eastern Mediterranean. *Journal of Environmental Management* 114, 548–556.

Studies of sewage and wastewater issues include:

Chan, W.W. (2005a) Partial analysis of the environmental costs generated by hotels in Hong Kong. *International Journal of Hospitality Management* 24 (4), 517–531.
Chan, W.W. and Lam, J.C. (2001) Environmental costing of sewage discharged by hotels in Hong Kong. *International Journal of Contemporary Hospitality Management* 13 (5), 218–226.
Chan, W.W., Wong, K. and Lo, J. (2009) Hong Kong hotels' sewage: Environmental cost and saving technique. *Journal of Hospitality and Tourism Research* 33 (3), 329–346.

A destination-based study that seeks to integrate both water use and wastewater issues is:

Cullen, R., Dakers, A., McNicol, J., Meyer-Hubbert, G., Simmons, D.G. and Fairweather, J. (2003) *Tourism, Water and Waste in Akaroa: Implications of Tourist Demand on Infrastructure.* Tourism Recreation Research and Education Centre (TRREC) Report No. 38, Lincoln: Lincoln University.

3 Measuring Water Use in Tourism

As has been outlined in Chapter 2, water consumption in tourism has usually been measured in hotels, focusing on water throughput (Styles *et al.*, 2015). For instance, early studies of water use in tourism (e.g. Gössling, 2001; Grenon & Batisse, 1991) assessed total water consumption divided by the number of guest nights to derive values of water use per tourist per day. Such measures of water consumption are still the standard, as hotels represent the main loci of water use and do not usually engage in more detailed measurements. However, as Chapter 2 demonstrated, water consumption is more complex when considering all the water that is needed to maintain the tourism system. Figure 3.1 distinguishes three main dimensions of water use, including direct water use, indirect water use and systemic water use. *Direct water use* refers to the water used on site at the hotel, i.e. including: the irrigation of gardens, lawns or golf courses; the filling of pools and filter backwash; in-room uses including showers and baths, toilet flushing and tap water; laundry and cleaning; as well as water used for food preparation in kitchens. *Indirect water use*, also called 'global' or 'embodied' water, refers to water that is imported in the form of foods, energy, hotel infrastructure, shopping, services, activities, marketing and sales (see Chapter 2). Finally, *systemic water use* refers to other aspects of the tourism production system that incur a water 'cost', for instance the construction of roads or marinas, or employee transport. The following sections provide more detailed information on water use in these categories.

Direct Water Use: Accommodation

Most studies of water use in tourism have summarised water use in accommodation on the basis of litres (L) per tourist per day (Gössling *et al.*,

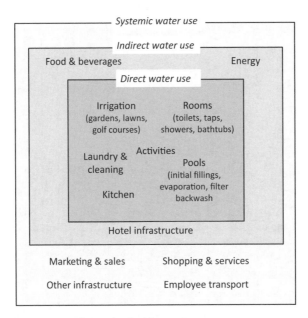

Figure 3.1 Water consumption embodied in tourism
Source: Authors.

2012), with the exception of one study by Deng and Burnett (2002), who calculated water use on the basis of a water use index, measured for one year as the consumption of m³ of water per m² of floor area. Where direct water use has been measured, a very large range in consumption has been identified, varying between 84 and 2425 L per tourist per day, including water use in rooms, for gardens and pool irrigation (for a complete overview of studies see Table 3.1). Whereas there is uncertainty regarding global averaged water use values, systemic reviews of summer destinations (Deyà Tortella & Tirado, 2011) or hotel chains such as Scandic or Hilton (Bohdanowicz & Martinac, 2007) have consistently reported direct mean water use values exceeding 300 L/guest night (see also WWF, 2004). Based on available evidence, average global direct water consumption values are estimated to be in the order of 350 L/day (Gössling, 2015).

A considerable share of this water use may be staff related. For instance, Lamei *et al.* (2009), in their work on hotels in Sharm El Sheikh, Egypt, reported staff water use values of 250 L per day per person in staff housing and 30 L per day for each member of staff during working hours. These values may be included in higher estimates of hotels, as in particular resort hotels in remote locations in developing countries may offer staff housing

Table 3.1 Water use per guest per day, various accommodation contexts

Country/region	Accommodation type	Water use per tourist per day	Reference
Mediterranean	Mostly hotels	250 L	Grenon and Batisse, 1991, quoted in GFANC, 1997
Mediterranean	Campsites	145 L	Scherb, 1975, quoted in GFANC, 1997
Mediterranean	All accommodation	440–880 L	WWF, 2004
Benidorm, Spain	Campsites	84 L	Rico-Amoros et al., 2009
Benidorm, Spain	1-star hotel	174 L	Rico-Amoros et al., 2009
Benidorm, Spain	2-star hotel	194 L	Rico-Amoros et al., 2009
Benidorm, Spain	3-star hotel	287 L	Rico-Amoros et al., 2009
Benidorm, Spain	4-star hotel	361 L	Rico-Amoros et al., 2009
Greece	5-star hotel	338 L	Gössling, 2014
Greece	5-star hotel	675 L	Gössling, 2014
Greece	4-star hotel	234 L	Gössling, 2014
Tunisia	Hotels	466 L	Eurostat, 2009
Morocco	Apartments	180 L	Eurostat, 2009
Morocco	3-star hotel, or villa	300 L	Eurostat, 2009
Morocco	4-star hotel	400 L	Eurostat, 2009
Morocco	5-star hotel	500 L	Eurostat, 2009
Morocco	Luxury 5-star hotel	600 L	Eurostat, 2009
Sarigerme, Turkey	4-star hotel	400 L – >1,000 L	Antakyali et al., 2008
Sharm El Sheikh, Egypt	Hotels/resorts	≤500 L (per bed)	Hafez and El Manharawy, 2002
Sharm El Sheikh, Egypt	5-star hotels	1410–2190 L (per room)	Lamei et al., 2006, in Lamei, 2009
Sharm El Sheikh, Egypt	Hotels	400 L	Lamei et al., 2009
Zanzibar, Tanzania	Guesthouses	248 L	Gössling, 2001

Zanzibar, Tanzania	Hotels	931 L	Gössling, 2001
Zanzibar, Tanzania	Hotels and guesthouses	685 L (weighted average)	Gössling, 2001
Jamaica	Unclear	527–1596 L (average 980 L)	Meade and del Monaco, 1999, quoted in Bohdanowicz and Martinac, 2007 and Antakyali et al., 2008
Thailand		913–3423 L (per room)	CUC and AIT, 1998, quoted in Bohdanowicz and Martinac, 2007
Philippines	4-star hotel	1802 L (per room)	Alexander, 2002
Philippines	Unclear	1499 L (per room)	Alexander and Kennedy, 2002, quoted in Bohdanowicz and Martinac, 2007
Hong Kong	Hotels	336–3198 L (per room)	Deng, 2003
Australia	Hotels	750 L (per room)	Australian Institute of Hotel Engineers, 1993, quoted in Bohdanowicz and Martinac, 2007
Australia	Large hotels	300 L (per room)	Smith et al., 2009a
Melbourne, Australia	Various	227–435 L	City West Water, 2006
USA	Unclear	382–787 L (per room)	Davies and Cahill, 2000, quoted in Bohdanowicz and Martinac, 2007
USA	National accommodation survey	545 L (per room)	1988 survey in Stipanuk and Robson, 1995
Las Vegas, USA	Hotels/resorts	303 L	Cooley et al., 2007
Seattle, USA	Hotels – various	378–1514 L (per room)	O'Neill and Siegelbaum and The RICE Group, 2002
Germany	Unclear	90–900 L (average 340 L)	Despretz, 2001, quoted in Bohdanowicz and Martinac, 2007 and Antakyali et al., 2008

(Continued)

Table 3.1 (*Continued*)

Country/region	Accommodation type	Water use per tourist per day	Reference
Germany	Unclear	275 L	Nattrass and Altomare, 1999, quoted in Bohdanowicz and Martinac, 2007
Scandinavia	Hilton chain	516 L	Bohdanovicz and Martinac, 2007
Scandinavia	Scandic chain	216 L	Bohdanovicz and Martinac, 2007
Coastal Normandy, France	Second home	102 L	Langumier and Ricou, 1995
Coastal Normandy, France	Campsite	92 L	Langumier and Ricou, 1995
Coastal Normandy, France	Hotel restaurant	259 L	Langumier and Ricou, 1995
Coastal Normandy, France	Hotel	175 L	Langumier and Ricou, 1995
Coastal Normandy, France	Other tourist accommodation	115 L	Langumier and Ricou, 1995
Coastal Normandy, France	Main home	114 L	Langumier and Ricou, 1995

Source: Based on Gössling *et al.* (2012), updated.

on site. As noted earlier, there is a general lack of disaggregated end-use water data for hotels, including specific water use for gardens, pools, rooms, laundry, food preparation (kitchens) and other purposes. This situation is further complicated by different studies collecting data on different dimensions of water use. Table 3.2 provides a breakdown of water consumption by mode of use in USA lodging facilities. The three largest water users are guest room activities, once-through cooling, and laundry. However, the study is also notable for its recognition of the role of leaks in water use (which is something that is surprisingly rarely assessed in water

Table 3.2 Breakdown of water consumption in USA lodging facilities

Consumption category	San Francisco[a] (% use)	Irvine[b] (% use)	New York[c] (% use)
Guest room			29.1%
Once-through cooling			17.4%
Laundry			16.2%
Cooling/heating			10.1%
Sanitation			6.4%
Landscape			3.8%
Kitchen			3.1%
Leaks			0.6%
Unaccounted for			13.3%
– of which landscape			3.8%
Cooling tower	13%	12%	
Landscaping		37%	
Kitchen		17%	
Laundry	13%	9%	
Showers/baths	47%	15%	
Toilets	16%	8%	
Room faucets	11%	2%	
Total	100%	100%	100%

Notes: [a]Water consumption for a 350-room downtown San Francisco hotel, which consumes an average of 123 gallons per day per guest. It is an older property with little public space and no restaurant as part of its meterage. It has unrestricted shower heads and five gallons per flush tank toilets.
[b]Water consumption for a 540-room, full-service hotel in Irvine, California. The hotel has 5 gallon per flush tank toilets and 3 gallon per minute shower heads. Water consumption averages 207 gallons per day per guest.
[c]The above are estimated figures for lodging properties New York-wide.
Source: Derived from Aulbach (1995) and Polansky et al. (2008).

management studies in tourism), as well as the fact that there was a substantial amount of water use that could not be clearly accounted for but of which 3.8% of total use was estimated as being used for landscape and grounds maintenance (Polansky *et al.*, 2008). This stands in stark contrast to some earlier American studies (Aulbach, 1995). However, even this study noted enormous variations in estimates of water use depending on the methodological approach that was used.

Text Box 3.1 1990 American Hotel and Motel Association survey of water use in hotels

One of the first studies of water use in the hospitality industry was undertaken by the American Hotel and Motel Association in 1990 (Stipanuk & Robson, 1995). The study was based on 408 valid responses out of 1800 questionnaires that were mailed out (Table 3.3 provides an overview of the characteristics of the hotels in the survey). Although somewhat dated, the results provide a significant benchmark against which to measure progress in water conservation both in North America and elsewhere in the world. The survey found substantial variability in American hotel properties with respect to water consumption patterns. In terms of median consumption the resorts/casinos/conference centre category was highest, followed by deluxe and luxury accommodation. There was a clear relationship between the size of the property with respect to the number of rooms and levels of water consumption, with the larger properties having the highest levels of water consumption per available room per day (Table 3.4). In 1990 the only conservation

Table 3.3 Summary of statistics of hotels in 1990 USA accommodation study

Total number of hotels	408
Percentage with a commercial kitchen	76%
Percentage with a pool	84%
Percentage with an on-site laundry	89%
Percentage with a central chiller	50%
Percentage irrigating landscaping	51%
Percentage using water conservation techniques	82%
Mean guests per occupied room	1.5

Source: Derived from Redlin and deRoos (1995).

Table 3.4 Water consumption per available room per day, USA, 1990

Accommodation category	25th percentile L	Median L	75th percentile L
<75 rooms	269	382	534
75–149 rooms	345	469	621
150–299 rooms	485	579	746
300–499 rooms	575	697	871
500+ rooms	621	787	961
Resort/casino/conference centre	670	961	1257
Convention/midmarket	473	579	715
Limited service/economy	257	356	511
Deluxe	742	878	1283
Luxury/first class	549	659	837
All-suite: economy and upscale	390	526	731

Source: Data derived from Redlin and deRoos (1995).

technology that had been widely adopted in the USA accommodation sector was the use of low-flow shower heads (77% of all hotels) and 33% of hotels used low water consumption toilets, while no hotels in the survey used grey water to supply toilets and only 2% were using grey water for irrigation (Table 3.5). Perhaps not surprisingly given their higher levels of water consumption per available room per day, larger properties

Table 3.5 Percentage of hotel properties using specific water conservation methods, USA, 1990

Conservation method	Number of rooms in property					
	<75	75–149	150–299	300–499	500+	All hotels
Low-flow shower heads	66%	70%	81%	83%	81%	77%
Low-consumption toilets	32%	27%	27%	37%	44%	33%
Reclamation of laundry wastewater	0%	0%	0%	5%	17%	4%
Grey water to supply toilets	0%	0%	0%	0%	0%	0%
Grey water to irrigate	0%	1%	2%	4%	3%	2%

Source: Derived from Redlin and deRoos (1995).

(Continued)

Text Box 3.1 1990 American Hotel and Motel Association survey of water use in hotels (Continued)

Table 3.6 Indicative examples of water consumption for various accommodation categories and types of consumption in USA 1990 hotel survey[a]

Hotel category[b]	On-site laundry		Kitchens		Irrigation			Cooling towers	Swimming pools
	L per kg range	% of total water use	L per meal range	% of total water use	Number of months irrigating	L/ha/day range	% of total water use	% of total water use	% of total water use
Centre city	9.43–35.72	5–30%	9.24–59.85	4–25%	4–12	10,102–70,155	1–11%	6–21%	0.01–0.86%
Resort	13.94–29.29	6–19%	25.29–58.67L	3–18%	7–12	36,490–61,025	16–44%	1–11%	0.26–13.10%
Convention	12.27–35.72	10–30%	9.24–58.60L	4–25%	4–12	10,102–70,155	1–11%	6–20%	0.06–0.12%
Midmarket	8.18–17.27	8–10%	–	–	12	30,559	25%	9%	0.34–0.86%
Luxury	9.43–19.44	5–22%	9.08–59.85L	10–22%	5–12	9,981–20,784	10–14%	6–19%	0.01–1.96%
Suburban	–	–	9.69–52.73L	–	12	20,784	14%	6–19%	0.20%

Notes: [a]Water consumption figures have been converted into metric from US units of measurement.
[b]Hotel categories are not mutually exclusive. In some categories data existed for only one property.
Source: Data derived from Redlin and deRoos (1995).

were also more likely to have adopted water conservation methods. Nevertheless, as Table 3.6 illustrates, there was substantial variation in water use per size of property and category. Although not indicated in the table, this was also a function of location and climatic conditions during the period when data were collected. Nevertheless, the different ranges of values that exist between properties is a theme that continues to the present day in research into water conservation and highlights the importance of each property requiring individual assessments, although broader data are extremely important for benchmarking purposes.

The 1990 study also noted changes in water use on a daily as well as a seasonal basis. Sundays and Mondays were high water consumption days, while Tuesdays and Wednesdays were low consumption days. Overall usage was reasonably stable, with less than 18% variance from day to day. In contrast, on a monthly basis water usage was at its lowest in December and highest in August. Depending on the location and the type of hotel, water use fluctuated between a minimum of 23% of average daily use and a maximum of 224% of average daily use (Stipanuk & Robson, 1995).

Although not noted in the 1990 USA accommodation study (and only rarely commented on since then in much of the tourism, hospitality and water conservation literature), not only is there variance in water consumption on a daily, weekly, monthly and seasonal basis, but also during the day. Indeed, the greatest variance for water and hot water consumption (with consequent energy demands) occurs as a result of demand for morning and evening showers and baths in which peak demand may be just under six times the average daily water flow (Lehr, 1995). Peaks in demand, however, will vary with the nature of the property and its clientele, i.e. time-constrained business travellers versus vacation tourists. Moreover, from a supply perspective, peak demand for water for showers, baths and washing (morning and night) also coincides with demands for hot water for hotel kitchens. Although there are some cultural differences in preferences for washing times and showers versus baths, the morning and evening periods of peak demand still remain. Table 3.7 indicates some of the potential differences in hot water use in USA lodging facilities.

Gardens and lawns

Where gardens, lawns and/or golf courses exist, water use for irrigation and reticulation will be substantial, although this will depend on the

Table 3.7 Hot water use in USA lodging facilities

Category	Average occupancy (persons per room)	Hot water characteristics	Peak periods of hot water use	Back-of-house requirements
Deluxe	1.2	Largest per capita water consumption.	Morning, evening peaks; more uniform usage throughout the day.	Full food service. Full laundry; three-sheet service; extra towel load.
Luxury/full service/ first class	1.2–1.3	High per capita hot water consumption. Defined sustained peaks.	Morning, evening peaks; lesser noon peaks; lower daytime usage.	Full food service. Full laundry. Possible concessions.
Mid-scale, full service	1.2–1.3	High per capita hot water consumption. Defined sustained peaks.	Morning, evening peaks; lesser noon peaks; lower daytime usage.	Full food service. Full laundry.
Convention	1.4–1.6	Peaks during conventions. Similar to luxury hotels.	Heavy morning and pre-dinner peaks.	Banquet facilities; multiple kitchens. Full laundry.
Limited service	1.1	Guestroom load dominant. Limited meeting space.	Morning guestroom peaks; low daytime use; moderate evening peak.	Limited food facilities; kitchenettes in suites. Sometimes uses outside services.
Upscale all-suites	2.0	Longer stays by guests; more apartment-like usage. Laundry units use more water/person.	Morning peaks; moderate daytime use; evening peak – similar to residential patterns.	Limited food facilities; kitchenettes in suites. Full laundry.
Economy all-suites	2.0–2.2	Longer stays by guests; more apartment-like usage. Lower consumption than upscale.	Morning peaks; moderate daytime use; evening peak – similar to residential patterns.	Limited food facilities; kitchenettes in suites. Laundry services vary from minimal to full.

Table 3.7 (Continued)

Category	Average occupancy (persons per room)	Hot water characteristics	Peak periods of hot water use	Back-of-house requirements
Resort	1.9–2.4	Higher consumption; more evenly distributed throughout day. Ski resorts produce special peak problems.	Less defined morning peak; larger evening peak.	Full food service; expanded beverage operation. Full laundry; extra towel load.
Conference centre	1.3–1.4	Use of facilities and back of house is not consistent.	Morning peaks; moderate daytime use.	Full food service. Full laundry.
Casino	1.3–1.4	Activity peaks in evening hours. Heavy hot water usage due to multiple baths/ showers.	Evening peak; heavy usage throughout the night.	Full food service; extensive beverage operations; concessions. Full laundry; heavy uniform laundering.
Economy	1.6–1.8	Short stays; low consumption; minimal services/ amenities.	Many peaks; little daytime use; evening usage spread out.	Limited or no food service. Many have no laundries.

Source: After Lehr (1995).

climate, rainfall, evapotranspiration and plant species. Water use will generally be highest in arid zones, and where high water demand plant species have been planted. Where gardens are extensive, water use for irrigation can make up 50% of total water use in hotels, with relative shares and absolute water use being considerably smaller in guesthouses and other small-scale accommodation (see also Figure 3.2, with results from a case study of 22 hotels and guesthouses in Zanzibar, Tanzania). In absolute numbers, a weighted average of 465 L per tourist per day for irrigation in hotels was found in Zanzibar, compared to 37 L per tourist per day in guesthouses (Gössling, 2001). This difference can be explained by the fact that guesthouses usually do not have gardens, other than a few potted plants, whereas hotels have to contend with the poor storage capacity of local soils, high

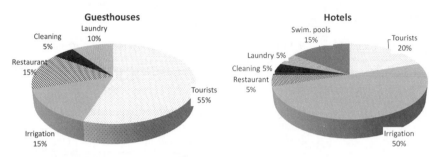

Figure 3.2 Distribution of water use by end-use, Zanzibar, Tanzania
Source: Gössling (2001).

evaporation and the use of flowering plant species not adapted to local climatic conditions. In another study of hotels in Rhodes, Greece, irrigation-related water consumption of 75 L per tourist per day was measured (Gössling, 2015).

It should be noted that a number of consultancies identified different distributions in water use, but it remains unclear whether these results are valid, given considerable uncertainties regarding measurements. For instance, Smith *et al.* (2009a) reported that in-room consumption was highest in hotels in Australia (42%), followed by kitchens (16%), laundry (15%), public toilets (12%), cooling towers (10%), irrigation (3%) and swimming pools (2%).

Plate 3.1 Large green areas in dry climates are water intense. Irrigation is, in resort hotels in warm climates, the most important direct or local water-consuming factor

Plate 3.2 A pond of grey water for lawn irrigation has been integrated into the landscape of the Sugar Beach Resort, Mauritius

Notably, no data on absolute water use were presented in this study. Likewise, a study of water use in the Iberotel Sarigeme Park Hotel in Turkey found that the kitchen and laundry together constituted the largest water use (30%), followed by swimming pools (20–25%), and guest rooms (12%) (Antakyali *et al.*, 2008).

Pools

Studies of water use in swimming pools typically fail to assess all aspects of water consumption, i.e. (i) the initial filling of the pool; (ii) evaporation and re-filling pools on a daily basis; and (iii) the cleaning of pool filters through backwashing (a process of reverse water pumping that cleans the filter). In a study of swimming pools in three hotels in Rhodes, Greece, Gössling (2015) found that initial fillings of hotel pools amounted to 7–40 L per guest night, i.e. dividing initial fillings (pool volumes) by the overall number of guest nights stayed in the hotel (Table 3.8). Spa indoor pool fillings were found to add very small amounts of water per tourist per guest night (approximately 1 L). Evaporation was difficult to assess, as it depends on various factors: pool water surface; whether the pool is undisturbed or occupied, with the number of people increasing water movement and evaporation surface; water transfer out of the pool on bodies and in swimsuits; pool water temperature; and air temperature, humidity and the vapour pressure of moisture in air (Shah, 2013).

Table 3.8 Water use for pools and spas, Rhodes, Greece

	Hotel A*****	Hotel B*****	Hotel C****
Pool area (m²)	1645 m²	2065 m²	425 m²
Pool volume (m³)	2301 m³	No data available	420 m³
Evaporation[a]	9870 L/day	12,390 L/day	2550 L/day
Filter number	15	12	6
Filter backwash[b] (estimate)	Backwash 1 × /day, exact volume unknown	2.3 m³/day	Backwash 1 × /day, sometimes 2 × /day, exact volume unknown
Spa indoor	56 m²/84 m³	80 m²/no data available	48 m²/41 m³
Pool area per bed (excluding spa)	10.7 m²/bed	10.2 m²/bed	2.1 m²/bed

Notes: [a]Assumed at 6 L/m²; dependent on temperature (water and air), humidity, wind and vapour pressure.
[b]Filters are sized based upon pool volume (m³), pool turnover rate (the time in hours required to completely cycle the total volume of water through the filter, typically 2–4 hours), and the particular flow rate for a given type of filter, such as sand media.
Source: Gössling (2015).

In one study of a swimming pool in Mallorca, Hof and Schmitt (2011) reported daily losses of 5 L/m²/day, and annual water losses of 1.83 m³/m². These values were averaged throughout the year, i.e. including a hot summer season and a comparatively cold winter. Moreover, it is unclear as to whether the year when measurements were made is representative of long-term averages: particularly under scenarios of global warming, variation in average values may increase. For an estimate, the Hof and Schmitt values would, if applied to Hotel A (Table 3.8) translate into daily water losses of 9870 L/day, or 33 L per guest night (at an average evaporation of 6 L/m²/day in summer, and an assumed 85% occupancy rate over the season). Again, the spa indoor pool would add about 1 L/tourist/day to this. Water use for filter backwashing is still insufficiently quantified. In the Rhodes study (Gössling, 2015), it amounted to 2.3 m³/day in one hotel, corresponding to about 7 L/guest night at 85% occupancy over the season, but further research is needed to confirm these values. Another trend observed in Rhodes and potentially relevant even more globally is the construction of private pools, which can significantly increase overall water consumption.

Plate 3.3 Pool filters need to be cleaned through backwash. Depending on the measure used, this can require considerable amounts of freshwater

Plate 3.4 Private pools are a new trend in many destinations, and can considerably increase overall water consumption

Text Box 3.2 Pool filter and treatment systems

A wide range of filter and treatment systems is in use for swimming pools. Depending on the model, these systems are more or less energy and water intense (backwash), and use more or less environmentally harmful chemicals for treatment. Together, filters and treatment systems are intended to ensure that microbial contamination is kept at acceptable levels from a health and safety perspective, as well as exposure to chemicals for the bathers. Microbial hazards stem from faeces released by bathers, contaminated water sources, animal contact with the water (e.g. birds) or other human body related contamination of the water (WHO, 2009). Where nutrient levels are sufficiently high, and where water is warm and aerated, viruses, bacteria, protozoa and fungi can grow, and involve, for example, adenovirus, hepatitis A, norovirus, echovirus (viruses), *Shigella* and *Escherichia coli* (bacteria), or *Giardia* and *Cryptosporidium* (protozoa). These can cause vomiting and fever, diarrhoea and nausea, as well as haemolytic uremic syndrome.

Disinfection using chemicals is intended to reduce these sources of illness in pools. Together with other additions to pool water, such as sweat, soap residues, cosmetics and suntan oil, these chemicals can affect swimmers through direct ingestion, inhalation and dermal contact, with children in particular being exposed to high levels of water ingestion (WHO, 2009). The most frequently used chemical disinfectants include chlorine, chlorine dioxide, bromochlorodimethylhydantoin (BCDMH), ozone and ultraviolet radiation. These treatment systems inactivate microorganisms chemically (chlorination) or physically (radiation). The relative intensity of disinfection measures is linked to various factors, such as the number of bathers, source water, size and location of the pool, and operational systems in place. As a general rule, it is important to minimise sources of contamination, and to dilute and filtrate pool water continuously. WHO (2009) recommends diluting pool water with no less than 30 L of freshwater per bather per day, which would considerably increase direct water consumption, irrespective of pool size or volume. As noted in other parts of this book, this is rarely a practice in most hotels, where pools are only 'topped up' to replace evaporated water, and represents an issue where environmental (water savings, eventually water-heating demands) and health issues (pathogen reduction) have to be weighed against each other. There is general consensus, however, that showering prior to entering pools can significantly reduce contaminant loads (e.g. Chowdhury *et al.*, 2014).

Filter systems are typically operated using media such as graded sand. Pressurised water is pumped through the sand, which holds back suspended particulates down to sizes of 7 μm (Korkosz *et al.*, 2012). More recently, 'crystal sand filters', containing crushed glass, appear to be being implemented on a broader basis, replacing sand. These filters are more effective and reduce backwash times by about 30% (personal communication, Mina Splagkounia-Zahariou, Sustainability-CSR Manager, Thomas Cook Concept Hotels, 17 July 2014). Other filter systems include cartridge filters or other media such as diatomaceous earth.

The treatment of pool water usually involves chlorine which, as a chemical, can affect swimmers and also pose a treatment problem, for instance when grey water is to be used for irrigation, or where pool water is to be treated. A number of novel systems have been developed in recent years including, for instance, a natural chlorine system that uses seawater containing sodium chloride (NaCl), which can be pumped through a chlorine generator, oxidising chloride ions through the electrolysis of NaCl. Such systems have, for instance, been used by the Sunwing hotels in Greece, with an installation cost of €1000 per 100 m^3 of pool water. According to Mina Splagkounia-Zahariou (personal communication, 17 July 2014), the natural chlorine system has reduced concentrated chlorine use by 40%, and is 50% less costly, with a running cost of €0.028 per hour per 100 m^3 of pool water. Other systems based on copper ionisation and oxidation of water have also been developed in recent years, and avoid the use of chlorine altogether.

Rooms

In-room water use includes showers, bathtubs, toilets and water taps. As outlined, very limited data appear to exist on water use for these. Data for in-room water consumption can only be generated on the basis of individual measurements of water flows for each water-consuming device in the room. It is rare, however, for hotels to engage in such specific measurements. Alternatively, it is possible, although less accurate, to interview tourists on water use, implying a greater degree of inaccuracy. Such data have been presented for one hotel in Rhodes, Greece (Gössling, 2015). The survey ($n = 101$) indicated flush-frequencies of three to 15 times per tourist per day (toilets inside rooms, as well as public toilets in the hotel). Cleaning by staff added two to three flushes per room per day, resulting in an average estimated value of 45 L per tourist per day for toilet use. As outlined, this value might vary depending on tourist behaviour (actual flush frequency), residence times in the hotel (guests may spend less time in city hotels than in resort hotels), as well as toilet technology (large/small flush options).

In the same study (Gössling, 2015), shower use was found to average 2.6 times per tourist per day ($n = 100$), with a range of one to seven showers being taken per day, including in-room showers, showers at pools, and showers in public areas. However, such installations may not exist in lower budget city hotels or small-scale accommodation, and is thus a characteristic of the resort-type hotel in warm climates. Shower times varied between one and 15 minutes, with an estimated average of two showers per day with an average duration of five minutes. At average measured water flows of 7–12 L/minute, depending on water pressure and showerhead, the result is an average water use of 70 L per day. Bathtub use has to be added to these values. In the survey conducted in Rhodes, only 28% of respondents reported using bathtubs at all. Of those using the bathtub, 68% used it only once, although there was also a share of 17% that used the bathtub every day. Overall, this resulted in an average bathtub-related water use value of 3 L per guest per day. The survey is not representative as results may vary depending on hotel type and standard (low-budget and bed-and-breakfast type accommodation may not have bathtubs at all, whereas 5-star hotels may offer jacuzzis), guest

Plate 3.5 Rain showers are the latest implementation in many luxurious hotels, causing considerable growth in water use. In comparison, low-flow showers use microholes and can reduce water use to 6 L per minute, while maintaining the impression of a generous water flow. Hotels also need to adjust water pressure to about 3–4 bar in order to reduce flow speeds. The example of a more luxurious low-flow showerhead in the photograph is, however, somewhat problematic, as metallic surfaces need to be cleaned carefully to become shiny, which is labour and potentially water intense

type (business/leisure), guest nationality and/or cultural/individual prefer-ence. Finally, with regard to water taps, daily water use values of 8 L per guest per day were determined, based on interviews and flow speeds of 4.5 L/min. Even these values are not representative.

Laundry

Laundry is an important aspect of water use, because many hotels exchange towels and bed linen every day. Only one single study, Bodhanowicz and Martinac (2007), reports specific laundry values. These vary, for the Scandic and Hilton chains, between 0.7 and 3.1 kg/guest night (Scandic hotels: mean 2 kg/guest night), and 0.7–16.2 kg per guest night (Hilton hotels: mean 4.1 kg/guest night). Bodhanowicz and Martinac (2007) do not report to which water use values this corresponds. More detailed data are provided in Table 3.9 (Mina Splagkounia-Zahariou, personal communication, 22 July 2014) for two 5-star hotels in Greece. The table shows that there is a consider-able range of laundry items, including bed sheets, pillow covers, bathrobes, various towels, kitchen towels and sofa pillow covers. In total, 20 items need to be washed, generating 618,230 items of laundry in hotel A (307,196 guest nights) and 228,492 items of laundry in hotel B (49,379 guest nights). This corresponds to 0.74 kg of laundry per guest night in hotel A, and 1.33 kg in hotel B. Note that laundry in the two hotels studied need to be seen as low, as both hotels engage in a wide range of environmental measures, actively trying to reduce laundry volumes. In other 5-star hotels in Greece, laundry volumes may consequently be higher, with an estimated 30 L of water needed per guest night for laundry, at 11 L of water per kg (Gössling, 2015). Higher laundry volumes per guest per day are a result of sport and health centres, as well as being affected by textile quality and/or weight of laundry items, including very large towels for spa facilities or beach use.

Cohen et al. (2009) reported on the water use implications of different laundry technologies in California. Standard washer extractors look and operate similarly to residential front-loading machines, but hold between 30 and 800 pounds of laundry and use 3–4 gallons of water per pound of laun-dry (gpp; 1 gallon = 3.785 L). However, water-efficient washer extractors have built-in water recycling systems that lower water use to less than 2.5 gpp. Cohen et al. (2009) suggest that the average Californian hotel with 125 rooms and a 70% occupancy rate will use more than 604,000 gallons of water every year (approximately 2.42 million L) just to wash bed sheets and towels with a standard commercial washing extractor (4.0 gpp). Therefore, if such a hotel installs a water-efficient washing extractor, it can potentially save close to 38% of its water consumption. For larger properties with a

Table 3.9 Laundry items, unit numbers and weight at two Rhodes hotels, 2013

	Unit use, hotel A	Unit use, hotel B	Weight per unit (kg)	Hotel A, total weight (kg)	Hotel B, total weight (kg)
Bed sheets, single	72,407	18,282	0.50	36,204	9,141
Bed sheets, double	5,925	150	0.85	5,036	128
Mattress protection	44	52	0.90	40	47
Pillow covers	108,556	27,015	0.15	16,283	4,052
Pique blankets, single	112	270	1.00	112	270
Quilt covers	70,313	12,861	0.90	63,282	11,575
Bath robes	9,410	5,923	1.20	11,292	7,108
Bath towels	39,284	24,215	0.60	23,570	14,529
Face towels	11,522	25,362	0.15	1,728	3,804
Bathmats	6,733	15,441	0.20	1,347	3,088
Make up towels 30 × 30		5,070	0.12	0	608
Beach towels	61,971	12,141	0.74	45,859	8,984
White tablecloths	5,104	38	0.32	1,633	12
Naperons 1 × 1	6,621	223	0.60	3,973	134
Round naperons	1,049		0.74	776	0
Linen restaurant towels	190,709	22,584	0.06	11,443	1,355
Kitchen towels	20,468	5,190	0.10	2,047	519
Runners	499	28	0.50	250	14
Covers	2,012	315	0.98	1,972	309
Sofa pillow covers	5,491	10	0.30	1,647	3
Grand total	618,230	175,170		228,492	65,680
Units/kg per guest night	2.01	3.55		0.744	1.330

Source: Mina Splagkounia-Zahariou, Sustainability – CSR Manager, Thomas Cook Concept Hotels, Rhodes, Greece (personal communication, 22 July 2014).

throughput of more than 800 pounds per hour, tunnel washers become cost-effective laundry options. They are designed to be more water efficient (typically using 2.0 gpp) and use 30–60% less water per pound of laundry than traditional washer extractors (Cohen *et al.*, 2009).

Kitchens

Kitchens in hotels and restaurants use water for thawing, food preparation and cooking, to fill pot and pan soak sinks, dishwashers, cleaning

Plate 3.6 Laundry is water and energy intense. In many hotels, towels and bed linen will be changed on a daily basis, even though many guests may change these only once per week or even less often at home. Most hotels no longer wash and iron their own laundry, and have outsourced this to external service providers. In such cases, laundry becomes an aspect of indirect water use

cooking equipment and for garbage disposal. In the study in Rhodes (Gössling, 2015), it was estimated that kitchen uses accounted for 25 L per guest per day. Water use for cleaning was negligible as marble floors are dry-cleaned. Together with styles of cooking, the plumbing requirements are often a key factor in the amount of water used in commercial kitchens. Gleick et al. (2003) estimate that a medium-sized commercial kitchen serving approximately 250 meals per day draws between 1722 L (455 gallons) and 2233 L (590 gallons) of water through the kitchen's faucet daily.

Building and plumbing codes can be a major factor affecting water flows in kitchens and in other parts of hotel operations. Current national standards and plumbing codes in the United States set the maximum flow rate for commercial faucets at 2.2 gallons per minute (gpm; approximately 8.3 L per minute). In contrast, in public restrooms, the faucet flow rate is limited to 0.5 gpm. Commercial sinks in kitchens generally require the full 2.2 gpm flow for operation. Traditional commercial faucets use 4–7 gpm. However, installing a faucet aerator can reduce water use by combining air with water as it comes out of the tap. The common aerator flow rates are 0.5, 1.0 and 2.2 gpm. Depending on the aerator and faucet use, installing a commercial low-flow faucet aerator can reduce a faucet's water flow by 30–50% without affecting performance or water pressure. Low-flow aerators also reduce the energy cost of heating faucet water by up to 50%. Although the water savings from low-flow faucet aerators is small in comparison to installing a high-efficiency toilet, the low cost of commercial faucet aerators, less than US$5 on average, make them a cost-effective water-saving device (Cohen *et al.*, 2009).

Text Box 3.3 Spray valves in California's restaurant kitchens and other water-saving technologies

California is one of the American states that is coming under the most pressure from climate change and is being affected by frequent droughts. It is estimated that in 2000 approximately 185,023,000 m³ (150,000 acre-feet) or 6% of total commercial, industrial and institutional water use in California was consumed by commercial food service operations (Gleick *et al.*, 2003). Typically, washing dishes consumes up to two-thirds of all water used in restaurants (Alliance for Water Efficiency, in Cohen *et al.*, 2009). The easiest and most cost effective way for restaurants to reduce their water consumption is to improve the efficiency of their dishwashing and pre-rinse spray equipment. Depending on their size, food service dishwashers use anywhere from just over 3 L to more than 80 L of water per rack of dishes. In the United States the average commercial dishwasher uses approximately 15 L (4 gallons) of water per rinse (Cohen *et al.*, 2009). Upgrading to a more water efficient dishwasher can reduce water and energy use by 25% annually, with the payback period for installing some smaller, more efficient commercial dishwashers ranging between one and four years (Cohen *et al.*, 2009).

Pre-rinse spray valves, which are used to rinse dishes before they are put into a commercial dishwasher, usually use between 1 and 5 gpm (1 gallon = 3.785 L). The California Urban Water Conservation Council, a partnership comprised of 396 water suppliers, environmental groups, and other stakeholder groups, implemented a 'Rinse 'n' Save' pre-rinse spray valve installation programme that replaced nearly half of all hot water pre-rinse spray valves in the state (50,000 of the estimated 102,000). Installing a water-efficient pre-rinse spray valve reduces water use from 3 gpm to 1.6 gpm or less (Santa Clara Water District, in Cohen *et al.*, 2009) and led to a 15–30% reduction in annual water, energy and sewage costs. The Alliance For Water Efficiency (in Cohen *et al.*, 2009) estimated that installing just one pre-rinse spray valve could save a business almost 190,000 L of water and 7,629 kWh per year. Table 3.10 provides details of a range of water-saving technologies applied in California in kitchens and other commercial, industrial and institutional water uses.

Table 3.10 Available technologies and potential water and energy savings in California's commercial, industrial and institutional (CII) sector

Area	Water use in California's CII sector	Water-efficient technology	Water and energy savings potential	Additional information and savings
Commercial landscaping	• 1/3 of total water use in the sector (approx. 1,000,000 acre-feet (AF) of water per year.	• Xeriscaping. • Smart controllers and sensors.	• Xeriscaping reduces water use by 50% or more. • Smart controllers cut 20–40% of annual water use.	• Reduces dry-weather runoff and waterborne contaminants. • Can improve the appearance of the landscape.
Commercial faucets	• Urinals account for 15% of the sector's total restroom water consumption. • Faucets account for 4% of total restroom water consumption (approx. 14,400 AF per year). • Medium-sized commercial kitchen faucets use 455–590 G per day.	• Low-flow faucet aerators (0.5, 1.0 and 2.2 gpm).	• Reduces faucet water flow by 30–50% (range is based on aerator type and faucet use). • Low-flow aerators also reduce the energy costs of heating faucet water by up to 50%.	• Faucet aerators cost less than US$5 on average, making them very cost effective.

(Continued)

Text Box 3.3 Spray valves in California's restaurant kitchens and other water-saving technologies (*Continued*)

Area	Water use in California's CII sector	Water-efficient technology	Water and energy savings potential	Additional information and savings
Showerheads	• Showers account for 7% of sector's total bathroom consumption (approx. 25,200 AF per year).	• Low-flow showerhead (2.0 and 2.5 gpm).	• 2.5 gpm flow can save 2 G per shower. • 2.0 gpm flow can save 3.5 G per shower.	• Low-flow showerheads can be purchased in bulk quantities for US$5–12 each.
Toilets	• 15% of water used in CII facilities is used in restrooms. • Toilets account for 72% of total restroom water consumption (approx. 259,200 AF per year).	• Ultra low-flow toilets (ULFT) (1.3–1.9 gpf). • High-efficiency toilet (HET) (1.28 gpf) (Composting toilets even lower).	• ULFT can save 15,000 G per year, depending on the facility. • HET can save up to 19,000 G per year.	• Overall reduction in wastewater.
Urinals	• Urinals account for 15% of total restroom water consumption in the sector.	• High-efficiency urinals (HEU) (0.5 gpf or less); • Waterless urinals.	• Each HEU can save 20,000 G of water per year. • Each waterless urinal can save 45,000 G of water per year.	• Overall reduction in wastewater.

| Commercial kitchen dishwashers | • 6% of total CII water consumption (150,000 AF) occurs in commercial kitchens.
 • Commercial dishwashers use 24% of water used in commercial kitchens (approx. 36,000 AF each year). | • Water-efficient commercial dishwasher. | • Reduces water and energy use by 25% per year. | • Payback period for installing small efficient commercial dishwasher ranges between one and four years.
 • Larger flight-type machines have a much longer payback period. |
| Commercial kitchen pre-rinse spray valves | • 6% of total CII water consumption (150,000 AF) occurs in commercial kitchens.
 • Pre-rinse spray valves account for 14% of water consumption in commercial kitchens (21,000 AF per year). | • Water-efficient pre-rinse spray valve (1.6 gpm or less). | • Saves up to 50,000 G of water and 7629 KWh of electricity per year (26–80% less water and energy compared to standard valves). | • Replacing a traditional pre-rinse spray valve that is used three hours per day with a water-efficient pre-rinse spray valve can save 180 G of water per day and up to US$1050 in water and energy costs per year. |

(Continued)

Text Box 3.3 Spray valves in California's restaurant kitchens and other water-saving technologies *(Continued)*

Table 3.10 *(Continued)*

Area	Water use in California's CII sector	Water-efficient technology	Water and energy savings potential	Additional information and savings
Clothes washers	• Industrial and on-premises laundries use approx. 30,000 AF of water per year. • Approx. 3000 additional coin-operated clothes washers in California each use up to 45 G of water per load.	• High-efficiency commercial clothes washers (HEW) (common-area laundries). • Water-efficient washer extractors (on-premises laundries). • Tunnel washers (industrial laundries).	• HEWs can reduce water consumption by 35–50% and achieve energy savings of up to 50%. • Efficient washer extractors can reduce water consumption by up to 40%. • Tunnel washers can reduce water consumption by 30–60%.	• More efficient washers can reduce energy bills by up to 50% and water and sewage costs by 35–50%. • HEWs require 50% less detergent.

Notes: acre feet (AF) = 1 US survey acre foot ≈ 1,233.4892384681 m³; gallon (G) = the US gallon is equal to exactly 3.785411784 L; gpf = gallons per flush; gpm = gallons per minute.
Source: Adapted from Cohen *et al.* (2009).

Activities

Various tourist activities also add to water use on site, even though 'activities' are part of the systemic water footprint of tourism, for example with regard to marketing and sales, or infrastructure involving water use during manufacturing. The most relevant examples of water-related infrastructure are golf and skiing, i.e. where irrigation of greens and snowmaking are needed. Most data appear to currently exist on water consumption by golf courses, where water consumption depends on course size, soils, climate and irrigation system efficiency and course management type (public, private or premier course) (Baillon & Ceron, 1991; Ceron & Kovacs, 1993; Peister & Scott, 2014; Throssell et al., 2009). Estimates of annual consumption include: 10,000–15,000 m³ per ha in Cyprus (Mangion, 2013); 80,000–100,000 m³ per golf course in the north of France to 150,000–200,000 m³ in southern France (Ceron & Kovacs, 1993); 60,000–94,000 m³ per 18-hole course in southern Ontario (Canada) (Peister & Scott, 2014); to a range of 52,000–566,000 m³ per 18-hole course in the diverse climatic zone of the USA (Throssell et al., 2009). Even higher values were reported for golf courses in sand dune systems, with one estimate by van der Meulen and Salman (1996) suggesting water consumption of 0.5–1 million m³ per year for an 18-hole golf course.

These examples suggest that golf courses are highly water consuming. In 2004, it was estimated that 9.5 billion L of water was used each day to irrigate the world's golf courses (Wolbier, 2004), although how robust this estimation is remains highly uncertain. According to Hudson and Hudson (2010) there now exist 32,000 golf courses in 140 countries, covering areas of up to 15 km². With the global golf industry and golf tourism markets expanding rapidly around the world over the past two decades (i.e. from 2005 to 2010 alone the number of golf courses has increased by an estimated 15%; Berenberg, 2012), tourism-related water consumption from this growing market will continue to increase.

Although less obvious, another increasingly water-intense tourism activity is skiing. According to skiresort.info (2013) there are now 4874 ski resorts worldwide, with up to 650 km of slopes per resort. As skiing and other winter sports activities are increasingly utilising snowmaking, the corresponding water use – and embodied energy – is considerable. For instance, in France snowmaking accounted for 19 million m³ of water use in 2007 (Badré et al., 2009). However, only 30% of this water may be used consumptively. In the United States, snowmaking was estimated to have used 60 million m³ in the season 2004–2005 (Scott et al., 2012b), an estimate that does not include energy use and its embedded water use. Visitation to concerts, events and attractions can also increase water demand (e.g. Meyer & Chaffee, 1997;

Sebake & Gibberd, 2008; Zaizen *et al.*, 2000) with, for example, each visitor to the Millennium Dome in London using on average 22 L of water (Hills *et al.*, 2002). It has been estimated that activities may add 10–875 L of water per guest night, the higher value including golf, potentially the most water-intense activity in tourism (Deyá Tortella & Tirado, 2011; Gössling *et al.*, 2012; Hadjikakou *et al.*, 2013a).

Overall, the chapter indicates that where gardens, lawns or golf courses need to be irrigated, and where spas and large or multiple swimming pools exist, water consumption will increase substantially. Higher standard accommodation and specifically resort hotels in warm climates are thus likely to consume significantly higher water volumes than small-scale accommodation or city hotels, which is a water management challenge as these hotels tend to have higher profit margins that allow them to continue with inefficient water use practices (Tortella & Tirado, 2011). Geographical location (urban–rural), climate zone (arid–humid), hotel structure (high-rise, resort style) and comfort standard (campsite to 5-star) were also identified as factors that influence relative shares of water use as well as overall water consumption (Gössling *et al.*, 2012). These are relevant insights for water management and will be returned to several times in Chapters 4 and 5.

Indirect (Embodied) Water Use

Indirect water use includes the water that is consumed to provide the services of the accommodation establishment, including the construction of the hotel, energy use, and food and beverage consumption. The locus of consumption of foods and beverages can also occur outside the accommodation, for instance when people eat at nearby restaurants. As identified earlier, a share of the consumption associated with indirect water use might also have occurred if people had not travelled. Yet there is some evidence that tourism increases levels of individual consumption, as will be outlined in the following sections.

Construction

With regard to the water embodied in construction, Rosselló-Batle *et al.* (2010) report that use and construction of buildings accounts for 17% of global water consumption. According to Low (2005) concrete is, after water, the second most consumed material in the world. The use of concrete is in itself water consuming, and it has been estimated that cement hydration consumes 1 km^3 of water per year (van Oss & Padovani, 2003). Tourism's contribution to this total is unknown and is difficult to define, due to the often multiple uses of infrastructure. It has been suggested that end-uses of concrete include residential buildings (31%), highways and roads (26%) and industrial and commercial buildings (18%) (Low, 2005).

To better understand water consumption in construction, Rosselló-Batle *et al.* (2010) analysed cement use in three hotels in the Balearic Islands. They found that for each 1 m^2 of floor space, 85–97 L of water were required. These values can be used to estimate water consumption per guest night over an assumed lifetime of 50 years of a hotel. For instance, a hotel with an average floor space of 20 m^2 per bed (including public and administrative areas), 200 guest nights per bed per year, and an average of 90 L/m^2 of water used during construction, would consume 0.2 L/guest night over the hotel's lifetime (Gössling, 2015). Construction-related water use thus appears negligible, even though also including other infrastructure for tourism, e.g. airports, ports, roads, constructions for activities (e.g. ski lifts), events, museums and restaurants would increase values. Nevertheless, careful construction and site development can sometimes have other benefits for the water system. For example, low-impact development – strategically placed beds of native plants, porous surfaces for parking lots and roads, and other tools – to retain rainfall on site and allow it to soak into the ground can enhance water supply, protect water quality and reduce greenhouse gas emissions.

Low-impact development is a cost-effective way to save water with total capital cost savings estimates ranging from 15% to 80% (Chapman & Horner, 2010; Horner, 2007). For example, in the Californian context, using low-impact development at a single restaurant with a 30-car parking lot could capture enough water to meet the needs of a family of four for almost an entire year (Cohen et al., 2009; Horner, 2007). By offsetting energy-intensive imported water in like amounts, and after accounting for average energy requirements associated with pumping groundwater in these areas, low-impact development would also contribute to savings in greenhouse gas emissions (Cohen et al., 2009).

Fuel production

Fuel and electricity production and distribution is water intense. To calculate the water footprint of indirect water consumption related to energy use would have to consider all energy use throughout the tourism value chain, based on a lifecycle analysis. This has so far not been attempted (cf. Gössling & Peeters, 2014), and the water footprint related to energy use can thus only be assessed on the basis of energy consumption for transport (to/from the destination), and energy use at the hotel as a proxy value for energy throughput.

This omits, for instance, energy use for goods or food production and transport, car rentals, as well as energy-intense activities such as water skiing or diving, helicopter flights or scenic drives, all of which would have to be assessed with regard to the water intensity of the different energy sources involved in production (see Chapter 1). Most energy use in tourism, however, will be based on fossil fuels (UNWTO, UNEP & WMO, 2008). Globally, it has been estimated that each guest night (accommodation only) involves energy use (throughput) in the order of 272 MJ (see case study on energy use in hotels and embodied water demand), or the energy equivalent of about 75 kWh, or 7 L of diesel. At an estimated 10 L of water per 1 L of diesel, a conservative estimate only considering production, this would result in an additional 70 L of freshwater per tourist per day embodied in energy use for accommodation. It needs to be noted, however, that energy use in accommodation varies hugely, with values of 3.5–1536 MJ reported in the literature (Gössling, 2010), or the equivalent of 0.1–42.2 L diesel (1 L diesel: 36.4 MJ) per guest night. At 10 L water per 1 L of fuel, this translates into an energy-related water use range of between 1 L and 420 L per guest night. Energy use for hotel construction would have to be added to this, which can be the equivalent of 20% of annual operational energy use (Rosselló-Batle et al., 2010).

Plate 3.7 Potatoes shipped from the Netherlands for consumption in a resort hotel in a small island in the Seychelles. Food production is not only water and energy intense, but it also requires considerable energy in order for foodstuffs to be distributed. In the words of a manager in the Seychelles (quoted in Gössling et al., 2011): 'Everything I fly. Even the coffee I fly. In terms of fuel, this hotel is terrible. We place the order for Christmas stuff now: it will be coming from Dubai, by container. If I order now, I don't have to fly it here. Christmas for me is August latest. You have to plan in a lot of advance if you don't fly the things here'

Text Box 3.4 Energy use in hotels and embodied water demand

Energy use was studied in more detail in three hotels in Rhodes, Greece. Notably, this does not include the transport component of the trip to the island, and is thus lower than the 272 MJ (75 kWh) of energy required on global average per guest night (UNWTO, UNEP & WMO, 2008). Moreover, the hotels studied are comparably new, and all have installed thermal solar capacity to support warm water production. The mix of solar thermal installation, use of air conditioning, the relative comfort standard of the hotels as well as their occupancy rates/total number of guest nights during the season from April to October result in different outcomes with regard to energy demand, with reported energy equivalent values of 17–42 kWh/guest night (Table 3.11). Using an average assumption of 0.8 L of freshwater per kWh (Gössling, 2015), this results in a water footprint of between 14 and 34 L per guest night, i.e. considerably lower values than global average estimates. Even though A/C use in Greece is considerable, solar thermal warming of water in combination with relatively new technologies may be responsible for reducing energy requirements in Greece in comparison with global averages.

Table 3.11 Energy use at hotels in Rhodes, Greece

Energy use	Hotel A*****	Hotel B*****	Hotel C****
Energy consumption per guest night (2012)[a]	19 kWh + 0.5 L oil	32 kWh + 0.338 L diesel + 0.597 m³ gas	16 kWh + 0.05 L diesel
Energy equivalent from above	25 kWh/guest night	42 kWh/guest night	17 kWh/guest night
Energy water footprint (0.8 L water/kWh)	20 L/guest night	34 L/guest night	14 L/guest night
Solar thermal installed	370 m²	248 m²	104 m²
Solar thermal per room	0.8 m²/room	1.4 m²/room	0.5 m²/room

Note: [a]The Electric Company at Rhodes Island produces electricity with generators running on fuel oil and diesel.
Source: Gössling (2015).

Table 3.12 Foodstuff use in kg per guest night in Greek case study hotel

Foodstuff	kg per guest night	Foodstuff	kg per guest night	Foodstuff	kg per guest night
Meats		*Dairy & eggs*		*Seafood*	
Cold cuts	0.063	Yoghurt	0.080	Lobster	0.001
Pork	0.115	Cream	0.040	Calamari	0.009
Rabbit	0.002	Butter & margarine	0.010	Shrimps	0.011
Beef	0.066	Cheese	0.086	Shellfish	0.009
Chicken	0.084	Eggs	0.078	Octopus	0.007
Duck	0.008	*Subtotal*	0.294	Squid	0.004
Turkey	0.018			Caviar	0.000
Lamb	0.029	*Carbohydrates*		Other seafood	0.003
Subtotal	0.385	Flour	0.025	*Subtotal*	0.044
		Cereals	0.059		
Vegetables & fruit		Sugar	0.024	*Fish*	
Dry fruits	0.016	Pasta	0.034	Smoked fish	0.005
Frozen vegetables	0.148	Mashed potatoes	0.002	Pangasius	0.022
Frozen potatoes	0.082	Semolina	0.001	Shark	0.020
Fresh fruit	0.571	Pastry	0.017	Cod	0.005
Fresh vegetables	0.773	Bread	0.064	Swordfish	0.004
Lemon	0.010	Croissants	0.013	Perch	0.014
Olives	0.013	Cookies & biscuits	0.014	Salmon	0.011
Subtotal	1.613	Rice	0.018	Tuna	0.002
		Subtotal	0.271	Sardine	0.000
Other				Bream	0.002
Pulses	0.005	*Sweet foods & spices*		Other	0.010
Oils	0.113	Traditional sweets	0.003	*Subtotal*	0.095
Nuts	0.020	Ketchup[a]	0.022		
Vinegar	0.041	Jam	0.010	*Beverages (L)*	
Soup	0.001	Spices	0.069	Soft drinks	0.037

(Continued)

Table 3.12 (*Continued*)

Foodstuff	kg per guest night	Foodstuff	kg per guest night	Foodstuff	kg per guest night
Snails	0.001	Salt	0.007	Refreshments	0.038
Stock	0.037	Honey	0.010	Juices	0.072
Subtotal	0.218	Ice cream	0.081	Milk	0.300
		Subtotal	0.202	Tea	0.612
				Coffee	0.114
Subtotal foodstuffs	**3.122**			Wine	0.288
Subtotal beverages	**1.784**			Beer	0.280
Total	**4.906**			Spirits	0.043
				Subtotal	**1.784**

Notes: ^aItem 'ketchup' includes ketchup, mustard and mayonnaise.
Food consumption values include peels, stones, bones or other parts of the food that have to be discarded.
Source: Gössling (2015).

Energy demand and embodied water use for transport is related to transport distances and the transport modes used. For instance, Peeters (2013) calculates that the average global return travel distance was 1898 km in 2010 and energy use was 1.123 MJ/pkm (domestic and international tourism). This translates into water use of approximately 130 L per guest night on global average, although there are considerable differences between, for instance, a longer trip by train and a shorter long-haul flight involving a cruise. Water use values for these different forms of holiday can vary between 5 L and 2500 L per guest night (Gössling, 2015). Energy for desalination, distribution or the lifecycle energy use for water networks would have to be added to these values.

Transport energy use is a significant problem for sustainability in tourism (Gössling *et al.*, 2013), for which few technological solutions are currently available. Biofuels are increasingly advocated as an alternative energy to replace fossil fuels (e.g. IATA, 2013). However, this would also significantly increase the water footprint of tourism. UNESCO (2009) reports that 44 km^3 or 2% of all irrigation water is already used for biofuel production, suggesting that the production of 1 L of biofuels may currently require 2500 L of water. Only a share of this is consumptive, however. Were the world's current commercial aircraft fleet to use biofuels, this would require approximately an additional 180 km^3 of irrigation water if De Fraiture et al.'s (2008) estimates for biofuel and agricultural production were to be applied. Further research into the water implications of biofuels is therefore warranted.

Food

Food use in accommodation has not been studied in great detail, possibly due to the difficulty in cooperating with hotels on what may be perceived as time consuming and a source of business advantage. It is generally acknowledged, however, that tourists consume a greater share of higher order foods, such as meats, which have greater water footprints (Gössling, 2015; Gössling et al., 2011). Estimates of daily requirements to support human diets have been estimated at 2500 L of water per person per day, considering UNESCO's (2009) estimate of 1 L of water per 1 kcal of food. Hadjikakou et al. (2013a) demonstrated, however, that in tourism, water footprints per kcal were greater (1.38–2.34 L/kcal), due to the use of higher order foods.

The only assessment of water embodied in food consumption that considered actual consumption values is by Gössling (2015) for a hotel in Greece. In this study, 150 foodstuff items as well as 60 categories of beverages were considered. Averaged per tourist per day, the use of some foodstuffs was found to be small, but when multiplied by more than 180,000 guest nights per season, absolute volumes included several tons of each of the foodstuffs considered. In this study, an average weight of 3.122 kg of food was consumed per guest per day (Table 3.12), as well as 1.784 L of beverages, including 0.611 L of alcohol. Total consumption values were multiplied by the amount of water embodied in the various foodstuffs, based on data by Mekonnen and Hoekstra (2011a, b), indicating that in this hotel daily average water consumption embodied in food and beverages is 4557 L for foodstuffs and 940 L for beverages, i.e. 5497 L per guest night in total. The share of blue water in these estimates is about 15–20% (Figure 3.3), ranging from 4.4 L water per 1 L of beer to 512 L of water per 1 kg of olives. Notably, these values do not include the energy needed to transport or process foods. The study confirmed a significant share of higher order foods, including meats (0.385 kg per tourist per day), seafood and fish (0.139 kg) and dairy products and eggs (0.294 kg). Three-quarters of the tourists in this study also agreed that they had eaten 'more than at home'. Meat consumption, at 2.65 m^3 of water per tourist per day, is the most relevant aspect of food use (Figure 3.4). In contrast, carbohydrates (e.g. bread, rice) are less water intense, and fruit and vegetables also have more favourable weight-to-water ratios.

Plate 3.8 An unconventional way of reducing plastic waste, saving energy for transport and distribution and enhancing guest quality perceptions: Water bottled at the Sentido Apollo Blue Hotel, Greece. The hotel decided to reduce considerable amounts of plastic bottles in need of disposal. The glass bottle is reusable, easy to clean, and is perceived by guests as vastly superior in design and quality to plastic bottles

Plate 3.9 Food management can help to reduce global water demand considerably. As a general rule, vegetarian choices are less water intense. However, as a manager cautions: 'The sure thing is that the vegetarians get more and more. But if clients do not see a variety of meat, you are dead. They will kill you where they find you, specifically the Internet' (4-star hotel, Rhodes, Greece: Interview, 8 June 2014)

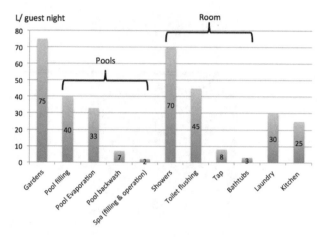

Figure 3.3 Direct water use in 4-star accommodation in Rhodes, Greece by end-use
Source: Gössling (2015), modified

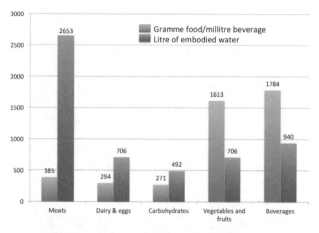

Figure 3.4 Weight of foodstuff groups consumed per guest night, and water use in litres
Source: Gössling (2015)

Systemic Water Use

Systemic water use is here defined as all water consumption associated with activities, shopping and services in transit to or in the destination. This will often involve other infrastructure, such as airports, roads, tracks or marinas/harbours, as well as the manufacturing of transport modes, or the treatment of wastewater, all of which involve water use. Furthermore, most holidays involve marketing and sales, and involve physical places for holiday transactions (travel agents and tour operators' headquarters). The water use embodied in these aspects of tourism has not been studied.

Conclusions

This chapter has provided an overview of knowledge regarding direct and indirect water use in tourism at an operation scale. As noted above, no

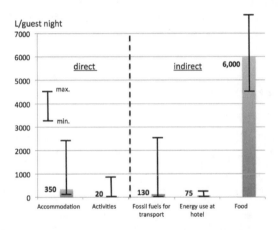

Figure 3.5 Globally averaged water footprint, litres per guest night
Source: Gössling (2015)

Table 3.13 Summary of resource use intensities in global tourism, 2010

Aspect	Range of estimates	Global average
Energy		
– per guest night	3.6–3717 MJ	272 MJ
– per trip (domestic & international average)	50–135,815 MJ	3575 MJ
Freshwater, L per tourist per day		
– direct (accommodation)	84–2425	350
– indirect (fuels, food)	4500–8000	6000
– combined	4600–12,000	6575
Food use, g per day		
– per tourist per day	2200–3100 g	1800 g

Source: Gössling and Peeters (2014).

research on embodied systematic water use is available. Nevertheless a summary of direct and indirect water use is provided in Figure 3.5, with a range of 4600–12,000 L and an estimated average of 6575 L of water per tourist per day for direct and indirect water use in tourism. As noted, these values are conservative and exclude systemic water use, as well as water use associated with the lifecycle of tourism facilities and infrastructure. Results also show that food is by far the most important water-use factor, accounting for an estimated 85% of total water consumption. However, there are huge differences in minimum and maximum water-use values depending on the nature of the tourism product that is being consumed (Table 3.13). These differences in consumption, also referred to as resource use intensities, open up opportunities for defining strategies to reduce water use in tourism. The next chapter of the book is thus devoted to the management of water consumption.

Further reading

On direct water demand see

Bohdanowicz, P. and Martinac, I. (2007) Determinants and benchmarking of resource consumption in hotels – case study of Hilton International and Scandic in Europe. *Energy and Buildings* 39 (1), 82–95.

Hof, A. and Schmitt, T. (2011) Urban and tourist land use patterns and water consumption: Evidence from Mallorca, Balearic Islands. *Land Use Policy* 28 (4), 792–804.

Stipanuk, D.M. and Robson, S. (eds) (1995) *Water Resources for Lodging Operations*. East Lansing, MI: Educational Institute of the American Hotel and Motel Association.

Styles, D., Schoenberger, H. and Galvez-Martos, J.L. (2015) Water management in the European hospitality sector: Best practice, performance benchmarks and improvement potential. *Tourism Management* 46, 187–202.

WHO (World Health Organization) (2009) *Guidelines for Safe Recreational Water Environments. Vol. 2. Swimming Pools and Similar Environments.* Geneva: WHO. See http://apps.who.int/iris/bitstream/10665/43336/1/9241546808_eng.pdf?ua=1 (accessed 29 July 2014).

Useful papers on some of the indirect aspects of water consumption in tourism include:

Gössling, S. and Hall, C.M. (2013) Sustainable culinary systems. In S. Gössling and C.M. Hall (eds) *Sustainable Culinary Systems: Local Foods, Innovation, Tourism and Hospitality* (pp. 3–44). Abingdon: Routledge.

Gössling, S., Garrod, B., Aall, C., Hille, J. and Peeters, P. (2011) Food management in tourism: Reducing tourism's 'carbon foodprint'. *Tourism Management* 32 (3), 534–543.

Rosselló-Batle, B., Moià, A., Cladera, A. and Martínez, V. (2010) Energy use, CO_2 emissions and waste throughout the life cycle of a sample of hotels in the Balearic Islands. *Energy and Buildings* 42 (4), 547–558.

4 Managing Water in Tourism: Effective Business and Destination Environmental Management Systems

Introduction

As previous chapters have discussed, it is clear that pressure on freshwater resources will increase in the future, while tourism's share in consumption will continue to grow. To conserve and efficiently use water is thus of growing importance. This chapter provides an overview of the measures that can help to serve this purpose, including management, marketing, behavioural change, policy and technology. Notably, all of these have in common the fact that they are either economical, i.e. saving financial resources, or can be communicated in a way that increases the added value of these measures to tourists and to other stakeholders. It is generally acknowledged that tourist facilities can reduce water consumption by at least 10–50% without jeopardising guest comfort or experience (e.g. Bohdanowicz & Martinac, 2007; Cooley *et al.*, 2007; O'Neill & Siegelbaum & The RICE Group, 2002). Relative efficiency gains are dependent on the standard already implemented, as well as absolute water consumption levels and the amortisation periods deemed acceptable.

It is important to recognise that water quality issues and water management in tourism and hospitality are often part of broader environmental and water management issues and procedures (Figure 4.1). Many businesses set their water management parameters in such a way as to comply with

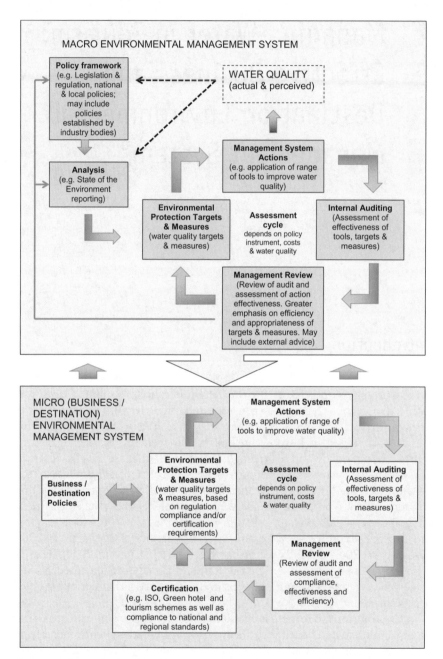

Figure 4.1 Interrelationships between macro- and micro-environmental systems

national or local standards and policies. Therefore, although this chapter focuses on what businesses can do, it is important to recognise the wider regulatory context and the role of improved governance. Tourism businesses and organisations increasingly utilise an environmental management system (EMS) as part of their overall management system. The EMS provides the framework for organisational environmental policy, and is a means to demonstrate consistent environmental performance and satisfy environmental regulatory requirements. Although the term 'environmental management' is somewhat of a misnomer in that it is not about managing the environment per se, it is about managing the activities of businesses, industries and individuals that affect the environment (Thompson, 2002). While there is no one single definition for an EMS, it is generally recognised as being a formal set of policies, procedures, objectives, targets and activities that outline an organisation's structure, procedures and resources for implementing, evaluating, managing and tracking its overall environmental policy and impacts, of which water and energy are usually the most important parts.

One key element of an EMS is continual improvement of the system, including incorporating feedback mechanisms from actual results. Although some organisations have used an EMS as a vehicle for greenwashing through setting easy-to-achieve targets in place of overriding ethical environmental practices, they are nevertheless an essential element of strategic environmental and water management (Barrow, 2006). In order to overcome setting too low an environmental target it is important that an organisation's EMS should be benchmarked, transparent and, where appropriate, externally audited. Such an approach can help ensure that businesses are aware of current best practice that can help them reduce environmental impacts and the costs of resource use. Standardised approaches to EMSs include certification through the International Organization for Standardization (ISO 14001; Chan, 2009) and industry-specific approaches in the case of the tourism industry, but generally organisations utilise an EMS voluntarily (Barrow, 2006; Hitchcock & Willard, 2009). For example, in 2005 as part of a larger environmental programme in the build-up to the hosting of the 2006 Commonwealth Games, all lodging facilities in Melbourne, Australia, implemented a water-saving programme called the Strategy Act Verify Enhance (SAVE) cycle. The water management plan involved six steps: (1) decide on key personnel; (2) develop water balance, baseline and benchmarks; (3) undertake a water audit; (4) identify water conservation measures; (5) conduct a cost-benefit analysis; and (6) introduce water-saving measures (City of Melbourne, 2007; Harris, 2013).

As noted throughout this book, in order to effectively manage water resources, it is important to distinguish direct and indirect water use. Most destinations and accommodation establishments will be more concerned with direct water use, as the most visible and tangible component of the total water footprint. Direct water management will also be more often relevant because destinations in dry climates are more vulnerable to the overexploitation and cost of water use, as well as competing uses. Furthermore, sewage and wastewater need to be treated, which is costly, also making reductions in water use a priority. The following sections consequently focus primarily on direct water use, including demand-side management (reducing water demand) and supply-side management (increasing sustainable water provisions).

Water management should always include energy and food management as the two most important indirect water-consuming subsectors. Energy is an important factor in water consumption, because most hotels have a huge potential to reduce energy, in the same order of magnitude as water (i.e. 10–50%). Specific solutions for energy savings have been discussed elsewhere (Gössling, 2010), but considering water and energy management together greatly increases the profitability of improved resource management, as energy is considerably more expensive than water. For instance, as shown in the case study on Cyprus (Text Box 4.1), a 1% reduction in energy use may generate financial savings almost 10 times greater than a 1% reduction in water use, given the considerably higher cost of energy. Food management is important, because water consumption for food production dwarfs all other water consumption. As an indirect part of the water footprint of tourism, it is less likely to be high on the management agenda in hotels. However, food is important because it is increasingly seen as the one aspect of a holiday that distinguishes otherwise unified packages, i.e. it has great and increasing importance for guest perceptions, provides added value to their holiday, and can positively influence regional economies (Hall & Gössling, 2013). Moreover, vegetarian choices, which as has been discussed are far less water intense than, for instance meats, can also be considerably cheaper. Providing a greater choice of non-meat choices can thus meet environmental and financial objectives, while also meeting guest expectations. Supply chain management for food and beverage source can therefore make a significant difference to tourism water use. The following sections will discuss management opportunities in greater detail.

Management

Water management requires action by all stakeholders, i.e. local and national governments, hotel managers and tour operators, as well as staff and tourists. Generally speaking, water management approaches are best guided when they are based on frameworks that allow managers to efficiently engage in resource conservation, with a focus on cost savings. This will increase the interest in resource savings and, given the vast potential to save water, also be a suitable approach in environmental terms. Yet few such management frameworks for tourism have been presented so far. Even though not fully comprehensive from the viewpoint of the insights presented in this book, one useful framework that has been developed comes from the Swiss tour operator, Kuoni (2013). Kuoni developed a 'Skills Map' consisting of seven steps to water management, including planning, data collection, cost-benefit analyses, action plan definition, monitoring, staff training and increasing customer awareness (Table 4.1). All of these aspects are covered in the following sections. This management section sets out an overview of the steps needed to engage on the basis of a 'skills map', i.e. representing an internal action plan. An alternative way of pursuing water management strategies would be to engage in programmes (e.g. Travelife, The Travel Foundation) or to hire companies for this purpose.

Planning

Water management needs to be embedded in the context of the destination, even though there is always an opportunity for accommodation businesses to engage in water management on their own. The destination context is of importance, however, because it determines whether water management is of interest to a greater number of stakeholders, whether collective action is needed, and the regulatory and policy context within which water management occurs. The case study in Text Box 4.1 presents the example of Cyprus, where acute water stress forced actors to engage in water management measures. Some islands, such as Mallorca, are dependent on water imports by ship (Clarke & King, 2004), indicating that water management in some destinations may only become an issue when costs for water provisions become significantly higher. Clearly, this is likely to be unsustainable from social, environmental and economic viewpoints. Prudent destination and accommodation managers would seek to avoid such a situation, and to build networks for water management before water scarcity becomes severe. This is also particularly relevant for the construction of hotels and other tourism infrastructure, which constitutes water 'lock-in', i.e. water consumption that will be difficult to reduce in the medium-term future. However, the reality is that individual business planning often occurs separately from destination-wide cumulative water planning, with consequent potential issues for both operators and the broader destination.

Table 4.2 shows how planning for water management might be embedded within accommodation, possibly also involving cooperation at the

Table 4.1 Kuoni's skills map for water management

Section	After completing this section, you will:
(1) Planning	• Have an understanding of the steps involved for successful water management in your hotel; • Be able to form a water management team in your hotel; • Know the skills required to run a water management programme.
(2) Data collection	• Know where water is supplied from; • Know where and how water is used and in what quantities; • Know the importance of logging water consumption by using several meters throughout the hotel property; • Know what costs are associated with the current system.
(3) Cost benefit analysis	• Know what water and cost savings are achievable throughout your water systems; • Have an overview of which plumbing fixtures can work as cost-effective replacements for outdated systems; • Be familiar with the benefits of installing a water treatment system.
(4) Defining the action plan	• Understand how to choose the right water consumption reduction targets for your business; • Have an overview of what kinds of improvements can be achieved in what time frame.
(5) Monitoring	• Understand why continuing to monitor your water consumption in the long term is key to successful water management.
(6) Training staff	• Know which departments in your hotel would benefit from a training session on water management; • Know what training resources are already available.
(7) Creating customer awareness	• Have an overview of how to communicate your sustainable water management with clients; • Gather ideas on how to include your clients in water-related local community projects.

Source: Kuoni (2013).

Plate 4.1 Pool size and volume are important factors in 'water lock-in'. Initial fillings at the beginning of the season can significantly increase direct per tourist per day water demand (volume), while larger pool area sizes increase evaporation. This requires hotel developers already to consider water lock-in at the planning stages

destination level to identify common scenarios for long-term water security, based on a comprehensive set of indicators (see discussion below). As indicated, it is essential for hotels to engage at various levels, involving top management. As outlined by Kuoni, it is vital that company boards, managing directors and hotel managers understand the objectives of such programmes. This poses a key challenge, as top management is not usually concerned with resource use, and in some contexts the massive use and waste of resources is even understood as a signifier of quality (Gössling *et al.*, 2005). Besides hotel management, technical staff need to be involved in data collection and measurement, while accountants may provide feedback on the economics involved and savings made (see also cost-benefit analysis). Staff involving housekeeping, kitchens and grounds keeping also need to be tasked with specific roles.

Data collection

A primary challenge for water management is to understand water use: only where detailed audits exist, can opportunities for conservation and efficient use be identified and potential savings calculated (Bohdanowicz-Godfrey & Zientara, 2014). Direct water use is easier to audit and monitor, and will usually be more attractive to management as a result of cost savings.

Table 4.2 Planning for water management

Position	Role	Experience required
Managing director/ board of directors	Understand programme objectives, define timing and expected results	Able to motivate staff and approve changes/spending
Hotel manager	Coordination of data, plan necessary training	Attention to detail with data received, analytical thinking to formulate action plan
Technical/ maintenance manager	Data collection, placement of meters, physical measurements, etc.	Good numeracy, ability to complete worksheets and cost-benefit calculations
Accounts	Budget spending on water-saving devices, provide bednight and other financial relevant figures	Budget planning
Head of housekeeping and laundry	Data collection, target setting, monitoring	None
Head of kitchen	Data collection, target setting, monitoring	None
Head of grounds keeping	Data collection, target setting, monitoring	None

Source: Adapted from Kuoni (2013).

To measure where water is consumed within the hotel is thus a first and crucial step, as most hotels will, if at all, have only a crude understanding of their overall water use. Unless there are particular regulatory and policy constraints, e.g. a period of prolonged drought that has led government to initiate water-saving measures, it is even rarer for hotels to audit water use by different divisions or areas of flow, i.e. to have meters installed at all abstraction points, including irrigation, pools (filling, replenish, backwash), laundry, spa, kitchens and in-room consumption (potentially with meters for toilet, shower, bathtub and tap), and also to control hot/cold water use, flow rates/water pressure or per-guest consumption of towels and bed linen. As outlined, management should also consider indirect water use, as this can make economic sense, especially in terms of energy. Moreover, at the destination, regional or national level, in some sense all water use is now global, as economies are interconnected and interdependent (see Chapter 5). To save 'destination' and 'global' water thus reduces future vulnerabilities. Table 4.3 shows the suggestion approach to water audit by tour operator Kuoni (2013). This audit has a focus

Table 4.3 Aspects to be considered in a water audit

No.	Sheet/record title	Use this sheet/record to:	Required data	Estimated time needed
(1)	Per capita consumption	Calculate volume of water used for one bednight and how this varies from month to month	Monthly water consumption from borehole, municipal, rainwater and water tanker sources, monthly bednight figures	2 hours
(2)	Base water cost	Calculate the actual cost of 1 m³ of water from different sources (groundwater, municipal, tanker, rainwater, treated water)	Local water costs (e.g. water rates, tankers, rainwater infrastructure cost and collection potential), pump power requirement, groundwater treatment and maintenance costs	2 hours
(3)	Hot water cost	Calculate your heating costs for 1 L of water from different sources (solar, electric, boiler)	Capacity, installation costs and running costs of all water-heating devices	1 hour
(4)	Laundry cost	Calculate the unit cost of washing one item of laundry such as a bed sheet or towel	Laundry washer, dryer and presser power, water ratings and purchase costs, monthly laundry logs, detergent and labour costs	2 hours
(5)	Flow rate measurement	Record and calculate flow rates from different parts of the hotel (such as showers, sinks)	This is a physical measurement, so it can be collected directly	1 hour
(6)	Water balance	Compile your water budget, factoring in water consumed in different departments using measurements or estimations	Water volumes used in different areas of hotel (sub-metering)	2.5 hours
(7)	Towel reuse record sheets	Monitor with housekeeping staff number of towels reused throughout one week and calculate % reuse	This is a record sheet so data can be collected directly	0.5 hour intro; 0.5 hour compiling

Notes: In situations where there are significant fluctuations in occupancy rates and/or climatic conditions, analysis may be better conducted weekly rather than monthly.
Source: Adapted from Kuoni (2013).

on cost, combining meter readings (municipal and borehole) with assessments of unit costs. Neither fuels nor food are considered in this audit, although such aspects could potentially be integrated into an audit. Indeed, hotels often audit food purchasing; however, this is not done from an environmental perspective but rather a cost control basis. Nevertheless, there is no practical reason why such approaches could not be integrated.

Cost-benefit analysis

There is a general understanding that the management in most hotels will not engage in any management measures if this does not lead to cost savings or is not otherwise required, e.g. by law. However, most water management measures will be cost effective, with payback periods as short as a few months. Even simple measures can generate considerable efficiency gains. For instance, installation of water-efficient fixtures replacing old standards can reduce in-room consumption by 30% (O'Neill & Siegelbaum & The RICE Group, 2002). As an example, data compiled by Sydney Water (2001, quoted in Smith *et al.*, 2009a) demonstrate that in-room water-saving measures entail costs of a few hundred US dollars with payback periods of less than three years (Table 4.4). Such measures are thus highly cost efficient. Where the economic outcome of a planned measure is uncertain, its costs can be calculated and compared to savings, considering payback periods and discount rates as deemed acceptable by management. Potentially more difficult to implement will be larger scale technical restructuring, for instance considering the replacement of a chiller-based air conditioning system with one that is based on geothermal cold water use.

Text Box 4.1 Measuring, auditing and monitoring in Cyprus

It took three years of drought, considerable water losses through leaks in the supply system, the consistent disinterest of the government in addressing the problem and, finally, the introduction of water rationing to convince the hotel industry in Cyprus that they had to act on water scarcity. Water cost was also possibly a factor, as 100,000 m³ of water per day was already provided through costly desalination.

To raise awareness, compile information on water- and energy-saving measures and practices in the hotel industry, monitor consumption and calculate water savings, a project was initiated in November 2008 in cooperation with the Cyprus Sustainable Tourism Initiative, with the support of the Travel Foundation (UK) and the Cyprus Tourism Organisation.

A major challenge was to approach hotel managers, who were hesitant about providing information in the early stages of the project. However, a total of 106 hotels were enrolled in the project, of which 63% collected data and participated in the project. These also carried out a wide range of saving measures after the data collected had been evaluated and concerns addressed. In particular, these included the fear of loss of revenue during the period when water- and energy-saving measures were introduced, as well as the costs of installing new equipment. Measures finally implemented included:

- installation of low-flow showers and tap output reducers;
- reduction of the volume of water in the toilet cisterns;
- installation of refrigerator air curtains;
- installation of motion sensors in the less frequently used areas;
- water flow reduction valves in bathrooms;
- auto-cut units for pool showers;
- delayed action sensors fitted in refrigerators so that compressors do not start the moment doors are opened;
- magnetic rings on diesel pipes that aid the efficient burning of fuel;
- replacement of 1.5 L bottled water with the 1 L bottle;
- tent cards in bathrooms that display linen change options;
- key cards for all the rooms.

Overall, the project was considered a success. From May to October 2008, the project recorded water savings of 131,833 m^3, corresponding to a 10% decline in water consumption, and cost savings of €260,000. Notably, the project also achieved a reduction in energy use of more than 900,000 kWh, saving €345,000, even though this only corresponds to a 1% reduction in consumption.

It was concluded that, in terms of the lessons learned from the project, all hotels can save water and energy, often through very simple measures. However, it takes committed hotel managers to achieve results that are more significant and the realisation that reducing resource use will mean financial savings. An additional important lesson was that, even when hotels were considered best practice, further savings were still possible. The Cyprus Sustainable Tourism Initiative also concluded that a project manager is key for the success of the project. Furthermore, projects become more far-reaching when they create competition. This can for instance be initiated on the basis of water use benchmarks,

(Continued)

Text Box 4.1 Measuring, auditing and monitoring in Cyprus (*Continued*)

which can be anonymised where individual or independent hotels are involved, or published internally where chains engage in such projects.

Source: The Travel Foundation (2009).

Where chains manage a large number of hotels, benchmarks can help to initiate competition for water-efficient management. Accor (1998) published, for instance, benchmarks for hotel managers that define target uses, notably with the implication that it is possible to under- or over-perform (Table 4.5). Similar benchmarks have been published by Hilton and Scandic hotels as well as a range of other hotels (Bodhanowicz-Godfrey & Zientara, 2014). Depending on the area and relative water abundance, benchmarks can also be absolute, i.e. defining what is sustainable for a given area and forcing management to achieve specific goals (see below).

Action plans

Through action plans, key priorities for management can be developed. For this purpose, it is essential to identify the most important water- and energy-consuming areas. As outlined above, these will usually include gardens and pools, in-room consumption, laundry and kitchen. Energy consumption is likely to be particularly associated with air conditioning or room heating, depending on the climate and season of the year. Where the most important water-consuming subsectors have been identified, options to reduce water use can be discussed based on behavioural, marketing and technical measures, also considering the economics of the suggested changes. An example of how the assessment of costs can be carried out is provided in Table 4.6 for a resort hotel in Kenya (Kuoni, 2013).

The action plan itself would then consist of four different management steps:

(1) Define the areas where water can be saved at a reasonable cost reduction.
(2) Develop a monitoring regime to control water consumption over time.
(3) Define best practice measures involving guests and staff.
(4) Define overall reduction targets for water consumption, and priorities for implementation as well as implementation times, including short-term, medium-term and long-term goals.

Table 4.4 Typical water saving per guest room in a hotel in Australia

Component	Best practice	Existing usage	Saving per room kL/year	Saving per room US$/year	Supply and installation cost	Description	Estimated payback period (years)
Showers	9 L/min (AAA rated)	15 L/min	28	US$100	US$50–120	New showerhead, plus option of flow control	0.5–2
Toilet	6/3 dual flush	11 L	17	US$30	US$400	New pan and cistern	>5
Basin	6 L/min	12 L/min	5.3	US$15	US$20–40	Flow control in spout or on taps	1.3–2.6
Cleaning	–	–	3.7	US$10	0	Typical saving	0
Total:			54	US$155	US$470–560	–	0–2.6

Source: After Sydney Water (2001), quoted in Smith *et al.* (2009a).

Table 4.5 Benchmarks for hotel managers, Accor

Consumption (m³ per day)	Per occupied room	Per meal	Gardens (per m²)
Formule 1	0.14	n.a.	0.3
Etap	0.20	n.a.	0.3
Ibis	0.26	0.05	0.3
Mercure	0.34	0.08	0.3
Novotel	0.31	0.08	0.3
Sofitel	0.58	0.15	0.3

Source: Accor (1998).

Monitoring

Monitoring is a key element of any approach to reducing resource use. For instance, initial efforts to reduce consumption in tourism may not last (e.g. staff behaviour and/or staff turnover), and require continued training. The objectives of certain projects may not have been met, resulting in greater costs than anticipated. In other areas, greater savings may have been achieved than anticipated. Monitoring thus allows managers to understand where efforts have to be renewed and where reductions have been comparably easy. Monitoring will also allow for the identification of leaks, which are often a cause of considerable water loss entailing economic losses.

Staff training

Staff are integral to sustainable management because they are in contact with customers, which gives them an opportunity to positively frame environmental actions to guests, and because they monitor rooms (e.g. cleaning), monitoring leakages or other problems with water fixtures. Cleaning staff can also considerably increase water consumption, for instance when flushing toilets more than once per room cleaning. In order to empower staff in their role as controllers and mediators of environmental performance, it is important for them to understand the underlying reasons for water management, and to provide them with knowledge about the hotel's activities in this regard.

An example of a successful staff training campaign was run by Hilton between 2006 and 2008, with environmental workshops organised for a total of 16,000 employees to develop their knowledge of environmental issues by participating in ecoLearning courses (Gössling, 2010). These courses were designed in a way as to include a series of quizzes and games covering

Table 4.6 Action plan summary sheet for a hotel in Kenya, Kuoni

(1) Per capita consumption

Your average daily consumption is	577	m³/day
Your average consumption per bednight is	1.07	m³/bednight
Your maximum was	1.22	m³/bednight
Your minimum was	0.88	m³/bednight
The industry average is	0.95	m³/bednight
Your average value is	1.12	times greater than the industry average
Best practice	0.9	m³/bednight
Your average value is	1.18	times greater than the industry average

(2) Base water costs

Primary supply of water is	groundwater	
This constitutes	94.5%	of your total supply
Average overall cost of water	18	kshs/m³
Softened water	59	kshs/m³
Desalinated water	38	kshs/m³
Rainwater	4.5	kshs/m³

(3) Hot water costs

Hot water – solar cost	0.18	kshs/litre
Hot water – electric heater cost	0.38	kshs/litre
Hot water – fuel boiler cost	0.18	kshs/litre

(4) Laundry costs

Laundering one towel cost you	32.0	kshs
– and uses	9.6	litres of water per item
Laundering one sheet cost you	42.0	kshs
– and uses	9.6	litres of water per item

(5) Flow measurements from fittings

Average flow rates in the following areas are

– guest bathroom sink	2.7	times greater than optimal flow
– guest bathroom shower	2.1	times greater than optimal flow
– staff washroom sink	0.95	times less than optimal flow
– staff washroom shower	2.5	times greater than optimal flow

(Continued)

Table 4.6 *(Continued)*

(6) Water budget analysis

Water is used in departments as follows (estimate)	m³/day	% of total
– laundry	38	8%
– guests	185	37%
– staff	66	13%
– health club/spa	1	0.1%
– irrigation	180	36%
– kitchen	27	5%
– pool	4	1%
– other (water sports, golf club, etc.)	0	0%
Total average daily consumption (estimate)	502	m³/day

(7) Towel re-use

Current re-use of towels is	16%	
This is	14%	less than best practice

(8) CBA laundry

With an improves re-use figure of	35%	
You will reduce items laundered by	55,822	per year
Saving a laundry cost of	1,783,591	kshs/year
With a water saving of	535,886	L/year
Which is equivalent to	0.25%	of total water consumption

(9) CBA plumbing fixtures

The total water wasted by fittings is	43,014	m³/year
Which is equivalent to	20%	of total consumption
Which costs an extra	2,939,485	kshs/year
The total cost of replacing all wasteful fittings is	7,460,400	kshs
The payback period for all fittings is	2.5	years
The fittings wasting the most amount of water are	guest showers	m³/year
– which waste a total of	19,057	
The fittings costing the most in wasted water are	guest showers	kshs/year
– which cost an extra of	2,514,259	
The fitting with the fastest payback period are	staff showers	Years
– with a payback period of	0.4	

Table 4.6 *(Continued)*

The fittings with the longest payback period are	guest toilets	Year
– with a payback period of	63	

(10) Wastewater treatment system

Type of system proposed	Constructed wetland – proposed	
Reduction in water required from other sources	65,754	m³/year
Which is equivalent to	31%	of total consumption
Equivalent cost	724,545	kshs/year

Note: kshs, Kenyan shillings.
Source: Kuoni (2013).

specific areas, such as kitchen or cleaning. To encourage team members to engage in pro-environmental activities and to reduce resource use, competitions were organised over three years, rewarding the teams in the best performing hotels with a mountain bike. In total, this helped the chain to reduce energy use by 15% and water use by 8% in Europe, also avoiding energy and water costs of €11 million. More than half of the savings were related to behavioural changes by staff members resulting out of the training provided. Hilton in continental Europe concluded that the success of the programme was partially embedded in the competitive element involving rewards, having fun, a focus on resource-use reductions (not costs), and support from top management. However, the lessons learned also included that ecoLearning programmes should have achievable goals and should be a continuous effort that has to be kept alive, while empowering staff. The Hilton initiative to conserve water and energy also generated worldwide attention and a positive media response, with positive repercussions for staff and guest loyalty.

Creating customer awareness

There are divided opinions as to whether guests on holiday can be involved in environmental initiatives, though evidence suggests that a large majority of guests are open to a moderate degree of involvement (e.g. Gössling, 2015). An important aspect of this is how hotels communicate their engagement, i.e. whether they openly and proudly announce their environmental ambitions and achievements or whether such action is 'hidden' from the view of the guests. Where communication is open, it is likely to result in 'crowding-in' effects; that is, guests will support the initiatives of an agent (the hotel) perceived as acting positively on such issues (see Plates 4.1 and 4.3). As discussed in greater detail below, guests can be involved in pro-environmental initiatives that consider psychological and sociocultural contexts. In some cases, it may even be possible to involve guests very pro-actively. One such example is Kuoni's (2013) 'Be a Water Champion with us' campaign. In this campaign, Kuoni provided water-saving tips for their customers, asking them to keep taps closed when brushing teeth, to re-use towels and to inform housekeeping about any leaks in the bathrooms. Kuoni even encouraged guests to develop and share their own ideas for water savings. To emphasise their commitment to the Water Champion campaign, Kuoni communicated the cost of washing one towel and vowed to donate the money saved from washing towels to local community water projects. Each day guests did not ask for a new towel, they were rewarded with a blue sticker corresponding to one credit point. The money saved this way was added up after the stay and donated to the projects.

In presenting this strategy, Kuoni (2013) underlines the idea that 'Water Champions' stand to gain from their initiatives and are encouraged by the

Plate 4.2 Entrance area of the Sunwing Kalithea Hotel in Rhodes, Greece. Open and proactive communication of environmental goals frames environmental performance as a quality aspect of the hotel, facilitating support by guests

Linen Change

Lady Elliot Island Eco Resort
GREAT BARRIER REEF

Linen Changes are done after the 3rd day of your stay upon request. Your room will also be serviced.

If you require your linen changed, please hang this card on the door by 9am.

eco CERTIFIED Advanced Ecotourism

Plate 4.3 Where guests are provided with a given option, in this case linen replacement after three days, they will often accept this as a suitable standard, particularly in eco-tourism (see here Lady Elliot Island, Australia). This card offers the opportunity to ask for a more frequent linen change, if desired

tour operator to maintain their engagement, based on 10 guidelines that conveniently summarise the above sections:

(1) Commit to a long-term engagement on sustainable water management.
(2) Purchase and install water meters in strategic locations in order to define water consumption throughout the hotel (e.g. laundry, kitchen, pool, gardens/lawns, guest rooms, staff rooms, spa, etc.).
(3) Collect basic water consumption data and complete simple calculations through the worksheets detailed within this manual.
(4) Log water consumption over a period of a few weeks and analyse consumption per guest night.

(5) Implement water-saving practices (technical solutions, staff training, etc.).
(6) Continue logging consumption data and calculate savings achieved.
(7) Report on your success and action plan.
(8) Commit to 'access to water' (or improved quality of water) related community project.
(9) Demonstrate an increased level of guest awareness and participation.
(10) Show off your Water Champion Award! (Kuoni, 2013)

Management opportunities: Irrigation, pools, kitchens and bottled water

Irrigation is one of the main factors in water use. From a management perspective, this raises the question as to how the interaction of soils, hydrology and plants can be improved. As an example, many small island developing states may have soils that are porous, draining irrigation water rapidly and hence making continuous irrigation a necessity. For such soils, the amelioration of the humus content of topsoils may improve water storage capacities. Humus can be generated from compost, i.e. returning food waste into organic compounds that can be used to improve soil characteristics and closing nutrient cycles. Furthermore, landscaping can considerably reduce water consumption. For instance, Smith *et al.* (2009a) suggest that 30–50% of water can be saved through measures such as choosing drought-resistant plants and grasses, mulching garden beds to reduce evaporation, the use of drip irrigation with electronic controllers and moisture sensors, or the use of grey water or harvested rainwater for irrigation. Sprinkler systems for lawns should always be operated pre-dawn in order to reduce evapotranspiration. The use of indigenous plants for landscaping may in many areas reduce the need for irrigation altogether (Carmody, 2007; Harris & Varga, 1995; Thompson, 2008), while in some locations the use of roof gardens may be a valuable way to enhance water recharge, help maintain biodiversity and provide a means of insulation.

Pools are the second most water consuming factor where these exist, and it is thus of importance to consider their size and volume when hotels are designed and planned. While deep pools increase the overall amount of water needed, pool size is important in terms of evaporation (e.g. Smith *et al.*, 2009a). Fountains, waterfalls and other features keeping water in motion increase evaporation. Smaller pools may be covered at night, although this may not be an option for irregularly shaped pools that also constitute part of the night-time attraction of a hotel (illumination). Measures to reduce water use for pools are thus limited, except for options to reduce water for backwashing (see Technology section) and the replacement of freshwater with seawater. Various options exist in this context. For instance, the Sunprime hotel in Rhodes, Greece reports that it fills its pool with seawater at the beginning of the season, and subsequently 'tops up' evaporated water with freshwater. In this way, no freshwater is used for the initial filling. Plate 4.4 shows another solution, i.e. where two pools exist, one may contain freshwater and the other seawater, to cater for different guest tastes while simultaneously reducing freshwater demand. A general consideration may also be as to whether freshwater pools can be replaced with seawater pools altogether. Where this is done, the seawater may possibly have to be circulated constantly, in order to avoid an accumulation of salt and algae growth.

Plate 4.4 Double pool containing freshwater (left) and seawater (right). Saltwater pools appear to be well accepted by many guests, and can replace one freshwater pool where different pools exist. This can help to significantly reduce freshwater consumption

Kitchens are directly involved in water consumption, for instance when food is washed, prepared, thawed and cooked, and when the kitchen, cooking implements, crockery and cutlery are cleaned. Various technological options to reduce water use are discussed further below. However, for chefs and hotel managers, there also exist many options to reduce water use on the basis of cost-benefit analyses. Generally, few hotels appear to consider the implications of food management, other than the cost of the foodstuffs purchased. There appears to be a general understanding that food purchases are costly, in the order of 30–50% of turnover, and that regional, organic or otherwise sometimes more expensive foods have to be weighted carefully against potential benefits in added consumer value and sales. In order to better understand these food management issues, a 5-star hotel in Rhodes, Greece provided a list of the purchases made, as well as per-kg costs for each of the foodstuffs used. These are shown in Figure 4.2 for 70 foodstuffs, i.e. only a selection of the most important of a total of 150 different foodstuffs purchased during the year.

Figure 4.2 shows that there are huge differences with regard to per-kg purchase costs. Dairy products, certain fish and seafood as well as meats are comparably expensive, while fruit and vegetables as well as carbohydrates are cheap. This opens up opportunities to create menus offering a greater variety of, for instance, non-meat alternatives. This is also depicted in Figure 4.3, which shows the quantities purchased of each of the products in relation to their total cost. Meats and cold cuts have considerably greater quantity to cost ratios than, for instance, dairy products, while fruit and vegetables have considerably lower costs in comparison to the amounts purchased. Depending on the hotel and its current meat plans, but also the guest types found, menus can be adjusted to better reflect tastes, while also being less water consuming and being economically more attractive for management.

In more general terms, a number of rules for low energy and low water food management have been suggested in the literature (Gössling *et al.*, 2011, 2012). These rules consider purchases, preparation and presentation:

Purchases
(a) Buy as little as possible policy
- Buy as little as possible vegetables grown in heated greenhouses;
- Buy as little as possible foods involving air transport;
- Buy as little as possible specific species, such as giant, king and tiger prawns, lobster;
- Buy as little as possible imported beef;
- Buy as little as possible aluminium foil.

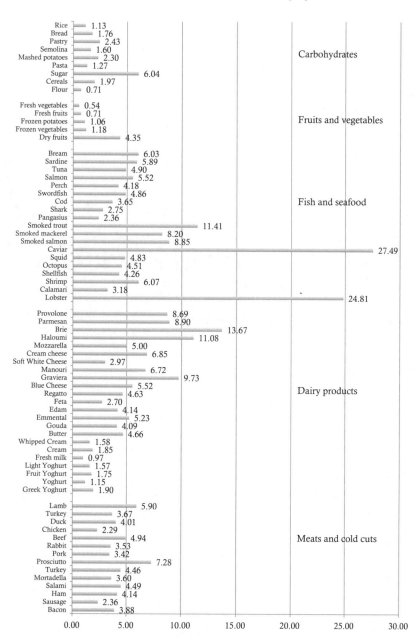

Figure 4.2 Per kg prices of different foodstuffs
Source: Nikos Portokallas, general manager, personal communication, October 2013.

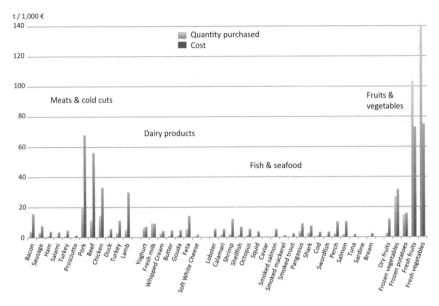

Figure 4.3 Food quantity to purchase cost ratios
Source: Nikos Portokallas, general manager, personal communication, October 2013.

(b) Buy less policy
- Buy less beef;
- Buy less deep-sea fish (e.g. cod);
- Buy less farmed carnivorous fish (e.g. salmon);
- Buy less rice;
- Buy less seasonal foods out of their season.

(c) Buy more policy
- Buy more locally produced foods, if transported over short distances;
- Buy more potatoes;
- Buy more grains (including pasta);
- Buy more pelagic fish;
- Buy more pork;
- Buy more chicken;
- Buy more foodstuffs with longer shelf lives.

Preparation
- Purchase energy from renewable sources;
- Use more energy-efficient cooking routines;
- Put dishes on the menu that use less meat and more vegetables;

- Plan purchases to avoid waste;
- Separate food waste from general waste.

Presentation
- Always present as many as possible attractive vegetarian alternatives;
- Reduce portion sizes at buffets, with more regular replenishment;
- Reduce plate size at buffets;
- Arrange buffets so that less water-intensive foods are at the centre;
- Train staff to recommend less water-intensive dishes (à la carte);
- Avoid single-use packaging.

One further aspect related to food management is bottled water, which has a considerable energy footprint (Gleick & Cooley, 2009), and is particularly problematic in terms of waste. Many destinations, particularly in the tropics, are not ready to handle the huge numbers of empty plastic bottles disposed of by tourists. Yet plastic bottles contain just plain water, and can thus be easily replaced with the glass bottle systems which are now readily available. An example is Scandic Hotels, one of the pioneers of more environmentally friendly accommodation practices. The chain decided to phase out plastic bottles in 2008, and had their own bottles designed and made from recycled glass in Spain. Since then, Scandic provides its guests with filtered and, where requested, carbonated tap water, which is monitored regularly with regard to its quality. Despite high investment costs for glass bottles, it has been economically profitable for Scandic to introduce the system, and guests generally appear to favour stylish glass bottles replacing plastic ones (see also Plate 3.8, showing a glass bottle example from Greece). Finally, in-room management considerations may include:

- Reduce laundry volume and weight (use medium towel quality, medium towel size; avoid thick linen napkins in restaurants);
- Room cleaning: flush toilet only once, when leaving hotel room;
- Staff to report running toilets and taps, etc.;
- Technician: check piping/cranes/taps/toilets, etc. for leakages twice a year (beginning and end of high season).

Social Marketing and Behaviour Change

Social marketing is the use of commercial marketing concepts and tools to create behavioural change (Hall, 2013a). Social marketing – 'the use of marketing principles and techniques to influence a target audience to voluntarily accept, reject, modify or abandon a behaviour for the benefit of individuals, groups or society as a whole' (Kotler *et al.*, 2002: 5) – is an area of marketing that is continuing to grow in significance, particularly as governments seek to use non-regulatory mechanisms to change individual and group behaviours and businesses and organisations strive to change their own customers' behaviour in some cases. Yet 'despite widespread attention being given to the importance of changing the behaviors of both tourists and tourism businesses' (Truong & Hall, 2013: 1), especially in the context of sustainable tourism, there is surprisingly little attention given to the potential of social marketing in the field of water conservation and tourism. Nevertheless, social marketing and behavioural change are inseparable from technical or structural changes to water provision (Hall, 2013a, 2013b). Businesses and destinations may seek to change the nature of supply in order to reduce water consumption, but tourists also need to be accepting of that change and, in some cases, change their own behaviour as well. However, importantly, it must be recognised that behaviour change in isolation from some of the technical suggestions also made in this book will, by itself, only have limited results. Social marketing to change tourists' and, in some cases, businesses' use of water must therefore go hand in hand with technical and regulatory change.

It is generally recognised that knowledge of environmental issues as well as guidance on the 'right' actions is important for encouraging pro-environmental action. Commonly used mechanisms may be soft policy instruments, such as ecolabels, which are widespread in tourism (Gössling & Buckley, 2015), or the provision of information to guests that a hotel is engaging in environmental programmes. However, importantly, social marketing is more than just education or the provision of information. Just providing information and expecting people to behave 'rationally' leads to a very limited behavioural change. Instead, social marketing is based on a systematic approach to a problem that requires a change in a targeted market's behaviour and is part of a continuum of behavioural change approaches (Figure 4.4) that have also been described as constituting 'lessons', 'hugs', 'shoves', 'nudges' and 'smacks' (Hall, 2013a; Thaler & Sunstein, 2008):

- *Lesson*: The provision of information with respect to a particular behaviour, e.g. on wasting water, and its negative effects (externalities) in the belief that individuals will change in their own self-interest.
- *Hug*: This covers a wide range of incentives for improved water behaviours – although these are not usually directly financial to individuals but may include vouchers or discounts, but may be for businesses. An example would be encouraging the adoption of water-efficient technologies by hotels in return for a reduction in property taxes, or providing a reward

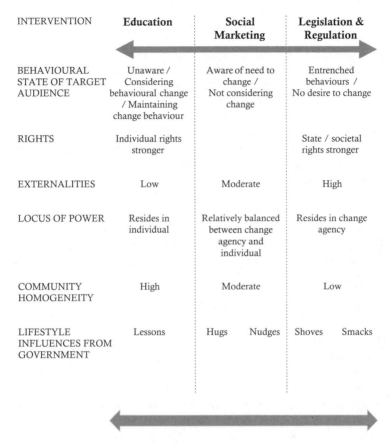

INTERVENTION	Education	Social Marketing	Legislation & Regulation
BEHAVIOURAL STATE OF TARGET AUDIENCE	Unaware / Considering behavioural change / Maintaining change behaviour	Aware of need to change / Not considering change	Entrenched behaviours / No desire to change
RIGHTS	Individual rights stronger		State / societal rights stronger
EXTERNALITIES	Low	Moderate	High
LOCUS OF POWER	Resides in individual	Relatively balanced between change agency and individual	Resides in change agency
COMMUNITY HOMOGENEITY	High	Moderate	Low
LIFESTYLE INFLUENCES FROM GOVERNMENT	Lessons	Hugs Nudges	Shoves Smacks

Figure 4.4 A continuum of behavioural interventions

like a bowl of fruit in the hotel room for high reuse of towels or for providing the hotel with an idea for environmental improvement.

- *Nudges*: Based on the idea that behaviour can be changed voluntarily without using compulsion. Nudges can include enticing people to take up activities by using financial or time incentives or disincentives or the use of social marketing. For example, stressing social norms or desired social status may encourage people to change behaviour because they want to be perceived in a particular way or think of themselves in a certain way. A very relevant piece of research on this issue was conducted by Goldstein *et al.* (2008). In two field experiments they found that appeals employing descriptive norms (e.g. 'the majority of guests reuse their towels') were superior to a traditional appeal widely used by hotels that focused solely on environmental protection, e.g. an educational message that appealed to rational behaviour (a lesson). Moreover, normative appeals were most effective when describing group behaviour that occurred in the setting that most closely matched individuals' immediate situational circumstances (e.g. 'the majority of guests in this room reuse their towels'), which Goldstein *et al.* (2008) refer to as provincial norms. This research is discussed in more detail later in the chapter.

- *Shove*: More deliberate than a nudge and is a mildly regulatory approach. For example, some planning departments may restrict particular types of accommodation and facilities in some locations because of their demands on groundwater supply but not ban the activity altogether. Similarly, some types of activities, such as overnight camping near streams, may be banned in some locations in a water catchment because of concerns over their effects on water quality but not in others.
- *Smack*: The most coercive of all government regulatory measures by banning something outright or imposing large financial penalties, e.g. for water pollution.

In brief, the stages of the social marketing process are:

- Define problem.
- Conduct marketing research.
- Segment and target market.
- Establish goals/objectives for intervention and/or programme.
- Design appropriate marketing strategy that includes consideration of the five Ps: product (service), price, place, promotion and politics.
- Implement and monitor intervention programme.
- Evaluate the programme.
- Start again! (Re)define problem.

As with commercial marketing, social marketing is still substantially founded on concepts of exchange and competition (Andreasen, 2012). However, social marketing extends the exchange concept of commercial marketing by framing social marketing as the voluntary exchange of behavioural change in the target audience for direct and indirect benefits to that audience. The costs associated with behavioural change can therefore take a number of forms, not only monetary but also such things as forms of pleasure and status among peer groups as well as, in the case of environmental behaviours, doing the 'right thing'. Ultimately, the perceived benefits of the new behaviour must outweigh the perceived costs in order for people to try it. In order to do that, focus may be put on:

- Increasing and highlighting the benefits to the target audience;
- Decreasing or de-emphasising the barriers to the adoption of new behaviours;
- Changing the product, place, price or promotion to meet the exchange.

The competition concept in social marketing means that the new behaviour being offered to the target audience competes with existing behaviours and/ or other potential new behaviours that could be adopted:

> *behavioral change* is the process of altering, maintaining or encouraging the cessation of a specific activity undertaken by the *targeted audience*. Behavioral change is achieved through the creation, communication, delivery and exchange of a competitive *social marketing offer* that induces voluntary change in the targeted audience, and which results in *benefit* to the social change campaign's recipients, partners and the broader society at large. (Dann, 2010: 151, emphasis in original)

The offer to the target audience may therefore be used to make competing behaviours less attractive, for example, in terms of economic or time cost, or with respect to their social acceptability, status or individual benefit. Social marketing therefore aims to develop products, services and messages that provide people with an exchange they will value. A good example of such a campaign is encouraging people to improve water quality in Chesapeake Bay by limiting harmful environmental behaviour.

Text Box 4.2 Exchanging new behaviours for water quality in Chesapeake Bay: 'Save the crabs, then eat 'em!'

Chesapeake Bay is the largest estuary in America, but a rapidly growing population around the bay had contributed to increased pollution, often in the form of agricultural chemicals from sewage and lawn fertiliser runoff. Although regulation had meant a reduction in pollution levels by the local industry, environmental campaigning had failed to achieve any sustainable behaviour change from the residents of the bay and visitors from the wider area. A social marketing approach was taken to find a way to motivate them into action and a suitable exchange was needed in order to get around resident scepticism and inertia.

(Continued)

Text Box 4.2 Exchanging new behaviours for water quality in Chesapeake Bay: 'Save the crabs, then eat 'em!' (*Continued*)

The focus of the exchange proposition became the blue crab, a seafood favourite, which was found to be under threat from the pollution because of habitat change. Local residents and holiday home-owners were therefore asked to change their behaviour by viewing fertiliser runoff as a culinary rather than an environmental problem. The focus was not to completely stop people from fertilising their lawns but to persuade them to fertilise in the autumn instead of spring, when heavy rains washed fertiliser into the bay. A humorous, 'Save the crabs, then eat 'em!' campaign ran in the media which promoted how people could go about looking after their lawns in a more effective way as well as looking after the bay overall. This was an initiative of the Chesapeake Bay Program – a regional partnership of federal and state agencies, local governments, non-profit organisations and academic institutions. After the intervention, there was increased awareness of lawn-care behaviours that contribute to pollution, and a corresponding decrease in intent to fertilise in the spring. No data were available on how many crabs were eaten! As Merritt *et al.* (2011) conclude:

> This is a great example of how social marketing was able to identify an exchange that changed the behaviour of people jaded by decades of message-based appeals.
> Whether consciously or not, people analyse costs and benefits at some level before they decide to act. By taking a social marketing approach and developing an exchange, you can ensure that the benefits offered are ones your audience value.

Chesapeake Bay Program: http://www.chesapeakebay.net/.

Andreasen (2012) highlights that the 'value proposition' of social marketing is not necessarily embedded in a specific product or service, although this may be a practical and attractive outcome for many organisations and businesses. Instead, it lies in behaviour. Therefore, he highlights a number of behavioural objectives that lie at the heart of what social marketing is trying to achieve

- *Start a behaviour*: e.g. label local foods on menus;
- *Switch or substitute a behaviour*: e.g. use reusable glass bottles for water in restaurants, cafés and hotels rather than plastic bottles;

- *Stop a behaviour*: e.g. make sure that air conditioning is turned off in a room when it is not occupied;
- *Not start a behaviour*: e.g. do not pollute lakes and rivers when camping and hiking;
- *Continue a behaviour*: e.g. continue to reuse towels rather than put them out for collection for washing;
- *Increase a behaviour*: e.g. use more local food on restaurant menus;
- *Decrease a behaviour*: e.g. have a shorter hot shower therefore using less energy and water.

Andreasen's behavioural focus provides a useful framework to understand not only the broader sphere of marketing but also the application of social marketing to changing behaviour in a tourism context.

Changing Behaviours

Guest behaviour and interventions to stimulate cooperative behaviour make up an area that has received growing interest in the literature in recent years, specifically in the context of climate change and pro-environmental behaviour (e.g. Goldstein *et al.*, 2012; Steg & Vlek, 2009; Stoll-Kleemann *et al.*, 2001). Tourism is generally seen as a hedonic space in which behaviour is particularly difficult to change (Hall, 2014). Schahn (1993) identified a wide range of excuses with which the impossibility of behavioural change would be justified:

(1) Metaphor of displaced commitment: 'I protect the environment in other ways.'
(2) To condemn the accuser: 'You have no right to challenge me.'
(3) Denial of responsibility: 'I am not the main cause of this problem.'
(4) Rejection of blame: 'I have done nothing so wrong as to be destructive.'
(5) Ignorance: 'I simply don't know the consequences of my actions.'
(6) Powerlessness: 'I am only an infinitesimal being in the order of things.'
(7) Fabricated constraints: 'There are too many impediments.'
(8) After the flood: 'What is the future doing for me?'
(9) Comfort: 'It is too difficult for me to change my behaviour.'

Stoll-Kleemann *et al.* (2001) developed these excuses into four 'denial' categories, including comfort, tragedy-of-the-commons, managerial fix and government distrust. More specifically, 'comfort' refers to an unwillingness to give up habits or favoured lifestyles, which importantly are associated with a sense of self-identity. 'Tragedy-of-the-commons' essentially means that the cost of action to self is considered greater than the value of such action to others, reflecting an unwillingness to act altruistically. 'Managerial fix' considers all problems as either irrelevant, or resolvable by third parties, for instance through the development of technology or regulation. Finally, 'government distrust' refers to a belief that others do not engage in action, and that one's own action thus becomes irrelevant. Steg and Vlek (2009) thus suggested that in order to change behaviour, it is important to understand the underlying factors, including perceived costs and benefits, moral and normative concerns, affect, contextual factors and habits.

In tourism studies, the general question has been raised as to whether it is meaningful to involve tourists in pro-environmental behaviour, given the hedonic character of leisure and business travel, and anticipated even greater psychological barriers that need to be overcome than with regard to 'at home' consumption. For instance, in a study of air travellers, it was found that only one-third of respondents assumed *any* responsibility for the emissions caused by their flight, with most air travellers suggesting that either airlines, manufacturers or governments needed to take action (Gössling *et al.*, 2009). It has thus been argued that it may be more effective to restructure industry, rather than to try design interventions to influence consumption.

This book takes the perspective that influencing guest and staff behaviour is of great importance for various reasons. First of all, many studies now exist that show that tourist behaviour can be influenced, if only to a modest degree (Hall, 2013a). However, as tourists come to perceive 'pro-environmental' activities by industry as a sign of quality, this may increasingly change in the future. Ideally, tourists may even take with them a wide range of ideas and positive ideas as to how to become more environmentally friendly at home. In short, to act in line with environmental concerns is no longer a contradiction, as there appears substantial public support in the EU and elsewhere for pro-environmental activities (Eurobarometer, 2011), and environmental knowledge is generally increasing (Barr *et al.*, 2010). From a business perspective, informational campaigns and strategies are not costly and, if framed positively, will help to increase customer loyalty, while at the same time saving costs. This, however, requires that such information needs to incorporate declarative, procedural and effectiveness knowledge, i.e. not only describing the problem, but also indicating as to how behaviour can be changed, and which difference this behavioural change will make (van der Linden, 2014).

As water consumption is embedded in energy and food consumption, virtually all stages of a holiday are important areas in which to influence pro-environmental change. This includes: the choice of the destination, with

Plate 4.5 Clearly communicated flush option for toilets. Best practice models will use as little as 1–2 L for a small, and 6 L for a large flush, and the state-of-the-art design will appeal to tourists

more distant destinations requiring significantly greater energy resources for transport; the transport mode, where surface-bound transport is an option (trains and buses being less energy intense than cars); and the choice of accommodation, with luxurious hotels generally being far more resource intensive than smaller ones. The following sections study two areas of consumption in greater detail in order to outline the complexities and difficulties involved in intervening with behavioural choices, i.e. food choices and towel and bed linen change.

Food choices

Food is one of the most important sustainability issues in a hotel, due to the range of social and environmental implications that arise during production, distribution and preparation, as well as the large quantities of water needed to produce food. As outlined in the previous sections, it is thus of importance to reduce the share of meats, and to offer larger quantities of vegetables and fruit. As much of the food in hotels is offered as a buffet, it is also important to reduce food waste resulting out of leftovers that have to be discarded (Plate 4.6). Generally, there is evidence that vegetarian choices are increasingly appreciated, as are regional and organic food choices. The case study in

Text Box 4.3 shows the results of a survey among tourists in a 4- and 5-star hotel in Rhodes, Greece, indicating that there is considerable room for adjusting food alternatives, considering food management rules as outlined above. To minimise food waste, various strategies can be employed. For instance, in the Maritime pro Arte Hotel, Berlin, small plates with a diameter of 26 cm are offered to guests, so that 'overloading' of plates is kept at a minimum (Gössling, 2010). Deep dishes on the buffet may also have smaller diameters of only 18–26 cm and be filled with a maximum of 10 portions. This helps avoid guests feeling that buffets have already been 'plundered', and the share of food that needs to be discarded after buffets is also minimised. At the same time, frequent re-filling generates an effect of all foods being freshly cooked, coming directly out of the kitchen. Upon refilling deep dishes, staff

Plate 4.6 Leftovers from a breakfast table by tourists at Tangalooma Island Resort, Australia. Food production has a wide range of environmental implications, and food waste significantly increases indirect (global) water consumption

can at the same time control how guests perceive the buffets, and whether they are generally happy with the food offered. The Maritime pro Arte also places meats at the periphery of buffets rather than in the centre, to encourage vegetarian choices. All of these measures have an appreciable effect on consumer behaviour.

Text Box 4.3 Sustainable food choices, Rhodes, Greece

Food is one of the most sensitive issues in tourism. From an environmental viewpoint, there are few issues that are connected to such a range of problems as food production, including the use of pesticides, clear cutting of forest areas for plantations (e.g. soy production to feed cattle), or animal welfare. Food production is also the major factor in water consumption, accounting for an estimated 85% of the overall direct and indirect water footprint of a holiday. The consumption of food, on the other hand, is one of the most central aspects of tourism and hospitality, is increasingly becoming a signifier of the quality of a holiday and has a huge potential to affect holiday perceptions. In particular, large buffets offering dozens of choices have become a sought-after aspect of a holiday, guiding perceptions of destination and holiday quality (see also Plate 4.6).

In order to better understand which aspects of food are of specific importance, an international sample of 103 tourists in a 4- and a 5-star hotel in Rhodes, Greece, were interviewed in June 2014. Questions included the importance of national specialities, regional foods (rather than imported foodstuffs), organic food, meat, fish, giant (tiger) prawns and overall eating habits. In order to evaluate the relative importance of these aspects, a Likert-scale (1 – 'very important' to 5 – 'not important at all') was used (Table 4.7). Results indicate that a considerable majority rate the importance of national specialities either very high or high (79%), with only 4% not considering Greek dishes as important for their holiday. Two-thirds (68%) also consider the purchase of regional or local foodstuffs as important, again with a minority (5%) believing that this has no importance. The situation is somewhat different for organic food purchases: half (49%) of respondents indicate that they are indifferent to the issue, with about equal shares stating that organic food is important (24%) or not important (28%). Finally, with regard to one environmentally harmful foodstuff, giant prawns, only 22% perceive these as being very important to their holiday, while 46% consider these as unimportant; one-third (32%) is indifferent.

(Continued)

Text Box 4.3 Sustainable food choices, Rhodes, Greece (*Continued*)

Table 4.7 Importance of different foods, Rhodes, Greece

Likert scale	Very important	– – – –		Not important at all
	1	2	3	4	5
How important are Greek specialities?	62%	17%	18%	0%	4%
How important is it that foodstuffs are local/regionally purchased?	47%	21%	28%	2%	3%
How important is it that foodstuffs are organically produced?	16%	8%	49%	9%	19%
How important are giant prawns?	19%	3%	32%	9%	37%

Source: Authors.

Results indicate that local dishes are important, and that it is also important to buy regional foodstuffs to prepare these. Organic purchases are important for about a quarter of respondents and can be considered an added value for these guests. Giant prawns are highly relevant to a share of guests. The potential to replace these, for instance with shrimp or local crustaceans, should consequently be further investigated.

Guests were also asked whether there were foods that they could 'not do without' (multiple answers possible). Almost half of the respondents (49%) valued chicken very highly, and almost as many respondents fish (48%), followed by beef (34%), pork (29%), as well as lamb and vegetarian choices (both 14%). In terms of food management, chicken production and (local) fish are less water and energy intense, and dishes with chicken could be favoured in food preparation. Beef, on the other hand, is the most energy- and water-intense food, and its use should be kept at a minimum. Non-meat choices might be made more attractive by offering a variety of dishes. Overall, it needs to be noted that the sample of tourists is small and shows considerable differences between the two hotels where interviews were carried out, and there are also considerable gender differences, with women being more interested in salads, fruit and vegetables. This indicates that different tourist populations may favour different foods, which has to be considered when buffets are adjusted to reflect issues of water and energy management.

Website: www.waterfootprint.org

Towel and bed linen change

As discussed in Chapter 3, towels and bed linen generate considerable amounts of laundry, which is a significant subsector of water and energy consumption in the hotel. Many hotels, because of perceptions of their guests' service expectations, have policies to change both towels (up to three per guest) as well as bed linen on a daily basis. In such hotels, encouraging guests to use their towels/linen for two days would cut laundry volumes, and thus water and energy use as well as detergents by 50%, while simultaneously reducing the workloads of cleaning staff. Recent research in the field has in particular addressed social norms, i.e. the effectiveness of signs encouraging hotel guests to reuse their towels based on normative appeals (Goldstein *et al.*, 2008, 2011; Shang *et al.*, 2010).

Goldstein *et al.* (2008) were the first to empirically test whether descriptive normative approaches to hotel conservation programmes would be more effective at encouraging towel reuse. The standard approach to towel reuse programme in hotels is currently based on largely identical statements along the lines of 'Help us save the environment', followed by some additional information as to how this can make a contribution to help nature, water consumption or the use of detergents (see also Plate 4.7). Goldstein *et al.* (2008) used this approach as well as an alternative descriptive norm message, informing guests that 75% of guests participated in the towel reuse

Plate 4.7 In-room environmental information is now widespread, but has often caused suspicions on the side of guests as to whether environmental engagement is genuine. Where towels are replaced even though guests wished to retain these, considerable frustration can result

programme by using their towels more than once, and encouraging guests to follow this good practice example by their fellow guests. Below this text, instructions were provided as to how to engage in the programme ('Please place towels on the floor') as well as information regarding the impact of the programme ('if most guests participated, ... this would save 72,000 gallons of water and 39 barrels of oil and 480 gallons of detergent'). Results from an *in situ* experiment in a hotel with 190 rooms indicated that this norm message yielded a considerably higher towel reuse rate, 44% rather than 35% as observed in the standard room.

In a follow-up experiment, Goldstein *et al.* (2008) designed five different messages asking guests to participate in towel reuse programmes, including: (i) the standard message, 'Help save the environment'; (ii) a descriptive norm 'Join your fellow guests in helping to save the environment', along with information that 75% of guests in the hotel already participated; (iii) the same norm, but information that 75% of guests in the specific room participated; (iv) a norm stating 'Join your fellow citizens in helping to save the environment', along with information that 75% of guests supported the programme; and finally, (v), a message with a gender identity norm, i.e. 'Join the men and women who are helping to save the environment', also stating that a slightly higher share of women (76%) than men (74%) supported this programme. Again, results indicated that all four descriptive norm messages achieved higher participation (44%) than the standard message (37%). Specifically successful was the 'same room identity norm', which yielded a 49% towel reuse rate.

Further research on towel and bed linen reuse was carried out by Shang *et al.* (2010), focusing on the general importance of reuse marketing campaigns, as well as the messages used in these. Shang *et al.* (2010) find that programmes help reducing towel and bed linen use, and their implementation is thus favourable to not involving guests. However, guests may perceive such programmes as having the purpose of saving financial resources for the hotel rather than achieving an environmental benefit, and requests for participation should thus be framed in a way that indicates how actual savings are redistributed. For instance, this may include an option to donate savings to charity, or to indicate that social compliance mechanisms are in place. While it was found that the type of charity (environmental or social) was of limited importance to guests, not engaging in donations may make the hotel appear to be less socially concerned.

More recent research on towel and linen reuse programmes focused on the importance of the distinction between reciprocity-by-proxy versus incentive-by-proxy strategies (Goldstein *et al.*, 2011). Incentive-by-proxy strategies encourage guests to reuse their towels on the basis of a donation to charity in exchange for the support of the guests. This essentially represents an *ex post* engagement, rewarding guests after they have supported the hotel's programme. In contrast, reciprocity-by-proxy represents an initial engagement of the hotel, i.e. a donation is made in the hope of the guests' compliance, thus creating a feeling of indebtedness on the side of the guests that they will try to reciprocate. Findings indicate that reciprocity-by-proxy messages are significantly more successful than standard environmental or incentive-by-proxy messages.

Overall, a number of conclusions can be drawn from behavioural change research as presented so far. First of all, engaging in towel and bed linen programmes represents an advantage over not engaging in them, and normative messages can be enforced through the use of hotel logos (Shang *et al.*, 2010). Furthermore, messages should highlight that a large share of guests *in the respective room where the information is provided* do support the towel/bed linen reuse program, and they should contain information indicating that the hotel is already supporting charity as a result of its financial profits from guest compliance, asking guests for reciprocal action (Goldstein *et al.*, 2011).

While research has yielded important insights, a number of significant issues remain unaddressed. For instance, as outlined, information should incorporate three dimensions of knowledge – declarative, procedural and effectiveness knowledge (van der Linden, 2014). Currently, it seems that none of the research engaging in field experiments has considered these. Furthermore, the importance of the length of the text provided has not been investigated, even though long texts may be a disincentive or prohibitive to actual reading, i.e. discouraging participation. Another aspect that may be of importance is the placement of information, with more prominent locations being potentially of greater importance in raising attention. Finally, the case study in Text Box 4.4 also indicates that there are considerable differences with regard to towel, pool towel and bed linen reuse, as well as the time of the year, with shoulder seasons being less 'towel intense' than hotter seasons. In this context, most hotels provide a variety of towels to guests, i.e. at least one larger and one smaller towel, and their use and perceptions of renewal needs may vary. This insight is potentially relevant with regard to considerable differences in temperatures between destinations: where guests are feeling hotter and sweatier, potentially also using more sun lotion, or in need of frequent showers to cool down, this may increase towel use and also have repercussions for perceptions of the need to change bed linen frequently. The case study also revealed that compliance might be guest type/culture specific, potentially related to the standard of the hotel with, for instance, expectations of daily changes of towels and bed linen being more likely in 5-star hotels than in bed & breakfast accommodation.

In contrast, irrespective of hotel standard, guests may react irritably when towels are exchanged even though guests wished to keep them for another day. In this context, the hotel's own engagement in environmental measures and their communication is potentially also of importance, as it may generate so-called 'crowding-in' effects, i.e. people supporting certain strategies because of a feeling that their engagement is matched by an agent, in this case the hotel. These aspects add further complexity to the design of messages. Figure 4.5, based on insights as outlined above, indicates how messages to encourage guests to reuse their towels may be designed, considering factual, procedural and effectiveness knowledge, as well as psychological insights on intervention design. Messages need to be placed in a central location in the room, for instance stuck against the bathroom mirror in a lower corner, so as not to be ignored.

Policy

A couple of years ago we had a very serious drought. To preserve water, the government sent out timers to all households. And that's how we all learned to take four-minute showers. (Resident, Brisbane area, Queensland, Australia, Interview, February 2014)

There is general consensus that resource use in tourism can only be broadly addressed through the development of appropriate environmental governance frameworks (e.g. Gössling et al., 2013; Higham et al., 2013; Scott et al., 2010). Various reasons have been outlined for this, with the more important ones including tourism's rapid growth and the usually considerable purchasing power of the sector in comparison to other competing sectors (e.g. agriculture, domestic uses in developing countries), as well as the fact that much of tourism's energy use is outside national policy frameworks (e.g. bunker fuels). Tourism also has strong lobbies due to the employment generated by the sector. However, these factors have often been barriers to the implementation of significant governance structures in tourism (e.g. Hall, 2011a, 2011b, 2013b; OECD & UNEP, 2011).

Compounding the need for well-articulated and focused environmental policies is the fact that tourism is becoming increasingly resource intensive, as a result of higher standards in hotels, with spas and multiple (heated) swimming pools, additional private pools, in-room jacuzzis, sports and health centres, expectations to change towels and bed linen on a daily basis, larger rooms, luxurious 'rain' showerheads, heated toilet seats and bathroom mirrors serving as examples of current developments that increase specific water consumption.

Help us protecting a precious resource!

Water is scarce in your holiday destination. For this reason, we would like you to help us minimizing our laundry volumes: each day you reuse your bathroom towels saves 15 L; and each day you keep your bed linen another 20 L of freshwater.

In 2013, 75% of all guests in room _____ reused their towels. As we expect a similar result this year, we have donated the equivalent of our savings from not having to wash the towels and bed linen to a charity, Blue Planet, which engages in providing safe water to people living in water-stressed areas.

Kindly note that towels will be changed every two days, bed linen every third day. If you wish to have these exchanged more often, please place them in the basket located in the bathroom for this purpose.

Thank you for supporting our environmental initiatives!

Let's go!

Figure 4.5 Example of a normative message to encourage towel and bed linen reuse
Source: Authors

Technology

Water consumption can be reduced through technology, but technology may also free up new water resources. From a supply-side viewpoint, it may thus be possible for hotels to abstract greater quantities of groundwater or water from inland sources or to desalinate seawater, but such options may often be unsustainable and incur a cost. Groundwater is vulnerable to overexploitation and coastal aquifers are vulnerable to salinisation as a result of

Text Box 4.4 Towel and bed linen policies

There are various unresolved questions with regard to normative messages and guests' willingness to support towel, pool towel and bed linen programmes. For example, it remains open as to whether there are significant differences in guest cultures, demanding specific messages tailored to these cultures, or default standards set to meet these guests' expectations – if these existed, a hotel may for instance have a two-, three-, or four-day towel change policy. There may also be important differences between countries, as well as between seasons, depending on temperatures. Furthermore, bed linen, towels and bed linen changes may be perceived differently, i.e. guests may be willing to use towels or linen for longer periods of time, demanding flexible management.

To address these issues, a study was carried out in Rhodes, Greece, in October 2013 and June 2014, including 101 guests in a 5-star hotel (October 2013) as well as 103 guests in a combined study of a 5-star and a 4-star hotel (June 2014). Results indicate that there are significant differences between seasons and with regard to towels in the room, towels used at pools and bed linen. Figure 4.6, referring to results from June 2014, shows that bed linen is the item that appears to be in least need of change, with only 7% of guests demanding a daily change. Another 29% are willing to keep their linen for at least two days, and 30% for three days. Another 14% would keep their linen four days and equally many for a whole week. The remainder would accept a change after five or six days. This indicates that a bed linen regime focusing on a change every three days will be acceptable to most guests, particularly when accompanied by a policy that allows for more frequent changes on demand (see also Plate 3.6).

The situation is somewhat different with regard to towels. About a quarter of respondents indicated that they would expect new towels every day, and half of all respondents every second day. There is a large majority requesting new towels in the room every day. The situation may be different in the shoulder season, when temperatures are lower, as results from the October 2013 survey indicated that only 12% of guests expected a towel change every day. Finally, pool towel perceptions are similar, although there is a significantly larger share of guests indicating that they are willing to use their pool towels for three or even four days. Other than in the case of in-room towels, pool towel management can be designed in different ways, however. Managers asked about their pool towels reported that they used different strategies to discourage frequent exchanges of particularly heavy and thick pool towels.

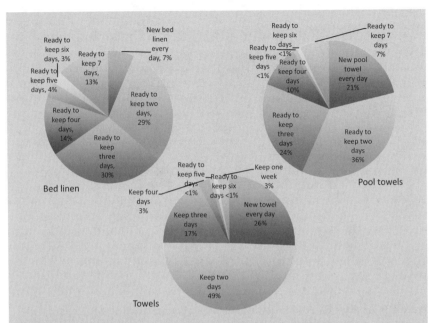

Figure 4.6 Willingness to reuse bed linen, towels and pool towels
Source: Authors.

These included: (i) pool towels were not part of the package booked, i.e. guests had to pay a fee to obtain a pool towel; (ii) pool towels were initially handed out to guests, but could only be changed against a fee, with even small amounts reportedly having a significant effect on exchange frequencies; and (iii) exchanges only during specific times or days of the week, in order to reduce the time frames within which new towels can be obtained. Depending on clientele, any of these measures may be used.

Various hotels in Rhodes reported that guests reacted with irritation when towels were exchanged even though guests wished to keep them. Conflicts often arose out of miscommunication, with staff being uncertain as to whether guests really wished to keep their towels, or whether they had simply forgotten to indicate this by putting the towel on the floor. Notably, guests might be reluctant to throw towels on the floor, which might be perceived as unethical behaviour, given that cleaning staff need to bend down to collect towels. In such situations, staff usually exchanged towels even when put up on racks as, in their experience,

(Continued)

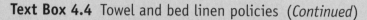

Text Box 4.4 Towel and bed linen policies *(Continued)*

Plate 4.8 A basket for used towels and linen. Rather than throwing these on the floor, guests are asked to deposit towels and linen in the basket if they request a change. This helps to avoid misunderstandings, as staff might decide to replace towels that guests wish to continue to use

this created less of a problem than a guest expecting a towel to be changed. In order to avoid misunderstandings, one hotel had introduced the simple solution of putting a basket in the bathroom, clearly communicating that if guests wished to replace towels, these should be thrown in this basket (Plate 4.8).

This hotel had also introduced a measure that, if guests wanted additional changes of linen, they were required to strip their beds and put the linen in the basket. No complaints had ever been received from the mostly Scandinavian clientele. Notably, this hotel communicated its environmental achievements and awards broadly in public spaces. In comparison, a majority of guests (55%) interviewed in June 2014 suggested that they would not deem it acceptable to have to strip beds of their linen in order to get these changed. This, however, referred to linen changes in general, i.e. not considering that these would be exchanged on a given basis (every second or third day), and that guests only had to strip their beds if they wanted additional changes. In contrast, 99% of guests stated that they found it acceptable to throw towels in the basket if they wanted to exchange these. In order to optimise the system, it would thus be advisable to introduce the following policies in the hotels where guests were interviewed:

(a) set up information in guest rooms regarding bed linen and towel change;
(b) exchange bed linen every three days, and offer additional exchanges on the basis of a card to be set up on the bed: 'Please exchange bed linen';
(c) replace in-room towels only when these are thrown in the basket in the bathroom;
(d) offer one pool towel in the beginning, and exchange these on demand, but potentially at restricted times (e.g. daily between 10.00 and 12.00).

ground subsidence due to groundwater abstraction. Such processes may be exacerbated by climate change in the future. Where water is already scarce, desalination is often regarded as the best alternative (Pombo *et al.*, 2008), although the technology is potentially unsustainable due to growing energy demand, emissions generation and high costs (Black & King, 2009; Gude *et al.*, 2010; Sadhwani & Veza, 2008). Using renewable energy sources for desalination may even be more costly, particularly when small-scale solutions are favoured (Gude *et al.*, 2010; see, however, also Bermudez-Contreras *et al.*, 2008; Kavanagh, 2002). Even though such technologies thus may have a role to play, using water more efficiently through technology will always be a priority.

Figure 4.7 provides an overview of the water-energy system in a hotel. Water is abstracted from municipal sources and/or from the hotel's own supply (e.g. groundwater extraction, rainwater collection) and used to provide rooms and kitchen and laundry facilities with potable water. A large share of this water is in need of treatment after use. Water is also needed for cooling and heating, which often requires substantial energy inputs, while energy is also often needed to move water around the property via pumping, as well as to send wastewater back into the larger hydrological system in which the property is situated.

A sustainable energy-water system would look different. Figure 4.8 provides a broad overview of a system that is based on sustainable use of both energy and water. In this system, local energy and water cycles are closed, with the exception of fossil fuels needed for transport, and water imported in

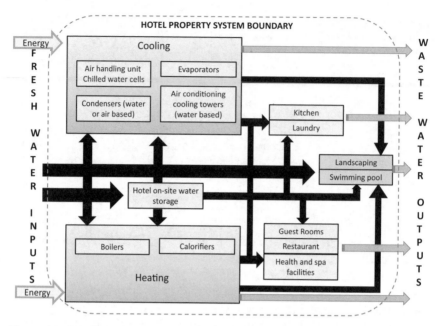

Figure 4.7 Overview of the water flows in the water system of a conventional hotel property. Note the importance of the inputs of energy into the heating and cooling of the system. Additional energy is required to assist in moving water around the system
Source: Authors

food/fossil fuels. The figure shows that energy is needed as electricity (lighting, cooking, cold storage, electric appliances), heating (warm water, heating of rooms, offices and public areas during cold seasons), and cooling (air conditioning in summer). The energy demand for these can be derived from solar (thermal and photovoltaic) installed, for instance, on rooftops. Wind energy may not be suitably produced on site, but there are opportunities to invest in wind power stations together with other businesses, from where the hotel's own energy is subsequently sourced. Additional electricity requirements are sourced from a green energy provider. These measures reduce emissions of greenhouse gases to a very low level, as well as water use for energy production. Heating requirements can be derived from wood pellets, where available, or alternatively involve heat pumps using green energy. As for cooling requirements, optimal systems would involve forms of geothermal cooling, which are vastly superior in terms of energy requirements to conventional cooling systems. Where these are not feasible, biogas (from composted waste) or natural gas may be used in combined cooling/warming systems.

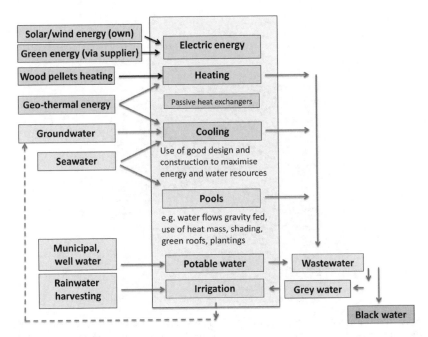

Figure 4.8 Maximising water-energy systems
Source: Authors.

With regard to water provisions, an optimal system may distinguish water use for rooms and kitchens (potable water), irrigation (grey water, rainwater) and pools (seawater, optionally combined with freshwater from wells or municipal sources). This helps to reduce overall direct water demand, while distinguishing different water types and only returning black water in need of treatment to a treatment facility. Importantly, facility design can also help in recharging groundwater (Plate 4.11).

The number of additional technical measures that can help to reduce water use are virtually unlimited, and can again be divided into energy- and water-saving measures. Technical measures to reduce energy use have been discussed at length in Gössling (2010), and in part include the general technical innovation cycle with, for instance, LED technology now replacing low-energy lighting systems, saving another 30% on electricity use. In public areas, hand dryers using pressurised air can help by avoiding paper and linen towels, reducing energy and water consumption directly and indirectly. Pool illumination can be shut down or reduced during the night, when guests sleep.

Regular replacement of all white appliances and other technology items is essential to save energy, including, for instance, air conditioning systems,

Plate 4.9 Warm water can be produced in many destinations with the help of solar thermal heat systems. Solar electric (photovoltaic) systems are also often profitable, particularly where limited amounts of energy are used. However, in spite of solar thermal and solar photovoltaic's economic feasibility in many areas of the world, these are often not implemented, requiring either subsidies or higher taxes on fossil fuels to increase the cost of 'polluting' energy

boilers, heat pumps, circulation pumps, filter technology, washing machines, dryers, fridges and freezers, stoves and ovens, TV sets, mini-bars and other infrastructure. Likewise, the use of pre-rinse spray valves with smaller nozzles helps achieve high water pressure with limited water use, while food can be steamed rather than boiled, and sinks and basins be equipped with flow control regulators. All such measures are highly economical (e.g. Cooley *et al.*, 2007; O'Neill & Siegelbaum and The RICE Group, 2002; Smith *et al.*, 2009a). New technologies also include 'crystal sand filters' for pools, which use crushed glass and can significantly reduce backwashing times by about 30%.

With regard to direct water consumption in rooms, there now exist many models of aerators and flow restrictors for showerheads and faucets, as well as dual flush options for toilets. Best practice standards for toilets are now as low as 1 L for a mini flush, 6.5 L for showerheads and 2.5 L for faucets (Hills *et al.*, 2002; Lazarova *et al.*, 2003). Urinals in public toilets can even be waterless.

Plate 4.10 Where water is regionally scarce, water management in tourism can be undertaken by both technical means and communication. This picture, taken at San Francisco International Airport in June 2014 at a time when California was experiencing a serious drought, illustrates not only an attempt to generate user awareness and response but also a sensor-activated tap system that helps save water

The Future: Novel Water Indicators

Throughout this book, it has been shown that water consumption in tourism is considerable, and that there is huge potential to reduce specific consumption. As most water – both direct and indirect – is consumed in or around accommodation, hotels in particular are key agents in water management. Yet analysis of current management approaches raises a number of problems, questioning the efficiency of these approaches (Gössling, 2015) and the overall readiness of stakeholders to address water management issues. For instance, even though World Tourism Day 2013 focused on water, the UNWTO *Background Paper on Tourism and Water* (UNWTO, 2013) contains virtually no guidance as to how to engage in water management. Even more problematic is the current situation with regard to indicators, which are needed to inform water management policies. A review of indicators in use by tourism organisations, advisory boards and consultancies as well as the scientific literature suggests that there are many indicators in use, although few appear to be comprehensive enough to consider the complexity of water management as outlined in this book. Chronologically, UNWTO (2004) was the first to publish a set of indicators in a manual for sustainable

Plate 4.11 Grey water systems for irrigation can help in reducing freshwater demand, particularly when efficient, timer-steered sprinkler systems for pre-dawn irrigation are used. Health issues need to be considered, however

tourism in destinations. Indicators focused on water availability, considering '% of annual supply in use', 'the number of days shortage per year' and the 'cost of new water'. Since no thresholds were defined for these parameters, which are also vague in terms of their relevance for sustainable water management, it remains unclear whether these would ever successfully address water management issues.

With regard to scientific reviews of water consumption in tourism, focus has usually been on direct water consumption in hotels, on the basis of the water pumped from wells or public water sources to the hotel, and divided by room number, guest nights or floor space (e.g. Bohdanowicz & Martinac, 2007; Deng & Burnett, 2002; Gössling, 2001). The first comprehensive review of assessments of water consumption in hotels was presented by Bohdanowicz and Martinac (2007), who summarised the results of reports and publications from the period 1990–2002, finding that all of them expressed water use as consumption in L per room, guest night or m² (although also see Stipanuk & Robson, 1995, for an early account of American studies). They built on this data to provide a dataset for 73 Hilton and 111 Scandic hotels,

Plate 4.12 Old and inefficient insulation of water pipelines. Many hotels in mature destinations have for decades neglected to replace insulation, circulation pumps and heating and cooling systems, as well as other machinery. For such hotels, energy efficiency gains exceeding 50% make investments in new water and energy infrastructure highly profitable

also focusing on indicators including freshwater use in 'm^3 per room and year' and 'L per guest night', and adding a 'laundry in kg per guest night' indicator. In virtually all studies presented since then, 'water use per guest night' or, synonymously, 'water use per tourist per day' has remained the key indicator (Gössling *et al.*, 2012; Table 4.8). One of the few exceptions to this rule appears to be Blancas *et al.* (2011), who suggested also assessing 'water savings', calculated as the volume of reused water. It is questionable, however, whether such an indicator is practical in terms of water management.

With regard to organisations concerned with the sustainable development of tourism, a set of indicators was developed by the European Commission (EC, 2013), called the European Tourism Indicator System TOOLKIT for Sustainable Destinations. The TOOLKIT contains four indicators for water management: 'Fresh water consumption per guest night compared to general population water consumption per person night'; 'Percentage of tourism enterprises with low-flow shower heads and taps and/or dual flush toilets/waterless urinals'; 'Percentage of tourism enterprises using recycled water'; and 'Percentage of water use derived from recycled water in the destination' (see also Table 4.8). These indicators are all relative, however, and not suitable for making statements regarding the sustainability of water use.

Among consultancies, various approaches have been developed. As an example, EarthCheck (2013) has presented a framework that considers

Table 4.8 Comparison of water use indicators: Scientific and corporate approaches

Indicator	Reference/organisation
• Water use per guest night.	Antakyali et al. (2008); Bohdanowicz and Martinac (2007); Eurostat (2009); Gössling (2001); Lamei (2009); Lamei et al. (2009); Langumier and Ricou (1995); Rico-Amoros et al. (2009); WWF (2004).
• Water use per room.	Alexander (2002); Cooley et al. (2007); Deng and Burnett (2002); O'Neill et al. (2002); Stipanuk and Robson (1995).
• m³ per room and year; • Laundry in kg per guest night.	Bohdanowicz and Martinac (2007).
• Total volume consumed per day; • Volume of reused water.	Blancas et al. (2011).
• The % of annual supply in use; • The number of days' shortage per year; • Cost of new water.	UNWTO (2004).
• Freshwater consumption per guest night compared to general population water consumption per person night; • Percentage of tourism enterprises with low-flow shower heads and taps and/or dual flush toilets/waterless urinals; • Percentage of tourism enterprises using recycled water; • Percentage of water use derived from recycled water in the destination.	EC (2013); Stipanuk and Robson (1995).
• How often does the organisation check for leaks? • What percentage of all toilets installed are low/dual flush? • What percentage of all tap fittings are low flow? • What percentage of all shower fittings installed are low flow? • Waste water treatment on site? • What percentage of water sprinklers are used/operated after dark? • What percentage of the landscaping requires minimal irrigation? • What percentage of total water consumption is from recycled/grey/rainwater sources?	The EarthCheck Company Standard (2013) (see also International Tourism Partnership and Green Globe 21, Green Key, American Hotel & Lodging Association, Considerate Hoteliers, Carbon Disclosure Project Reporting, UN Global Compact or the Global Reporting Initiative LEED, TraveLife, UK Green Tourism Business Scheme, TripAdvisor greenleaders). Accor, Scandic Hotels, Rezidor SAS, Marriott, Six Senses.

Text Box 4.5 Geothermal cooling

Air-conditioning is responsible for up to 70% of all energy use in hotels in warm climates, and cooling is consequently one of the major cost factors in hotels. Most hotels use chillers to generate cold, even though some also have individual A/C units which operate even more inefficiently. In recent years, two alternatives to conventional cooling systems based on the use of electricity or gas have been developed: seawater air conditioning (Figure 4.9) and groundwater air conditioning (Figure 4.10). Both systems are geothermal cooling systems that use temperature differences in water supplies to generate cold.

Cool seawater is available at depths of around 1000 m, where temperatures will drop to 5°C. This water is pumped up through pipelines, which can be several kilometres long, depending on geomophology and water temperatures. As pipelines are usually running for a distance on land, pipelines have an outside diameter of about 600 mm, with a second pipeline inside this bigger one, with a diameter of 400 mm. Cold water is pumped up in the inner pipeline, and insulated against outside temperatures of up to 30°C by the outer pipeline, which contains 'used' water flowing back into the sea with a temperature of about 12°C. Seawater is pumped through a heat exchanger, to keep salt- and freshwater cycles separate (Figure 4.9). Cold freshwater is used to air condition rooms, offices and public areas in the hotel. As an example of such an investment, Gössling (2010) reports that the InterContinental Resort Thalasso & Spa of Bora Bora, French Polynesia, with 83 bungalows, had investment costs of €6.6 million for a system generating 1500 kW of cold. This corresponds to a pumped volume of 270 m^3 of seawater per hour. Payback time in this case is about seven years. The system is estimated to reduce electricity consumption by 90% compared to conventional air conditioning.

Geothermal cooling based on cold groundwater is similar, although it uses freshwater and is a solution even for city hotels. The system contains two wells, one to pump up cold water and one to release the 'used' water back into the ground. Cold water is pumped through a heat exchanger, which then provides cold to the cold-water air conditioning system in the hotel (Figure 4.10). Water temperatures of groundwater should ideally be below 14°C, but it is still possible to use the system at a maximum of 16°C in temperate climates. At outside temperatures of around 25–30°C, it takes 4 kW of cold to cool 100 m^2 of floor space, corresponding to a

(Continued)

Text Box 4.5 Geothermal cooling (*Continued*)

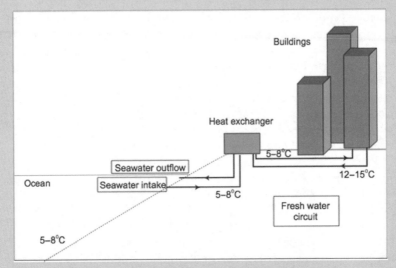

Figure 4.9 Schematic overview of a seawater cooling system
Source: Based on Gössling (2010).

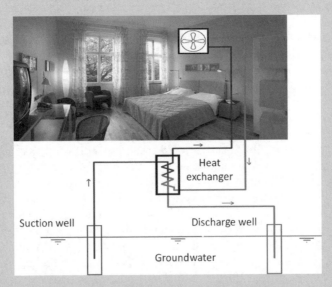

Figure 4.10 Geothermal groundwater system
Source: Bertram Späth, Hotel Viktoria, Freiburg, Germany.

pumped groundwater volume of 860 L per hour at 15°C. After the cold is 'used', warm water is pumped back about 4°C warmer, leading to longer term increases in the groundwater temperature. However, during winter the water cools down, and is ready to be used again in the following spring. The cost of a 100 kW system is about €50,000–75,000, i.e. considerably lower than the seawater system, although this also depends on location and experience. The remotely located InterContinental Resort claims to be the first hotel in the world using seawater for cooling, and initial costs may have been considerably higher. The groundwater cooling system is expected to save €4000 per 100 kW per year in comparison to conventional air conditioning. This corresponds to payback times of between five and 10 years, depending on electricity cost.

Text Box 4.6 Cruise ships and water inputs and outputs

Cruise ships are often regarded as floating hotels. Even though they are surrounded by seawater when in service, they have particular problems of water storage, use and waste (Johnson, 2002; Loehr et al., 2006). Moreover, the cruise ship industry as well as the cruise ships themselves are growing, with ships of 3000–7000 passengers not uncommon, making them, in effect, floating small towns. Water has to be either taken on board in large quantities from different ports and/or produced by on-board desalination plants that also require substantial energy inputs. A typical cruise ship discharges around one million litres of 'black water' (sewage) during a one-week voyage (US Environmental Protection Agency, 2000). A cruise ship of 3000 passengers can generate 340–960 m^3 of grey water daily (The Ocean Conservancy, 2002, in Guilbaud et al., 2012).

Grey waters are one of the largest liquid flows on board cruise ships and usually refer to wastewaters coming from cabin sinks, baths, laundry and galleys. These effluents occur in a wide range of pollutant forms (soluble, solid, biodegradable, non-biodegradable) and concentrations and contain a wide variety of pollutants such as bacteria, suspended solids, metals, detergents, oil and grease, food particles, hairs, lint and medical wastes (Johnson, 2002). Discharge of grey water is limited under national and international laws. The International Maritime Organisation (IMO) Convention prohibits the discharge of

(Continued)

Text Box 4.6 Cruise ships and water inputs and outputs (*Continued*)

black and grey waters into the sea without treatment less than 12 miles from shore. Therefore cruise companies are looking for ways to cost efficiently filter, recycle and dilute grey and black water. However, because of the limited space available, they are not necessarily able to adopt some of the procedures used on land. The most common procedures to treat grey and black waters are the use of immersed or external membranes in conjunction with a bioreactor. For example, Holland America treat laundry and accommodation waters by a bag filter system followed by reverse osmosis modules and UV treatment, with black and galley waters being treated by membranes and bioreactor (EPA, 2006, in Guilbaud *et al.*, 2010). However, the growth of the sector and criticisms of their environmental record means that cruise lines are looking for new technologies in order to improve the filtration of grey water as well as placing more effort into recycling and more efficient and safe water use (Mouchtouri *et al.*, 2012).

Text Box 4.7 Novel water management indicators

Area situation

Indicator 1: *Renewable water resources per guest night in peak season*

This indicator assesses a watershed or region's water supply system with regard to renewable water availability, considering the region's future development (additional beds planned) under different climate change scenarios. It focuses on renewable water resources, as neither the use of fossil nor desalinated water can be considered sustainable. The peak season is generally the driest season and is thus an indicator of pressure on water resources at the time of their most limited availability. The outcome of the calculation of this indicator determines benchmarks for the following indicators.

Planning accommodation

Indicator 2: *Area of irrigated land per bed*

Gardens have been identified as a major water-consuming factor in many destinations, even though it is acknowledged that many city hotels do not have gardens. Where gardens exist, their size and design, as well as the plant species chosen, influence water demand. A proxy for these variables is 'area of irrigated garden per bed', the general rule being that the smaller the irrigated area, the lower water consumption for irrigation.

Indicator 3: *Area of pool per bed*
Pools, like gardens, are major water-consuming factors. Both pool size and pool volume influence water consumption as a result of the initial filling, evaporation and backwashing. The design of pools consequently has great relevance for future water use and 'water lock-in', and can be assessed on the basis of a calculation of pool area per bed. Where no pools exist, this indicator is redundant. In some destinations/hotels, the use of seawater for pools may be accepted or even appreciated by guests.

Indicator 4: *Area of solar thermal and PV installed per bed*
Indirect water use is influenced by energy consumption. Hotels and virtually all forms of accommodation can in most climates reduce their indirect water demand by producing warm water via solar thermal installations and electricity from photovoltaic (PV) cells. Alternatively, various forms of geothermal cooling have been explored (Gössling, 2010). At the same time, accommodation should also be built in a way that minimises energy consumption.

Operating accommodation
Indicator 5: *Amount of meats and dairy products per guest night*
The importance of food in water consumption has been clearly outlined, and meat and dairy products have been identified as key food groups in water-intensive diets. For instance, Hadjikakou *et al.* (2013a) find in their analysis of different meal compositions that 75% of the food water footprint is related to meat and dairy products. Reducing the share of these foodstuffs is thus of great importance for reducing indirect water demand.

Indicator 6: *Energy use per guest night*
Energy used in accommodation can be produced by the hotel itself (Indicator 4), or be purchased from renewable sources. Where this is the case, the indicator becomes less relevant, even though reducing energy use is always relevant to improving environmental performance. Where energy use per guest night is high and costly, the indicator can help to

(Continued)

Text Box 4.7 Novel water management indicators (*Continued*)

identify major energy consumption subsectors, which are likely to include A/C systems (Gössling, 2010).

Indicator 7: *Share of rooms fitted with low-flow options*

Room-specific water use depends primarily on the showerheads chosen as well as low-flow toilets with dual flush options, and low-flow taps. The installation of Jacuzzis should generally be avoided, as these are water and energy intensive. A wide range of low-flow plumbing fixtures are now available, which can be chosen based on guest comfort perceptions and regional water availability (Indicator 1).

Indicator 8: *Kg of laundry used per guest night*

This indicator refers to both water and energy use for laundry. The general rule is that the less laundry produced, the lower will be the direct and indirect water consumption. Again, specific benchmarks have to be set against water availability (Indicator 1).

percentage low-water use technology implementation (toilet dual flushing, tap and shower fittings, timer-steered sprinklers), wastewater treatment on site, checking for leaks, low water landscaping, and recycled water use. Other standards have been developed by the International Tourism Partnership and Green Globe 21, Green Key, American Hotel & Lodging Association, Considerate Hoteliers, Carbon Disclosure Project Reporting, UN Global Compact or the Global Reporting Initiative LEED, TraveLife, UK Green Tourism Business Scheme, or TripAdvisor's greenleaders initiative. Links to many of these resources are provided at the end of the book.

Other indicators have been presented by industry itself including, for instance, the Accor and Kuoni groups. Accor (2011) is the first to include indirect consumption of livestock, and makes a meaningful distinction between rainwater and municipally sourced water. However, well water is also excluded from assessments, even though this might be relevant with regard to renewable groundwater resource use. In comparison, Kuoni (2013) has presented a comprehensive water management manual focusing on direct water use, including per capita consumption values, best practice, a differentiation between hot and cold water costs, laundry costs, and recommendations regarding flow measurements, towel reuse, wastewater treatment, and cost-benefit analyses for laundry and plumbing fixtures. The manual also proposes a 'water champion' scheme, which uses an economic argument to generate interest in water reduction. It thus creates interest in water management rooted in economics.

As outlined by Gössling (2015: 237), the review of indicators currently used by various stakeholders in tourism to manage water use reveals various weaknesses. These include:

(1) The most widely used indicator, water use per guest night, only considers direct water use, ignoring the importance of embodied water (food, fuels). In some assessments, such as by Accor, well water is not included, even though groundwater abstractions may be specifically relevant for sustainable water management (Gössling, 2001).

(2) 'Quantity [L/G] per guest night' is an indicator of relative use levels that can also be used for benchmarking purposes, but it does not indicate whether abstraction levels are sustainable in terms of aggregated (absolute) consumption, i.e. in comparison with available renewable water resources.

(3) Water use as measured in 'quantity [L/G] per guest night' may not be a sufficient criterion on its own for the purposes of informing water management. Only by combining it with an audit of subsectors can particularly water-intensive end-uses be identified and measures for water conservation implemented.

(4) A considerable share of water use is characterised by 'lock-in'. For instance, as fixed installations, pools need to be filled and require constant water replenishment. Indicators thus need to distinguish between the planning of tourism infrastructure and its operation, considering an embedded and an operational water footprint.

(5) There is evidence that water consumption in tourism is growing due to various trends, such as: growing interest in energy- or water-intensive activities; higher hotel standards with larger pools and gardens; higher quality standards including in-room jacuzzis; all-inclusive arrangements with large buffets; or the planned use of biofuels for transport. Such trends need to be addressed in water management.

To consider these insufficiencies, it has been suggested that managers should identify new indicators for water consumption and management (Gössling, 2015), adjusted to sustainable water abstraction levels both for direct and indirect consumption by end use, i.e. allowing a better understanding, planning, minimising and monitoring of water use. Water management also needs to consider water availability, and the level of sustainable renewable water abstractions that are possible without affecting water tables or groundwater levels. Such assessments also need to consider human development and climate change scenarios, including changes in rainfall patterns. Out of these considerations, novel water management indicators can be developed (Gössling, 2015; Text Box 4.6).

Consideration of these novel indicators is likely to help managers to prepare plans that are comprehensive, leading to real reductions in both direct and indirect water consumption. As shown in the following chapter, this again helps to address future challenges, including climate change and water insecurity.

Recommended reading

On behavioural change and social marketing see:

Hall, C.M. (2013a) *Tourism and Social Marketing*. Abingdon: Routledge.
McKenzie-Mohr, D. (2011) *Fostering Sustainable Behavior: An Introduction to Communitybased Social Marketing*. Gabriola Island: New Society Publishers.
Also refer to the extremely useful *Tools of Change* website, which has a wide range of social marketing material including case studies: http://www.toolsofchange.com/en/home/.
Goldstein, N.J., Cialdini, R.B. and Griskevicius, V. (2008) A room with a viewpoint: Using social norms to motivate environmental conservation in hotels. *Journal of Consumer Research* 35, 472–482.

On benchmarking see:

Bohdanowicz, P. and Martinac, I. (2007) Determinants and benchmarking of resource consumption in hotels – case study of Hilton International and Scandic in Europe. *Energy and Buildings* 39 (1), 82–95.
Chan, W.W. (2009) Environmental measures for hotels' environmental management systems: ISO 14001. *International Journal of Contemporary Hospitality Management* 21 (5), 542–560.
Gössling, S. (2010) *Carbon Management in Tourism: Mitigating the Impacts on Climate Change*. Abingdon: Routledge.

On the use of technology and efficiency approaches see:

Chan, W.W. (2005b) Predicting and saving the consumption of electricity in sub-tropical hotels. *International Journal of Contemporary Hospitality Management* 17 (3), 228–237.
Lo, J.Y., Chan, W.W. and Wong, K. (2011) A comparison of cold-water thawing options in Chinese restaurants. *Cornell Hospitality Quarterly* 52 (1), 64–72.
Mak, B.L., Chan, W.W., Li, D., Liu, L. and Wong, K.F. (2013) Power consumption modeling and energy saving practices of hotel chillers. *International Journal of Hospitality Management* 33, 1–5.

For a range of example of various approaches towards sustainability in tourism see:

Hall, C.M., Gössling, S. and Scott, D. (eds) (2015) *The Routledge Handbook of Sustainable Tourism*. Abingdon: Routledge.

5 The Future: Water Security and Tourism Development

As Chapter 1 outlined, water is a fundamental resource for economic and social development and one that has been going through unprecedented pressures over the last 30 years as rapidly growing populations and economies have increased demand and degraded supplies in many watersheds. Accumulating scientific evidence and policy analyses conclude that business-as-usual in the water sector is already no longer an option for many watersheds and countries and that the salience of water security will increase in the decades ahead (UNESCO, 2012; UN Water, 2014; World Bank, 2012). Indeed, the 2030 Water Resources Group (2009: 4) reached the sobering conclusion that:

> ... for water, arguably one of the most constrained and valuable resources we have, ... calls for action multiply and yet an abundance of evidence shows that the situation is getting worse. There is little indication that, left to its own devices, the water sector will come to a sustainable, cost-effective solution to meet the growing water requirements implied by economic and population growth.

A number of leading authorities on water futures further assert that the non-substitutable and regional nature of water resources will make it one of the most important and geopolitically contentious resources issues worldwide (Cooley *et al.*, 2012; Michel & Pandya, 2009; UN Water, 2014).

This chapter examines how the tourism–water nexus is anticipated to evolve over the next 20–40 years. It will outline the most important anticipated drivers of future water security and how they are expected to interact to create regional water security risks with implications for future tourism development. The chapter will then provide an overview of the evolving consideration of water resources by the global business community – away from conversations about environmental sustainability to those on strategic investment, operations and financial performance – and the place of tourism in this global dialogue on future water challenges.

Drivers of Future Water Security Challenges

Global freshwater consumption has tripled in the latter half of the 20th century (UN Water, 2014), as humans have been able to appropriate a greater and greater proportion of global freshwater resources (see Chapter 1). With fewer newly accessible sources of freshwater, a degraded freshwater supply (both in quantity and quality) in an increasing number of watersheds and a much accelerated demand, the future of the world's freshwater water supplies is expected to be under increasing stress in the first half of the 21st century (Ercin & Hoekstra, 2014; UNESCO, 2012; UN Water, 2014).

Studies that have explored alternative futures of the world's water and its use have indicated that the drivers of water resource challenges before 2050 are fundamentally tied to economic growth and development (population growth, economic growth and trade patterns and lifestyle/consumption changes), technological change (infrastructure), governance (including historical access and human rights) and also climate change and climate-related ecosystem change (Ercin & Hoekstra, 2014; UNESCO, 2012). In the early decades of the 21st century, additional stresses on freshwater resources are expected to arise predominantly from population and economic growth. With the global population estimated to reach 9.6 billion by mid-century (UN, 2013), the additional food and water requirements of 2.4 billion people even with current global dietary patterns are significant. However, the current dietary trends in many developing nations that are linked to economic development are resulting in higher per capita water requirements (different crops and higher consumption of meat). Similarly, the increased energy requirements associated with continued rapid economic growth in several highly populated developing economies imply major increases in water demand in these regions, and increased competition among water users (upstream-downstream, economic sectors, ecosystems).

The range of estimates for future freshwater water use all warn of a growing gap between supply and demand in an increasing number of highly populated watersheds. Global water withdrawals are estimated to increase between 65% and 75% between 2000 and 2030 (2030 Water Resources Group, 2009; Postel et al., 1996; UNESCO, 2012). The resultant gap in water supply and demand (even with assumed efficiency gains) would leave an estimated 1.7–1.8 billion people living in basins with chronic significant water stress (see definition in Chapter 1) by 2030 and 3.2–3.9 billion by 2050 (2030 Water Resources Group, 2009; OECD, 2012b; UNESCO, 2012). Notably, much of the increase in people living in watersheds with severe water stress is anticipated to be concentrated in Brazil, India, China and southeast Asia (Veloia-IFPRI, 2012; Schlosser *et al.*, 2014), regions where some of the strongest growth in domestic and international tourism is projected (UNWTO, 2014). The implications for intersectoral water competition are discussed at the end of this chapter.

In addition to the aforementioned non-climatic drivers of freshwater use, continuing anthropogenic climate change (ACC) is expected to become an increasingly important determinant of freshwater resource availability. Changes in water resources are one of the most direct ways that communities and countries will experience the impacts of ACC in the decades ahead and play a key role in successful adaptation to climate change (IPCC, 2014a).

The IPCC (2007, 2013, 2014b) has concluded that, even at the present +0.8°C above pre-industrial average temperatures, changes in the global water cycle have been observed, including more water vapour in the atmosphere, changing regional precipitation patterns, greater occurrence of extreme precipitation events and a decline in seasonal snow and glacial ice. Consequently, the IPCC (2007) has argued for over a decade that water resource planning using extrapolations of historical climate data is no longer valid. The observed patterns of a changing water cycle are expected to accelerate under greater ACC in the 21st century (IPCC, 2013), which will exacerbate regional water stress and scarcity in multiple ways.

First, because precipitation and potential evaporation are the main climatic drivers controlling freshwater resources, ACC will impact the reliability of annual and seasonal freshwater supply. Global mean precipitation will increase in a warmer world, although there will be substantial spatial variation with some regions receiving less annual rainfall. Generally, wet regions are anticipated to become wetter while dry regions become drier (IPCC, 2013), increasing the geographic contrast in available freshwater resources. Increased temperatures will contribute to greater evaporative losses from lakes and reservoirs. Inter-annual variability in seasonal precipitation and the frequently and intensity in extreme precipitation (extreme rainfall events and periods of drought) are also projected to increase in many regions of the world under ACC (IPCC, 2013). Changes in precipitation variability and extreme conditions (high- and low-flow conditions) have significant implications for disrupting the timing and reliability of water resources.

Secondly, ACC will adversely impact water quality in many regions, posing risks to drinking water even with conventional treatment (IPCC, 2014a). Increases in heavy rainfall and runoff events can increase nutrient and pollutant loadings in surface water bodies, requiring greater treatment and, in combination with water temperatures, creating conditions favourable to algal blooms and other pathogens. Lower flow conditions associated with increased drought conditions reduce the dilution of pollutants, degrading water quality and potentially increasing the likelihood of water-borne illness. Coastal areas and islands, where much of the world's tourism infrastructure and activity are concentrated, face an additional climate change related risk to freshwater resources. With several recent studies projecting global sea level rise as much as 1 m projected for the 21st century (Rahmstorf, 2010), the salinisation of coastal freshwater aquifers and inundation of essential coastal wetlands will substantially reduce locally available freshwater resources in many coastal destinations, creating what some have termed 'salinity refugees'.

Finally, higher average temperatures and increased periods of drought will increase demand for freshwater by a range of users, including irrigation, industrial and energy-related cooling, and ecosystems (e.g. minimum water levels or flow requirements).

The combined impacts of ACC on regional water resources will not be uniform, and Table 5.1 summarises the anticipated climate-induced impacts on annual runoff, drought and flooding hazards in some of the world's leading tourism regions. By mid-century increased water stress from population and economic growth in combination with climate change is expected in several mature tourism regions like the Mediterranean basin (Europe and African coasts), the Caribbean and Australia, but also many watersheds in northeast and southeast Asia, northern and central Africa and the Middle East that are expected to lead global growth in tourism through the 2030s and beyond. As indicated by Scott et al. (2012b), water stress, not increased temperatures (i.e. 'too hot for tourism') is likely to be the most salient climate change challenge to face the tourism industry throughout the Mediterranean region by mid-century and, without costly investments in desalination powered by renewable energy, may pose a barrier to further tourism development on the north African coast. The effects of climate change runoff and drought occurrence in the later decades of the 21st century are more pronounced in the key tourism regions of the Mediterranean basin (runoff −32%, drought occurrence +33%), central America (runoff −28%, drought occurrence +30%), southeast Asia (runoff −8%, drought occurrence +5%) and Australia (see Table 5.1). Particularly relevant are the projected increases in water stress in regions where significant growth in international tourism is a key strategy for future economic development strategy and poverty alleviation, including several countries in southeast Asia, Africa and many SIDS.

The costs of dealing with water scarcity under scenarios of serious climate change are likely to be considerable. Globally, Parry et al. (2009a)

Table 5.1 Future water stress in major tourism regions

Region	Growth in annual international tourist arrivals (2010–2030) (%)[b]	2050s Water stress level (% of total renewable water withdrawn)[c]	Change in water stress index from economic growth and climate change[d]	2071–2100[a] Change in annual runoff (%)[e]	Change in annual occurrence of days under drought conditions (%)[f]	Change in annual frequency of a 1-in-30 year flood event (%)[g]
Mediterranean basin						
• Europe	2.3	Moderate (20–40)	+50 to 75	−32	+33	−54
• North Africa	4.6	**High (>50)**	**+50 to 75**			
Northern Europe	1.8	Low (<20–40)	−10 to −50	−7	+13	−65
Northeast Asia	4.9	**High (>50)**	**−25 to +25**	+11	+12	+70
Southeast Asia	5.1	Low (<20)	**+10 to 75**	−8	+5	+77
Western North America	1.7	**High (>50)**	0 to −25	−2	+12	−52
Eastern North America	1.7	Moderate (20–30)	−25 to +100	+1	+16	−46
Central America	5.2	Low (<20)	**+25 to 50**	−28	+30	−53
• Caribbean	2.0	Moderate (30–40)	**+50 to 100**			
Northern Australia	2.4	Low (<20)	**+25 to 50**	−12	+16	+45
Southern Australia	2.4	Low (<20–30)	**+75 to 100**	−29	+20	+45
Middle East/Sahara				+16	+14	+47
• Middle East	4.6	**High (>50)**	**+150 to 300**			
• North Africa	4.6	**High (>50)**	**+100 to 600**			

Notes: [a]Change between present day (1981–2010) climate and 2071–2100 under a high emissions (RCP8.5) scenario.
Source: [b]UNWTO (2014); [c]Veloia-IFPRI (2012); [d]Schlosser et al. (2014) – BAU emissions scenario; [e]Davie et al. (2013); [f]Prudhomme et al. (2013); [g]Dankers et al. (2013). [e,f,g]Ensemble averages from Richardson and Lewis (2014).

estimate that the cost of climate change in terms of water provisions will be an additional US$9–11 billion per year. The cost for Spain alone, at additional water requirements of 1.1 billion m^3 per year, was calculated at €3.8 billion (Downward & Taylor, 2007). In Australia, costs of US$4.75 billion in the period 2001–2015 were calculated for national water initiatives, treatment plants to supply recycled water, pipelines and drought aid payments to communities (Bates et al., 2008).

A very important finding from the Fifth IPCC Assessment (IPCC, 2013, 2014b) is that the climate change impacts on water resources increase substantially under scenarios of greater temperature change. Under increases in global mean temperature of less than 2°C above pre-industrial temperatures expected through the mid-century, changes in population and economic growth were found to have a greater effect on changes in water resource availability than climate change. For example, a recent study by Schlosser et al. (2014) found that, by 2050, economic growth and population change alone could lead to an additional 1.8 billion people living in regions with at least moderate water stress. However, when the effects of climate change were integrated, an additional 1.0–1.3 billion people were projected to be living in regions with overly exploited water conditions (i.e. where total potential water requirements will consistently exceed surface water supply) by 2050. However, when global warming surpassed 2°C above pre-industrial temperatures, the influence of climate change relative to socio-economic drivers increased significantly. For example, Schewe et al. (2014) estimated that approximately 8% of the global population would see a severe reduction in water resources (a reduction in runoff either greater than 20% or more than the standard deviation of current annual runoff) with a 1°C rise in global mean temperature (compared to the 1990s), and this would rise to 14% at 2°C and 17% at 3°C. Similarly, Portmann et al. (2013) projected that 24% of the global population would suffer from a decrease in renewable groundwater resources (a loss of more than 10% compared to the 1980s) under a low GHG emissions scenario, but this would increase to 38% in a high emissions scenario. Unfortunately, international agreements and action to reduce GHG emissions have not appreciably slowed or reversed global emissions and, in the absence of effective near-term actions to reduce emissions, the likelihood of +4°C warming (above pre-industrial temperatures) being reached or exceeded this century continues to increase (IEA, 2012; IPCC, 2013; World Bank, 2012).

Tourism: Future water-use projections (to 2050)

The preceding discussion has revealed that several high-level expert commissions have concluded that the world's freshwater resources will be under increasing stress in the first half of the 21st century and that the tourism sector will face increased competition for access to freshwater in a growing number of water insecure regions. Within this global and regional context of increasing pressures on water resource allocation, it is important to understand how the tourism sector's water footprint is expected to change over the same time frame. Do trends suggest the tourism sector is becoming a more efficient water user? Will tourism be able to decouple growth in travel and international arrivals from water use? Could tourism be a 'water resilient' economic development strategy for water-scarce regions?

As shown in Figure 5.1, total water use in tourism has grown in line with global growth in the tourism system, and it continues to grow in both relative and absolute terms despite anticipated improvements in water efficiency. This is a result of globally growing tourist numbers, as well as changing diets towards higher order foods, and longer trips in terms of average distances travelled, contributing to growth in fuel use. Consequently, water consumption is expected to double over the next 40 years, from an estimated current consumption of 138 km³ in 2010 to 265 km³ by 2050 in a business-as-usual scenario (Gössling & Peeters, 2014).

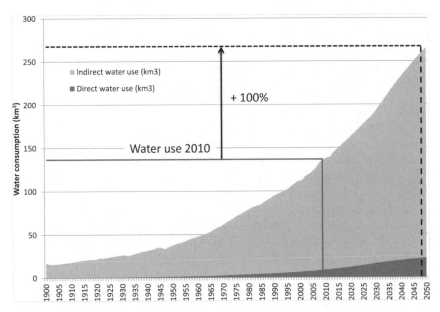

Figure 5.1 Past and future growth in water use for global tourism
Source: Adapted from Gössling and Peeters (2014).

Notably, these are the results of a component-based bottom-up analysis based on relative water-use intensities; input-output analyses as presented by Cazcarro *et al.* (2014) may arrive at significantly higher figures. Most of the projected growth in tourism sector water use is associated with indirect water use, including in particular food and fuels (see Chapter 3 for further details). Even though water use is expected to become more efficient in the future, overall consumption will increase significantly in both absolute and relative terms. Notably, these future water-use scenarios for the global tourism sector do not reflect the geographic concentration of tourism or the share of water that is partially abstracted in areas that are already facing water stress.

Text Box 5.1 Climate change, water and Great Lakes tourism

The United Nations Intergovernmental Panel on Climate Change (IPCC) declared that the warming of the global climate system is unequivocal (+0.85°C warming in global average surface temperatures between 1880 and 2012) and that human influence has been the dominant cause of observed warming since the mid-20th century (IPCC, 2013). Importantly, the IPCC (2013) also emphasised that human-caused global climate change has just begun, and additional warming will strongly depend on future greenhouse gas (GHG) emissions. Reviews of international GHG emission reduction commitments conclude that the policy goal of the international community to hold global warming to below +2°C (relative to pre-industrial temperatures) to prevent dangerous climate change is increasingly unlikely and the current trajectory is towards a warming of +4°C or greater by the end of the 21st century (Peters *et al.*, 2013). The World Bank (2012: xiii) has warned that 'A 4°C world is likely to be one in which communities, cities and countries would experience severe disruptions, damage, and dislocation, with many of these risks spread unequally', putting at risk many of the development gains made in the developing world over the last several decades. As scientific understanding of the potential scale of ACC and the far-reaching consequences for ecosystems, economies and society has advanced over the first decade of the 21st century, climate change has become increasingly considered by many high-level government and business decision makers to be among the most salient challenges facing humankind in the 21st century.

Tourism is considered a highly climate sensitive sector. The multifaceted interface between tourism and climate change, including climate policy, has been examined in detail elsewhere (see Gössling *et al.*, 2013;

Scott *et al.*, 2012a, 2012b). The projected changes in the spatial and temporal distribution of water resources will be one of the most direct, immediate and widespread impacts for the tourism sector. This chapter has provided an overview of how climate change will interact with other major drivers to exacerbate water security challenges in many water basins. The specific regional manifestations of these impacts for tourism will be diverse and importantly will not be restricted to water-scarce regions. This case study illustrates some of the climate change and water impacts in a region with one of the world's largest supplies of freshwater resources – the Great Lakes region of North America.

Rising temperatures and a decrease in natural snowfall due to climate change will make it more difficult for ski resorts in the Great Lakes region to maintain the length and reliability of current operating seasons. Scott *et al.* (2003) estimated that with current snowmaking capacities the average ski season in the 2050s would be reduced by 7% to 32% from the current average of 123 days. Snowmaking requirements to maintain these shortened seasons increased 60–240% above current levels (56 cm over all skiable terrain) and more than tripled under the warmer scenarios of the 2080s (an increase of 310% to 400%). The recent introduction of a water-use monitoring programme in the Province of Ontario (Canada) revealed that 17 ski areas used 1.6 million m^3 of water for snowmaking (approximately 1300 m^3 per acre of skiable terrain) during a winter with temperatures and snowfall close to the 1981–2010 normal. However, during the recent record warm winter (2011–2012), which serves as an analogue for normal winters in the 2050s, water use for snowmaking doubled to over 3.3 million m^3 or approximately 2700 m^3 per skiable acre. The sustainability of snowmaking as an adaptation has been questioned by several studies (see Scott *et al.*, 2012b, for a review) and this substantial increase illustrates the water cost of this primary climate change adaptation strategy in a relatively small ski tourism market.

In contrast to the diminished ski tourism season in the Great Lakes region, the season length and quality of weather conditions for golf tourism is projected to increase. In southern Ontario, warming spring-summer-fall temperatures are expected to lengthen the annual golf season by up to seven weeks in the 2020s and by up to 12 weeks in the 2050s (Scott & Jones, 2007). Increased evaporation during this extended and warmer operating season, combined with projections of reduced summer rainfall in the region, will increase course irrigation demands. A study of

(Continued)

Text Box 5.1 Climate change, water and Great Lakes tourism (*Continued*)

golf course water use in Ontario found that, during a climatically normal season (for the 1981–2010 period), turf grass irrigation for the Province's 848 18-hole equivalent courses required 50.5 million m³ of water (Peister & Scott, 2014). This volume increased by 58% to 80 million m³ during a season that was a 1.2°C warmer and 29% dryer than normal, indicating that water use by the golf industry would increase substantially due to climate change. Importantly, the comparison of water efficiency among courses of similar soil type, age and management type illustrated that, if golf courses in each category adopted technology and irrigation practices to become as efficient as courses in the 80th percentile of efficiency (not even best in class), water-use reductions of 35% were possible.

Recreational boating/sailing and sport fishing are an estimated US$4 billion tourism industry on the Great Lakes (US Army Corps of Engineers, 2008). Water levels on all of the five Great Lakes have fallen below historic averages during the 1998–2012 period and, in early 2013, Lakes Michigan and Huron reached their lowest levels since coordinated monitoring began in 1918. These low water levels have already had a substantial impact on marinas, boaters, some coastal hotels and wetland spawning areas (see Plate 5.1). Great Lakes water levels are projected to

Plate 5.1 Low water level impact on Lake Huron coastal tourism properties

decline further under climate change (Pryor *et al.*, 2014). A 2008 survey of marina operators on Lake Huron documented the impact of low water levels and found that a further water level decline of 45–60 cm (an analogue for some future water level scenarios under climate change) would result in closures of 40% of the currently operating marinas (Dawson & Scott, 2010). This would have important implications for tourism in communities where marina closures would be expected, while bringing tourism benefits to communities with new or expanded marinas.

In addition to lower water levels, thermal conditions on the Great Lakes would be altered by climate change. Recent massive algal blooms on Lake Erie have been linked to warmer water temperatures and excessive phosphorus running off of farm fields during extreme rain events. Warmer water temperatures are detrimental to cold-water sport fish habitat, with the US Environmental Protection Agency (1995) projecting losses of 50–100% in the Great Lakes region. An assessment of the economic implications of climate change induced low water scenarios by the Council of the Great Lakes Region (2014) found that the recreational boating and fishing sector would be one of the most impacted economic sectors, with losses of US$6.6 billion between 2010 and 2030 and over US$12.8 billion through 2050.

As the above examples illustrate, changes in water resource availability and quality from contemporary climate change are already affecting the tourism system of the Great Lakes basin. If the magnitude of climate change increases as projected, its influence on private and government investment and tourism operator decisions will only increase in the decades ahead.

Water Security as a Strategic Business Factor

The international community and the business world are increasingly turning their collective attention to the issue of water security as a strategic economic concern (Ceres, 2009; Ernst & Young, 2012; JPMorgan, 2008; Lloyd's, 2010; and see also Chapter 1 for a discussion of different concepts of water security). A recent corporate survey by the Water Disclosure Project (2013) found that a strong majority (70%) of the Global 500 companies responding identified water as a substantive business risk, with more than half (53%) reporting that their company had experienced detrimental impacts related to water in the past five years, and 64% indicating that they expected further water risks within the next five years.

The water-related risks companies report have been classified into four main types (2030 Water Resources Group, 2009; Ceres, 2009; Ernst & Young, 2012):

(1) **Operational risks** include the physical shortage (scarcity from drought, overuse or lack of infrastructure capacity), low quality (untreated, polluted, thermally unsuited), excessive amounts (flooding), or high cost of water, which can impact business operations in all sectors. The wide range of tourism-specific operational risks was discussed in Chapter 2 and 3.

(2) **Regulatory risks** can arise from a range of governance structures or changes. Legislated water-use restrictions (rationing) are a more common impact for businesses in water-scarce regions. For example, tourism operators have been prevented from irrigating golf courses or using snowmaking in times of drought or low reservoir levels/stream flow in a several states of the USA. Other risks can include the prioritisation of competing water users. In some jurisdictions, historical water access and/or government policies give priority access to certain water users and economic sectors. The prioritisation of economic sectors for water allocation will become increasingly important in the future as governments and the international community determine how better to manage water scarcity in an increasing number of watersheds. As outlined in Chapter 3, the tourism sector generally lacks the systematic water-monitoring information required to make a comparative case for economic productivity and water-use efficiency. Even within economic sectors, voluntary regulatory frameworks such as water stewardship standards or accreditation systems can pose a competitive risk to companies that have not assessed or disclosed their water use. Increased water-use monitoring and reporting requirements are likely to be inevitable in water-scarce basins as part of the basin-wide water management strategies recommended by several high-level expert panels (2030 Water Resources Group, 2009; UNESCO, 2012; World Bank, 2013).

(3) **Financial risk** is increasing as awareness of water resource risks and demands for water risk disclosure grow within the financial services sector. Some large institutional investors (for example, those with over US\$92 trillion in managed assets that support the Water Disclosure Project, 2013) and other financial services companies (banks, insurance) are beginning to consider water risks and management strategies as part of investment or credit risk assessments (Ceres, 2009; JPMorgan, 2008; Lloyd's, 2010). The US Securities and Exchange Commission (2010), having concluded that changes in the availability or quality of

water can affect the performance of companies, issued new disclosure guidance for public companies about the water- and climate-related risks and opportunities they face. Similar water disclosure requirements for companies publically traded on other global stock markets are highly probable.

(4) **Reputational risk** can result from inappropriate use or degradation (pollution or destruction of water sources such as wetlands) of the water resources where a company operates. Such actions negatively impact the public image of a company or sector so that they adversely influence the decisions of customers or investors. Furthermore, tensions between water users, particularly where water access by local communities or traditional livelihoods are accused of being supplanted by powerful multinational corporate interests, can create unstable business conditions, even jeopardising the social license to operate locally or adversely impacting the brand or company on a much broader scale. Reputational risk is an important factor for tourism companies that operate in destination communities to consider, because tourism competes with locals for water and its high per capita use (Chapter 2) has been the subject of strong criticisms by organisations (Tourism Concern, 2012). They contend that, in several developing country destinations, tourism is infringing on the human right to accessible water and sanitation as affirmed by the UN Human Rights Council in 2010. Tourism Concern (2012) has requested the UK government to provide operating guidance or regulate water use by UK-based tourism companies, regardless of which overseas country they operate in. The increased power of social media and consumer review platforms is also likely to elevate reputational risk where perceived inequalities or unsustainable water uses are documented.

Importantly, the geographical scale of water risk perception continues to evolve from a primarily local concern to one with regional implications for trade, long-term economic development and even geopolitical risk. Whereas the immediate impacts of too much or too little water are often local, recent high-profile examples of drought in Russia (2010) and California (2014) and massive flooding in Thailand (2011) have revealed the international ripple effects on the increasingly globalised economy and food system. Water security is increasingly recognised as a systemic global economic risk factor. For the past three years the World Economic Forum's (WEF, 2014) global risks survey with leading international decision makers has ranked water security as one of the top five risks to the global economy over the next decade.

The Place of Tourism in Water Futures Planning

How will the global community respond to the complex and evolving global water challenges in the decades ahead and what will be the implications for the tourism sector? A number of global multi-stakeholder water resource forums established over the last 20 years, including the Global Water Partnership (2014), the World Business Council for Sustainable Development's Water Task Force (2014), the World Bank's World Water Partnership Strategic Action Plan (WBCSD, 2014), the World Water Council (2014) and the World Economic Forum's Global Agenda Council on Water (WEF, 2014), have reached a similar conclusion – there will be no simple solution to the imminent and evolving water challenges. Each of these high-profile expert groups and the UN-WATER initiative have recommended significant, strategic and sustained investment in improving the water resource information base (both supply and demand side) and water management infrastructure, as well as a concerted reform of water governance. Each has also made it clear that successful water management will require much greater cooperation among the diverse network of public and private water stakeholders and institutions – from the local to the international scale.

Of particular relevance to the tourism sector is the consensus among these expert forums that water is a critical cross-sectoral resource that is integral to economic growth and sustainable development and that in water basins where water scarcity is a reality, water optimisation solutions will involve cross-sectoral trade-offs. The 2030 Water Resources Group (2009: v) emphasised that difficult sectoral trade-offs and policy choices will be required to achieve water security in many already stressed basins, concluding that, 'The conversation needed amongst stakeholders, then, is about a country's economic and social priorities, what water will be needed to meet those priorities, and which difficult challenges are worth tackling to deliver or free up that water'. Failure to do so will mean that water scarcity will hinder economic development. Water scarcity, competition and costs will therefore unreservedly become a more influential factor in long-term tourism development in these regions.

Where will tourism be ranked in the list of priority water users? How will tourism's position vary regionally and locally, and what are the implications for future tourism development? These are questions that remain largely unasked within the tourism sector. The reality for tourism, as for all economic sectors, is that business-as-usual water use is or will soon be no longer an option and tourism needs to better prepare itself for increased competition for water. As indicated, the tourism sector is generally ill-prepared to make an evidence-based case for water allocations based on relative water efficiency and socio-economic benefits. Addressing this information gap should be a priority of tourism scholars and practitioners, particularly in the light of the evolving economics of water as outlined in this book and the conclusions of the aforementioned global expert forums.

A concerted effort will also be required to elevate the status of tourism in regional and trans-boundary water planning as well as international negotiations related to programmes that will guide and finance the transformation of the water sector. Although the UNWTO is a participant in the UN-WATER initiative, tourism has had a very low profile in most of the multi-stakeholder forums mentioned above. For example, reports by the 2030 Water Resources Group (2009), UN World Water Assessment Programme (UNESCO, 2012) and the World Water Partnership Strategic Action Plan (World Bank, 2013) do not mention tourism at all. Tourism also has no representation on the Water Partnership Program headed by the World Bank. With water thought to become a more strategic, and in some regions more expensive, resource than oil in the 21st century (UN Water, 2014), there are risks associated with tourism remaining largely invisible in the international dialogue on the future of water and a failure to adapt to these evolving commercial realities.

Through supra-national organisations like the UNWTO and WTTC and key regional organisations like PATA, tourism must become a more active contributor to the evolving global and regional dialogue on water futures if it is to have an influential voice in the discussions about sectoral water access that will be important in order for the projected large-scale growth of domestic and international tourism to be realised. Innovative leadership and vision on this critical aspect of sustainable tourism is crucial in the near future. A major collaboration by government, industry and tourism scholars to improve the information base on the status of water use and document the water-use savings possible through best practices as part of a Declaration on Tourism and Water Security would be a major sectoral contribution to the end of the International Decade for Water Action ('Water for Life') in 2015.

Further reading

For general papers on water futures, including in relation to climate change, see:

Ercin, A. and Hoekstra, A. (2014) Water footprint scenarios for 2050: A global analysis. *Environment International* 64, 71–82.
IPCC (Intergovernmental Panel on Climate Change) (2013) Summary for policymakers. In *Climate Change 2013: The Physical Science Basis. Contribution of Working Group I to the*

Fifth Assessment Report of the Intergovernmental Panel on Climate Change. See www.ipcc. ch/report/ar5/wg1/#.Upyi_aUrTHg.

IPCC (Intergovernmental Panel on Climate Change) (2014a) Chapter 3 – Freshwater systems. In *Climate Change 2014: Impacts, Adaptation and Vulnerability. Contribution of Working Group 2 to the Fifth Assessment Report of the Intergovernmental Panel on Climate Change.* See http://ipcc-wg2.gov/AR5/images/uploads/WGIIAR5-Chap3_FGDall. pdf.

IPCC (Intergovernmental Panel on Climate Change) (2014b) Summary for policymakers. In *Climate Change 2014: Impacts, Adaptation and Vulnerability. Contribution of Working Group 2 to the Fifth Assessment Report of the Intergovernmental Panel on Climate Change.* See http://ipcc-wg2.gov/AR5/images/uploads/WG2AR5_SPM_FINAL.pdf.

OECD (Organization for Economic Cooperation and Development) (2012b) *Environmental Outlook to 2050: Key Findings on Water.* Paris: OECD. See www.oecd.org/env/indicators-modelling-outlooks/49844953.pdf.

Schewe, J., Heinke, J., Gerten, D., *et al.* (2014) Multimodel assessment of water scarcity under climate change. *Proceedings of the National Academy of Sciences* 111 (9), 3245–3250.

Schlosser, C.A., Strzepek, K., Xiang, G., *et al.* (2014) *The Future of Global Water Stress: An Integrated Assessment.* Cambridge, MA: Joint Program on the Science and Policy of Global Change, Massachusetts Institute of Technology.

Water Disclosure Project (2013) *Moving Beyond Business as Usual: A Need for a Step Change in Water Risk Management. Carbon Disclosure Project.* Global Water Report 2013. London: Carbon Disclosure Project. See https://www.cdp.net/CDPResults/CDP-Global-Water-Report-2013.pdf.

World Bank (2012) *Turn Down the Heat: Why a 4°C Warmer World Must Be Avoided.* Washington, DC: World Bank. See www.worldbank.org/en/news/feature/2012/11/18/Climate-change -report-warns-dramatically-warmer-world-this-century.

On tourism and climate change see:

Dawson, J. and Scott, D. (2010) Climate change and tourism in the Great Lakes region: A summary of risks and opportunities. *Tourism in Marine Environments* 6 (2–3), 119–132.

Gössling, S., Scott, D. and Hall, C.M. (2013) Challenges of tourism in a low-carbon economy. *Wiley Interdisciplinary Reviews – Climate Change* 4 (6), 525–538.

Peister, C. and Scott, D. (2014) *Water Use in Ontario's Golf Industry.* Waterloo: Interdisciplinary Centre on Climate Change.

Scott, D. and Jones, B. (2007) A regional comparison of the implications of climate change of the golf industry in Canada. *Canadian Geographer* 51 (2), 219–232.

Scott, D., McBoyle, G. and Mills, B. (2003) Climate change and the skiing industry in southern Ontario (Canada): Exploring the importance of snowmaking as a technical adaptation. *Climate Research* 23, 171–181.

Scott, D., Gössling, S. and Hall, C.M. (2012a) International tourism and climate change. *Wiley Interdisciplinary Reviews – Climate Change* 3 (3), 213–232.

Scott, D., Gössling, S. and Hall, C.M. (2012b) *Climate Change and Tourism: Impacts, Adaptation and Mitigation.* Abingdon: Routledge.

Online Resources

AHLA (American Hotel and Lodging Association), Green Resource Centre: www.ahla. com/green.aspx.

Alliance for Water Stewardship, a multi-stakeholder organisation dedicated to enhancing water stewardship capacity, and guiding, incentivising and differentiating responsible water use: www.allianceforwaterstewardship.org/.

AQUASTAT database, Food and Agriculture Organisation of the United Nations (FAO): www.fao.org/nr/water/aquastat/main/index.stm.

Ceres Water initiative: www.ceres.org/issues/water.

Energy Star, a US programme that although mainly focused on more efficient energy use also provides information on water management: www.energystar.gov.

Ernst and Young (2012) Preparing for water scarcity: Raising business awareness on water issues: www.ey.com/Publication/vwLUAssets/Preparing-for-water-scarcity/$FILE/Preparing-for-water-scarcity.pdf.

Global Water Partnership: www.gwp.org.

Green Hotelier: www.greenhotelier.org/know-how-guides/water-management-and-responsibility-in-hotels/.

Green Restaurant Program: www.dinegreen.com/.

IUCN water programme: www.iucn.org/about/work/programmes/water/.

SIWI (Stockholm International Water Institute): www.siwi.org/.

The Travel Foundation, Greener Accommodations: www.thetravelfoundation.org.uk/green_business_tools/greener_accommodations/.

Tourism Concern (2012) Water equity in tourism – a human right, a global responsibility: www.ecotourism.org/news/tourism-concern-water-equity-tourism-human-right-global-responsibility.

Travelife: www.travelife.org/Hotels/landing_page.asp.

UN Document Centre on Water and Sanitation: www.unwater.org/other-resources/documentation-center/en/.

UNEP, Water and Sanitation (focused on waste management): www.unep.org/ietc/Ourwork/WaterandSanitation/tabid/56240/Default.aspx.

UN Global Compact, the CEO Water Mandate: ceowatermandate.org/water-assessment-tools-methods/.

UN Water, the United Nations inter-agency mechanism on all freshwater related issues, including sanitation: www.unwater.org/.

UNWTO (United Nations World Tourism Organisation), as well as useful policy information the site also contains information on international tourism flows: www.unwto.org/.

WaterAid is an international non-profit organisation that was first set up as a response to the UN International Drinking Water & Sanitation decade (1981–1990). This is the global/US website: www.wateraid.org/.

WaterAid (UK): www.wateraid.org/uk.

WaterAid (Australia): www.wateraid.org/au.

Water Disclosure Project (2013) Moving beyond business as usual: A need for a step change in water risk management. Carbon Disclosure Project Global Water Report 2013. London: Carbon Disclosure Project: https://www.cdp.net/CDPResults/CDP-Global-Water-Report-2013.pdf.

Water Footprint Network: www.waterfootprint.org/.

WaterSense, a United States Environmental Protection Authority Partnership Program: www.epa.gov/watersense/commercial/challenge.html.

WBCSD (World Business Council for Sustainable Development), the WBCSD Global Water Tool: www.wbcsd.org/work-program/sector-projects/water/global-water-tool.aspx.

WEF (World Economic Forum) (2014) Global agenda council on water: www.weforum.org/reports/global-agenda-council-water-security-2012-2014.

World Bank (2013) World Water Partnership Strategic Action Plan: water.worldbank.org/node/84262.

World Economic Travel and Tourism Competitiveness Index (2013) *Data Analyser*: (www.weforum.org/issues/travel-and-tourism-competitiveness/ttci-platform.

World Resources Institute, Aqueduct: Measuring, mapping and understanding water risks around the globe: www.wri.org/our-work/project/aqueduct.

World Travel & Tourism Council, as well as details of organisation policies the site contains useful information on the economic dimensions of tourism: www.wttc.org/.

World Water Council: www.worldwatercouncil.org/.

WWF Water Risk Filter: waterriskfilter.panda.org/.

The Authors

C. Michael Hall: http://scholar.google.co.nz/citations?user=d5GFhXYAAAAJ&hl=en/ https://canterbury-nz.academia.edu/CMichaelHall.

Stefan Gössling: http://scholar.google.co.nz/citations?user=cQjZDXIAAAAJ&hl=en/ https://lu.academia.edu/StefanGossling.

Daniel Scott: http://scholar.google.co.nz/citations?user=jUz0p_QAAAAJ&hl=en/ https://uwaterloo.academia.edu/DanielScott.

Glossary

Acre-feet is a unit of volume used in the United States in reference to large-scale water resources. One acre-foot (43,560 cubic feet=1233.48183754752 m^3) is often taken in the United States to be the planned water usage of a suburban family household.

Benchmarking is the process of measuring environmental management performance, e.g. with respect to energy, water and waste management, for comparison with similar properties.

Biodegradable means capable of decomposing naturally within a relatively short period of time.

Blackwater (also referred to as *foul water* or *sewage*) is a term that describes wastewater containing faecal matter and urine. It is distinct from *grey water* (see below) or *sullage*, the residues of washing processes.

Blue water refers to surface and groundwater, i.e. water in its conventional sense found in rivers, lakes and aquifers and used for irrigation.

Consumption is the fraction of withdrawn water that is lost in transmission, evaporation, absorption or chemical transformation, or otherwise made unavailable for other purposes as a result of human use.

Data-tracking is the process of gathering environmental data, e.g. energy, water and waste data, for properties in order to track their performance over time.

Direct water use refers to the water used on site at a tourism infrastructure such as a hotel, i.e. including: the irrigation of gardens, lawns or golf courses; the filling of pools and filter backwash; in-room uses including showers and baths, toilet flushing and tap water; laundry and cleaning; as well as water used for food preparation in kitchens.

Environmental Management System is a formal set of policies, procedures, objectives, targets and activities that outline an organisation's structure, procedures and resources for implementing, evaluating, managing and tracking its overall environmental policy and impacts, of which water and energy are usually the most important components.

Eutrophication (also referred to as hypertrophication) is the response of aquatic ecosystems to the addition of artificial or natural substances, mainly phosphates and nitrates, through detergents, fertilisers or sewage. It is often associated with algal blooms.

Gallons are a liquid capacity measurement that is still used in the United States and some Commonwealth countries. The imperial (UK) gallon is defined as exactly 4.54609 litres, and was originally based on the volume of 10 pounds (approximately 4.54 kg) of water at 62°F (17°C). The US gallon is equal to exactly 3.785411784 litres and is legally defined as 231 cubic inches. The US liquid gallon of water weighs approximately 8.34 pounds or 3.78 kg at 62°F (17°C), making it about 16.6% lighter than the imperial gallon.

Green water stands for the precipitation on land that becomes soil moisture in the unsaturated soil zone that plants then use to grow.

Grey water is wastewater that does not contain sewage or faecal contamination and can be reused for irrigation after simple filtration.

Indirect water use, also called 'global' or 'embodied' water, refers to water that is imported in the form of foods, energy, hotel infrastructure, shopping, services, activities, marketing and sales.

Irrigation is the supply of water to plants.

Litre is a unit of volume occupying a volume of 10 cm^3 and is equal to one-thousandth of a cubic metre.

Natural flow is the amount of water that would flow in natural conditions, i.e. without human influence. It contrasts with *actual flow*, which takes into account upstream abstraction of water and legal agreements.

Non-conventional water resources are water generations (productions) that come either from desalination of sea and brackish waters or from wastewater regeneration for reuse.

Reclaimed water is wastewater (often sewage) that has been treated and purified for reuse, rather than discharged into another body of water (e.g. a river).

Renewable water resources are the total resources that are offered by the average annual natural inflow and runoff that feed each hydrological system (catchment area or aquifer).

Systemic water use refers to other aspects of the tourism production system that incur a water 'cost', for instance the construction of roads or marinas, or employee transport.

Water footprint is a concept developed to capture the full implications of human consumption on freshwater, and to subsequently compare the water embodied in consumption in a country as compared to the water embodied in production.

Water lock-in is the situation in which, once infrastructure that requires water has been developed, e.g. a swimming pool or golf course, then those water demands will become fixed as part of the demands of the tourism system.

Water scarcity is the excess of water demand over available supply.

Withdrawal is the total amount of water taken from a lake, river or aquifer for any purpose.

Details of Some of the Metrics Used in This Book

Unit	Symbol	Definition	Relation to international system (SI) of units
Acre-foot	ac ft	$\equiv$ 1 ac $\times$ 1 ft = 43,560 ft^3	= 1233.481 837 547 52 m^3
Cubic foot	cu ft (ft^3)	$\equiv$ 1 ft $\times$ 1 ft $\times$ 1 ft	$\equiv$ 0.028 316 846 592 m^3
Cubic metre (SI unit)	m^3	$\equiv$ 1 m $\times$ 1 m $\times$ 1 m	$\equiv$ 1 m^3
Gallon (US fluid)	gal (US)	$\equiv$ 231 cu in (in^3)	$\equiv$ 3.785 411 784 $\times$ 10^{-3} m^3
Litre (liter)	L	$\equiv$ 1 dm^3 (10 cm^3)	$\equiv$ 0.001 m^3
Gallon (US fluid) per minute	gpm	$\equiv$ 1 gal/min	= 6.30901964 $\times$ 10^{-5} m^3/s

References

2030 Water Resources Group (2009) *Charting Our Water Future: Economic Frameworks to Inform Decision-making.* Washington, DC: Water Resources Group. See www.2030 waterresourcesgroup.com/water_full/Charting_Our_Water_Future_Final.pdf (accessed 15 October 2014).

2hm and Associates (2012) Wirtschaftsfaktor Sportstätte – Präsentation der Ergebnisse 'Bäder'. Stuttgart: BMWi. See www.2hm.eu/documents/BMI-interbad-2012-20121010-SpSKIII-fin.pdf.

Accor (2011) The Accor group's environmental footprint. First Multi-criteria Lifecycle Analysis for an International Hospitality Group. See http://www.accor.com/fileadmin/user_upload/Contenus_Accor/Developpement_Durable/img/earth_guest_research/2011_12_08_accor_empreinte_environnementale_dp_bd_en.pdf (accessed 20 November 2013).

Alberts, B., Johnson, A., Walter, P., Lewis, J., Raff, M., Roberts, K. and Orme, N. (2007) *Molecular Biology of the Cell.* New York: Garland Science.

Alexander, S. (2002) *Green Hotels: Opportunities and Resources for Success.* Portland, OR: Zero Waste Alliance. See http://www.zerowaste.org/publications/GREEN_HO.PDF (accessed 20 November 2013).

Alexandratos, N. and Bruinsma, J. (2012) World agriculture towards 2030/2050: The 2012 revision. ESA Working Paper No. 12-03. Rome: FAO.

Allan, J.A. (1998) Virtual water: A strategic resource: Global solutions to regional deficits. *Ground Water* 36 (4), 545–546.

Amos, J. (2014) Algarve golf courses' growing thirst. *BBC News Science,* 28 April.

Anderson, D.M. (2009) Approaches to monitoring, control and management of harmful algal blooms (HABs). *Ocean and Coastal Management* 52, 342–347.

Andreasen, A.R. (2012) Rethinking the relationship between social/nonprofit marketing and commercial marketing. *Journal of Public Policy and Marketing* 31 (1), 36–41.

Anisfeld, S.G. (2010) *Water Resources.* Washington, DC: Island Press.

Antakyali, D., Krampe, J. and Steinmetz, H. (2008) Practical application of wastewater reuse in tourist resorts. *Water Science and Technology* 57, 2051–2057.

Arnell, N.W. (2004) Climate change and global water resources: SRES emissions and socio-economic scenarios. *Global Environmental Change* 14 (1), 31–52.

Aulbach, R. (1995) Conserving water resources. In D. Stipanuk and S. Robson (eds) *Water Resources for Lodging Operations* (pp. 43–68). East Lansing, MI: Educational Institute of the American Hotel and Motel Association.

Badré, M., Prime, J. and Ribière, G. (2009) *Neige de culture: etat des lieux et impact environnementeaux. Note socio-economique.* Paris: Conseil Général de l'Environnement et du Développement Durable.

Baillon, J. and Ceron, J. (1991) *L'essor du golf.* Grenoble: Presses Universitaires de Grenoble.

Ballantine, D.J. and Davies-Colley, R.J. (2010) Water quality trends at NRWQN sites for the period 1989–2007. NIWA client report (HAM 2009-026) for the Ministry for the Environment. See www.mfe.govt.nz/publications/water/water-quality-trends-1989-2007/index.html.

Ban, K.-M. (2008) At World Economic Forum, Ban Ki-moon pledges action on water resources. *UN News Centre*, 24 January. See www.un.org/apps/news/story.asp?New sID=25398andCr=davos#.U_714Vatudc.

Banerjee, S.G., Bhatia, M., Azuela, G.E., Jaques, I., Sarkar, A., Portale, E., Bushueva, I., Angelou, N. and Inon, J.G. (2013) *Global Tracking Framework, Vol. 3. Sustainable Energy for All.* Washington, DC: World Bank. See documents.worldbank.org/curated/en/2013/05/17765643/global-tracking-framework-vol-3-3-main-report.

Barr, S., Shaw, G., Coles, T. and Prillwitz, J. (2010) 'A holiday is a holiday': Practicing sustainability, home and away. *Journal of Transport Geography* 18, 474–481.

Barrow, C.J. (2006) *Environmental Management for Sustainable Development* (2nd edn). New York: Routledge.

Bates, B., Kundzewicz, Z.W., Wu, S. and Palutikof, J. (2008) Climate change and water. IPCC Technical Paper No. VI. Geneva: IPCC.

Beal, C.M., Hebner, R.E., Webber, M.E., Ruoff, R.S., Seibert, F. and King, C.W. (2012) Comprehensive evaluation of algal biofuel production: Experimental and target results. *Energies* (Special Issue: Algal Fuel) 5, 1943–1981; doi:10.3390/en5061943.

Beeton, S. (2005) *Film-induced Tourism.* Clevedon: Channel View Publications.

Bermudez-Contreras, A., Thomson, M. and Infield D.G. (2008) Renewable energy powered desalination in Baja California Sur, Mexico. *Desalination* 220, 431–440.

Berenberg, B. (2012) *Strong Growth Expected in Golf Club Market Web.* See About.com: http://composite.about.com/cs/sportinggoods/a/bpr_ecomp.htm (accessed 27 November 2012).

Black, M. and King, J. (2009) *The Atlas of Water: Mapping the World's most Critical Resource.* London: Earthscan.

Blancas, F.J., Lozano-Oyola, M., González, M., Guerrero, F.M. and Caballero, R. (2011) How to use sustainability indicators for tourism planning: The case of rural tourism in Andalusia (Spain). *Science of the Total Environment* 412–413, 28–45.

Blue Flag (2014) Beaches and marinas with Blue Flag. See www.blueflag.org.

Bohdanowicz, P. and Martinac, I. (2007) Determinants and benchmarking of resource consumption in hotels – case study of Hilton International and Scandic in Europe. *Energy and Buildings* 39 (1), 82–95.

Bohdanowicz-Godfrey, P. and Zientara, P. (2014) Environmental management and online environmental performance assessment tools in the hotel industry: Theory and practice. In C. M. Hall, D. Scott and S. Gössling (eds) *Handbook of Tourism and Sustainability.* London: Routledge (in press).

Bramwell, B. (2004) Mass tourism, diversification and sustainability in southern Europe's coastal regions. In B. Bramwell (ed.) *Coastal Mass Tourism: Diversification and Sustainable Development in Southern Europe* (pp. 1–31). Clevedon: Channel View Publications.

Briassoulis, H. (1991) Methodological issues: Tourism input-output analysis. *Annals of Tourism Research* 18 (3), 485–495.

Brooker, S. (2014) Deal 'like apartheid'. *Courier Country*, 6 August, 1, 3.

Carbon Disclosure Project (2012) *Water Disclosure Global Report 2011: Raising Corporate Awareness of Global Water Issues.* New York: Deloitte. See https://www.cdp.net/CDPResults/CDP-Water-Disclosure-Global-Report-2011.pdf (accessed 15 October 2014).

Carmody, J.A. (2007) Specialist accommodation operations in North Queensland: Environmental management, environmental attitudes and ecological sustainability. Unpublished PhD thesis, James Cook University.

Cazcarro, I., Duarte, R. and Sánchez-Chóliz, J. (2012) Water flows in the Spanish economy: Agri-food sectors, trade and households diets in an input-output framework. *Environmental Science and Technology* 46 (12), 6530–6538.

Cazcarro, I., Hoekstra, A.Y. and Sánchez Chóliz, J. (2014) The water footprint of tourism in Spain. *Tourism Management* 40, 90–101.

Ceres (2009) *Water Scarcity and Climate Change: Growing Risks for Businesses and Investors.* Boston, MA: Ceres. See www.ceres.org/resources/reports/water-scarcity-climate-change-risks-for-investors-2009.

Ceron, J. and Kovacs, J.C. (1993) *Golf et environnement: un aperçu des principaux problèmes. Le golf et le respect de l'environnement.* Les Arcs: Fédération française de golf.

Chan, W.W. (2005a) Partial analysis of the environmental costs generated by hotels in Hong Kong. *International Journal of Hospitality Management* 24 (4), 517–531.

Chan, W.W. (2009) Environmental measures for hotels' environmental management systems: ISO 14001. *International Journal of Contemporary Hospitality Management* 21 (5), 542–560.

Chan, W.W. and Lam, J.C. (2001) Environmental costing of sewage discharged by hotels in Hong Kong. *International Journal of Contemporary Hospitality Management* 13 (5), 218–226.

Chan, W.W., Wong, K. and Lo, J. (2009) Hong Kong hotels' sewage: Environmental cost and saving technique. *Journal of Hospitality and Tourism Research* 33 (3), 329–346.

Chapagain, A.K. and Orr, S. (2008) *UK Water Footprint: The Impact of the UK's Food and Fibre Consumption on Global Water Resources.* Godalming: WWF-UK. See www.waterfootprint.org/Reports/Orr%20and%20Chapagain%202008%20UK%20water footprint-vol1.pdf.

Chapman, C. and Horner, R.R. (2010) Performance assessment of a street-drainage bioretention system. *Water Environment Research* 82 (2), 109–119.

Chenoweth, J., Hadjikakou, M. and Zoumides, C. (2013) Review article: Quantifying the human impact on water resources: A critical review of the water footprint concept. *Hydrology and Earth System Sciences Discussions* 10 (7), 9389–9433.

Chenoweth, J., Hadjikakou, M. and Zoumides, C. (2014) Quantifying the human impact on water resources: A critical review of the water footprint concept. *Hydrological and Earth System Sciences* 18, 1–18.

Chowdhury, S., Slhooshani, K. and Karanfil, T. (2014) Disinfection byproducts in swimming pool: Occurrences, implications and future needs. *Water Research* 53, 68–109.

CIA (Central Intelligence Agency) (2014) *World Fact Book.* See https://www.cia.gov/library/publications/the-world-factbook (accessed 15 October 2014).

Clarke, R. and King, J. (2004) *The Atlas of Water.* London: Earthscan.

City West Water (2006) *Benchmarking Fact Sheets.* Melbourne: City West Water.

City of Melbourne (2007) *WasteWise Hotels Toolkit,* March. Melbourne: City of Melbourne.

Cohen, R., Ortez, K. and Pinkstaff, C. (2009) Increasing water efficiency in California's commercial, industrial and institutional (CII) sector. NRDC Issue Paper, May. New York: National Resources Defense Council.

Cole, S. (2012) A political ecology of water equity and tourism: A case study from Bali. *Annals of Tourism Research* 39 (2), 1221–1241.

Cole, S. (2013) Tourism and water: From stakeholders to rights holders, and what tourism businesses need to do. *Journal of Sustainable Tourism* 22 (1), 89–106.

Collins, A.Y. (1995) The origin of Christian baptism. In M.E. Johnson (ed.) *Living Water, Sealing Spirit: Readings on Christian Initiation* (pp. 35–57). Collegeville, MN: Liturgical Press.

Cooley, H., Hutchins-Cabibi, T., Cohen, M., Gleick, P. H. and Heberger, M. (2007) *Hidden Oasis. Water conservation and efficiency in Las Vegas.* Boulder, CO: Pacific Institute, Oakland, California, and Western Resource Advocates.

Cooley, H., Morrison, J., Donnelly, K. and Ha, M.L. (2012) *Water as a Casualty of Conflict: Threats to Business and Society in High-risk Areas.* Oakland, CA: Pacific Institute. See http://pacinst.org/wp-content/uploads/sites/21/2013/02/full_report39.pdf (accessed 15 October 2014).

Council of the Great Lakes Region (2014) *Low Water Blues: An Economic Impact Assessment of Future Low Water Levels in the Great Lakes and St. Lawrence River.* Toronto: Council of the Great Lakes Region. See http://councilgreatlakesregion.org/low-water-blues-economic-fallout-from-lower-future-water-levels-in-the-great-lakes-st-lawrence-region-could-total-more-than-18-billion-by-2050/(accessed 15 October 2014).

Cullen, R., Dakers, A., McNicol, J., Meyer-Hubbert, G., Simmons, D.G. and Fairweather, J. (2003) *Tourism, Water and Waste in Akaroa: Implications of Tourist Demand on Infrastructure.* Tourism Recreation Research and Education Centre (TRREC) Report No. 38, Lincoln: Lincoln University.

Dalin, C., Konar, M., Hanasaki, N., Rinaldo, A. and Rodriguez-Iturbe, I. (2012) Evolution of the global virtual water trade network. *Proceedings of the National Academy of Sciences* 109 (16), 5989–5994.

Dankers, R., Arnell, N.W., Clark, D.B., *et al.* (2013) First look at changes in flood hazard in the Inter-Sectoral Impact Model Intercomparison Project ensemble. *Proceedings of the National Academy of Sciences* 111 (9), 3257–3261.

Dann, S. (2010) Redefining social marketing with contemporary commercial marketing definitions. *Journal of Business Research* 63, 147–153.

Davie, J., Falloon, P.D., Kahana, R., *et al.* (2013) Comparing projections of future changes in runoff from hydrological and biome models in ISI-MIP. *Earth System Dynamics* 4, 359–374.

Dawson, J. and Scott, D. (2010) Climate change and tourism in the Great Lakes region: A summary of risks and opportunities. *Tourism in Marine Environments* 6 (2–3), 119–132.

Deans, N. and Hackwell, K. (2008) *Dairying and Declining Water Quality: Why Has the Dairying and Clean Streams Accord Not Delivered Cleaner Streams?* Wellington: Fish&Game New Zealand. See www.forestandbird.org.nz/files/file/Dairying_and_Declining_Water_Quality%283%29.pdf.

De Fraiture, C., Giordano, M. and Liao, Y. (2008) Biofuels and implications for agricultural water use: Blue impacts of green energy. *Water Policy* 10, 67–81.

D'Elia, C.F. and Wiebe, W.J. (1990) Biochemical nutrient cycles in coral reef ecosystems. In E. Dubinsky (ed.) *Ecosystems of the World, Vol. 25, Coral Reefs* (pp. 49–74). New York: Elsevier Science.

Deng, S. (2003) Energy and water uses and their performance explanatory indicators in hotels in Hong Kong. *Energy and Buildings* 35 (8), 775–784.

Deng, S. and Burnett, J. (2002) Water use in hotels in Hong Kong. *International Journal of Hospitality Management* 21 (1), 57–66.

De Stefano, L. (2004) Freshwater and tourism in the Mediterranean. Rome: WWF Mediterranean Programme. See http://awsassets.panda.org/downloads/medpotourismreportfinal_ofnc.pdf (accessed 15 October 2014).

Deyá Tortella, B. and Tirado, D. (2011) Hotel water consumption at a seasonal mass tourist destination. The case of the island of Mallorca. *Journal of Environmental Management* 92, 2568–2579.

Downward, S.R. and Taylor, R. (2007) An assessment of Spain's Programa AGUA and its implications for sustainable water management in the province of Almería, southeast Spain. *Journal of Environmental Management* 82, 277–289.

EarthCheck (2013) *White Paper on Tourism and Water*. Melbourne: EarthCheck Research Institute.

Energies Nouvelles (2011) Water in fuel production. Oil production and refining. Panorama. Rueil-Malmaison: Energies Nouvelles. See www.ifpenergiesnouvelles. com/actualites/evenements/nous-organisons/panorama-2011.

Englebert, E.T., McDermott, C. and Kleinheinz, G.T. (2008) Effects of the nuisance algae, *Cladophora*, on *Escherichia coli* at recreational beaches in Wisconsin. *Science of the Total Environment* 404, 10–17.

Ercin, A. and Hoekstra, A. (2014) Water footprint scenarios for 2050: A global analysis. *Environment International* 64, 71–82.

Essex, S., Kent, M. and Newnham, R. (2004) Tourism development in Mallorca: Is water supply a constraint? *Journal of Sustainable Tourism* 12 (1), 4–28.

Eurobarometer (2011) Attitudes of European citizens towards the environment. Available at: http://ec.europa.eu/environment/pdf/ebs_365_en.pdf (accessed 28 December 2013).

European Commission (EC) (2013) European tourism indicator system TOOLKIT for sustainable destinations. DG Enterprise and Industry. February 2013. See http://ec.europa.eu/enterprise/newsroom/cf/_getdocument.cfm?doc_id.7826 (accessed 7 November 2013).

Europetravel (2010) *International Arrivals at the Main Airports, Jan–Dec 2010/2009*. Rhodes: Europetravel. See www.europetravel.gr/userfiles/file/JAN-DEC%202010-9(bilin gual%20version).pdf.

Eurostat (2009) *MEDSTAT II: 'Water and Tourism' Pilot Study*. Luxembourg: Eurostat, European Commission. See http://epp.eurostat.ec.europa.eu/cache/ITY_OFFPUB/KS-78-09-699/EN/KS-78-09-699-EN.PDF (accessed 15 October 2014).

Fagan, B.M. (1998) *Clash of Cultures*. London: Alta Mira Press.

Falkenmark, M. and Rockström, J. (1993) Curbing rural exodus from tropical drylands. *Ambio* 22, 427–437.

Falkenmark, M. and Widstrand, C. (1992) Population and water resources: A delicate balance. *Population Bulletin* 47 (3), 1–36.

FAO (Food and Agriculture Organisation) (2011a) *'Energy-smart' food for people and climate*. Issue paper. Rome: FAO. See www.fao.org/docrep/014/i2454e/i2454e00.pdf.

FAO (Food and Agriculture Organisation) (2011b) *AQUASTAT – Water Use*. Rome: FAO. See www.fao.org/nr/water/aquastat/water_use/index.stm.

FAO (Food and Agriculture Organisation) (2012) *Coping with water scarcity. An action framework for agriculture and food security*. FAO Water Reports No. 38. Rome: FAO. See www.fao.org/docrep/016/i3015e/i3015e.pdf.

FAO (Food and Agriculture Organisation) (2013) *FAO World Hunger Map*. Rome: FAO. See http://faostat.fao.org/site/563/default.aspx (accessed 15 October 2014).

FAO (Food and Agriculture Organisation) (2014) *AQUASTAT, various documents*. Rome: FAO. See www.fao.org/nr/water/aquastat/main/index.stm.

Gago Pedras, C.M., Lança, R.M., Martins, F., Fernandez, H., Vieira, C., Monteiro, J.P. and Guerrero, C. (2014) Evaluation of water demand in golf courses of southern Portugal during the last three decades. *EGU General Assembly Conference Abstracts* 16, 16688.

Garrod, B. and Gössling, S. (eds) (2007) *New Frontiers in Marine Tourism: Diving Experiences, Management and Sustainability*. Amsterdam: Elsevier.

Gershwin, L.A., de Nardi, M., Winkel, K.D. and Fenner, P.J. (2010) Marine stingers: Review of an underrecognized global coastal management issue. *Coastal Management* 38 (1), 22–41.

GFANC (German Federal Agency for Nature Conservation) (1997) *Biodiversity and Tourism. Conflicts on the World's Seacoasts and Strategies for Their Solution*. Berlin: Springer-Verlag.

Gikas, P. and Tchobanoglous, G. (2009) Sustainable use of water in the Aegean Islands. *Journal of Environmental Management* 90 (8), 2601–2611.

Gleeson, T., Wada, Y., Bierkens, M.F.P. and van Beek, L.P.H. (2012) Water balance of global aquifers revealed by groundwater footprint. *Nature* 488, 197–200.

Gleick, P.H. and Cooley, H.S. (2009) Energy implications of bottled water. *Environmental Research Letters* 4 (1), 014009.

Gleick, P.H. and Palaniappan, M. (2010) Peak water limits to freshwater withdrawal and use. *Proceedings of the National Academy of Sciences* 107 (25), 11155–11162.

Gleick, P., Wolff, G.H. and Cushing, K.K. (2003) *Waste Not, Want Not: The Potential for Urban Water Conservation in California*. Oakland, CA: Pacific Institute for Studies in Development, Environment, and Security.

Global Water Partnership (2014) GWP website. See www.gwp.org.

Goldstein, N.J., Cialdini, R.B. and Griskevicius, V. (2008) A room with a viewpoint: Using social norms to motivate environmental conservation in hotels. *Journal of Consumer Research* 35, 472–482.

Goldstein, N.J., Griskevicius, V. and Cialdini, R.B. (2011) Reciprocity by proxy: A novel influence strategy for stimulating cooperation. *Administrative Science Quarterly* 56, 411–473.

Gössling, S. (2001) The consequences of tourism for sustainable water use on a tropical island: Zanzibar, Tanzania. *Journal of Environmental Management* 61 (2), 179–191.

Gössling, S. (2002) Global environmental consequences of tourism. *Global Environmental Change* 12 (4), 283–302.

Gössling, S. (2005) Tourism's contribution to global environmental change: Space, energy, disease, and water. In C.M. Hall and J.E.S. Higham (eds) *Tourism, Recreation, and Climate Change* (pp. 286–300). Clevedon: Channel View Publications.

Gössling, S. (2006) Tourism and water. In S. Gössling and C.M. Hall (eds) *Global Environmental Change, Ecological, Social, Economic and Political Interrelationships* (pp. 180–194). Abingdon: Routledge.

Gössling, S. (2010) *Carbon Management in Tourism: Mitigating the Impacts on Climate Change*. Abingdon: Routledge.

Gössling, S. (2015) New key performance indicators for water management in tourism. *Tourism Management* 46, 233–244.

Gössling, S. and Buckley, R. (2015) Carbon labels in tourism: Persuasive communication? *Journal of Cleaner Production*, DOI: 10.1016/j.jclepro.2014.08.067

Gössling, S. and Hall, C.M. (2013) Sustainable culinary systems. In S. Gössling and C.M. Hall (eds) *Sustainable Culinary Systems: Local Foods, Innovation, Tourism and Hospitality* (pp. 3–44). Abingdon: Routledge.

Gössling, S. and Peeters, P. (2015) Assessing tourism's global environmental impact 1900–2050. *Journal of Sustainable Tourism*, in press.

Gössling, S., Peeters, P., Ceron, J.P., Dubois, G., Patterson, T. and Richardson, R.B. (2005) The eco-efficiency of tourism. *Ecological Economics* 54 (4), 417–434.

Gössling, S., Hultman, J., Haglund, L., Källgren, H. and Revahl, M. (2009) Voluntary carbon offsetting by Swedish air travellers: Towards the co-creation of environmental value? *Current Issues in Tourism* 12 (1), 1–19.

Gössling, S., Hall, C.M., Peeters, P. and Scott, D. (2010) The future of tourism: Can tourism growth and climate policy be reconciled? A climate change mitigation perspective. *Tourism Recreation Research* 35 (2), 119–130.

Gössling, S., Garrod, B., Aall, C., Hille, J. and Peeters, P. (2011) Food management in tourism: Reducing tourism's 'carbon foodprint'. *Tourism Management* 32 (3), 534–543.

Gössling, S., Peeters, P., Hall, C.M., Ceron, J.P., Dubois, G., Lehmann, L.V. and Scott, D. (2012) Tourism and water use: Supply, demand, and security. An international review. *Tourism Management* 33 (1), 1–15.

Gössling, S., Scott, D. and Hall, C.M. (2013) Challenges of tourism in a low-carbon economy. *Wiley Interdisciplinary Reviews – Climate Change* 4 (6), 525–538.

Grenon, M. and Batisse, M. (1991) *Futures for the Mediterranean Basin: The Blue Plan.* New York: Oxford University Press.

Gude, G., Nirmalakhandan, N. and Deng, S. (2010) Renewable and sustainable approaches for desalination. *Renewable and Sustainable Energy Reviews* 14 (9), 2641–2654.

Guilbaud, J., Massé, A., Andrès, Y., Combe, F. and Jaouen, P. (2010) Laundry water recycling in ship by direct nanofiltration with tubular membranes. *Resources, Conservation and Recycling* 55, 148–154.

Guilbaud, J., Massé, A., Andrès, Y., Combe, F. and Jaouen, P. (2012) Influence of operating conditions on direct nanofiltration of greywaters: Application to laundry water recycling aboard ships. *Resources, Conservation and Recycling* 62, 64–70.

Hadjikakou, M. (2014) Measuring the impact of tourism on water resources: Alternative frameworks. PhD thesis, University of Surrey.

Hadjikakou, M., Chenoweth, J. and Miller, G. (2013a) Estimating the direct and indirect water use of tourism in the eastern Mediterranean. *Journal of Environmental Management* 114, 548–556.

Hadjikakou, M., Chenoweth, J., Miller, G. and Druckman, A. (2013b) Economic impact and water use trade-offs and synergies: A case study of the Cyprus tourism sector. *The European Conference on Sustainability, Energy and the Environment 2013, Brighton*, pp. 77–97.

Hafez, A. and El Manharawy, S. (2002) Economics of seawater RO desalination in the Red Sea region, Egypt. Part 1. A case study. *Desalination* 153, 335–347.

Hall, C.M. (2005) *Tourism: Rethinking the Social Science of Mobility.* Harlow: Pearson.

Hall, C.M. (2006) Tourism urbanization and global environmental change. In S. Gössling and C.M. Hall (eds) *Tourism and Global Environmental Change: Ecological, Economic, Social and Political Interrelationships* (pp. 142–156). Abingdon: Routledge.

Hall, C.M. (2008) *Tourism Planning* (2nd edn). Harlow: Pearson.

Hall, C.M. (2010) Tourism destination branding and its effects on national branding strategies: Brand New Zealand, clean and green but is it smart? *European Journal of Tourism and Hospitality Research* 1 (1), 68–89.

Hall, C.M. (2011a) Policy learning and policy failure in sustainable tourism governance: From first and second to third order change? *Journal of Sustainable Tourism* 19, 649–671.

Hall, C.M. (2011b) A typology of governance and its implications for tourism policy analysis. *Journal of Sustainable Tourism* 19, 437–457.

Hall, C.M. (2013a) *Tourism and Social Marketing.* Abingdon: Routledge.

Hall, C.M. (2013b) Framing behavioural approaches to understanding and governing sustainable tourism consumption: Beyond neoliberalism, 'nudging' and 'green growth'? *Journal of Sustainable Tourism* 21 (7), 1091–1109.

Hall, C.M. (2014) You can check out any time you like but you can never leave: Can ethical consumption in tourism ever be sustainable? In C. Weeden and K. Boluk (eds) *Managing Ethical Consumption in Tourism: Compromise and Tension* (pp. 32–56). Abingdon: Routledge.

Hall, C.M. and Gössling, S. (eds) (2013) *Sustainable Culinary Systems. Local Foods, Innovation, and Tourism & Hospitality.* London: Routledge.

Hall, C.M. and Härkönen, T. (2006) *Lake Tourism: An Integrated Approach to Lacustrine Tourism Systems.* Clevedon: Channel View Publications.

Hall, C.M. and Page, S.P. (2014) *The Geography of Tourism and Recreation* (4th edn). Abingdon: Routledge.

Hall, C.M. and Stoffels, M. (2006) Lake tourism in New Zealand: Sustainable management issues. In C.M. Hall and T. Härkönen (eds) *Lake Tourism: An Integrated Approach to Lacustrine Tourism Systems* (pp. 182–206). Clevedon: Channel View Publications.

Hall, C.M., Timothy, D. and Duval, D. (2004) Security and tourism: Towards a new understanding? *Journal of Travel and Tourism Marketing* 15 (2–3), 1–18.

Hall, C.M., Gössling, S. and Scott, D. (eds) (2015) *The Routledge Handbook of Sustainable Tourism.* Abingdon: Routledge.

Harris, R. (2013) An exploration of the relationship between large-scale sporting events and education for sustainable development: The case of the Melbourne 2006 Commonwealth Games. *International Journal of the History of Sport* 30 (17), 2069–2097.

Harris, R. and Varga, D. (1995) I Jemby-Ringah lodge. In R. Harris and N. Leiper (eds) *Sustainable Tourism: An Australian Perspective.* Chatswood: Butterworth-Heinemann.

Hau'ofa, E. (1997) The ocean in us. In S. Mishra and E. Guy (eds) *Dreadlocks in Oceania 1* (pp. 124–148). Suva: Department of Literature and Language, University of the South Pacific.

Hejazi, M., Edmonds, J., Clarke, L., *et al.* (2013) Long-term global water projections using six socioeconomic scenarios in an integrated assessment modeling framework. *Technological Forecasting and Social Change* 81, 205–226.

Hellenic National Meteorological Service (2014) *Climatology Rodos.* See www.hnms.gr/hnms/english/climatology/climatology_region_diagrams_html?dr_city=Rodos.

Higham, J., Cohen, S. A., Peeters, P. and Gössling, S. (2013) Psychological and behavioural approaches to understanding and governing sustainable mobility. *Journal of Sustainable Tourism* 21 (7), 949–967.

Hills, S., Birks, R. and McKenzie, B. (2002) The Millennium Dome 'Watercycle' experiment: to evaluate water efficiency and customer perception at a recycling scheme for 6 million visitors. *Water Science and Technology* 46 (6–7), 233–240.

Hitchcock, D.E. and Willard, M.L. (2009) *The Business Guide to Sustainability: Practical Strategies and Tools for Organizations.* London and Sterling, VA: Earthscan.

Hoekstra, A.Y. and Chapagain, A.K. (2007) Water footprints of nations: Water use by people as a function of their consumption pattern. *Water Resources Management* 21 (1), 35–48.

Hoekstra, A.Y. and Chapagain, A.K. (2008) *Globalization of Water: Sharing the Planet's Freshwater Resources.* Oxford: Blackwell.

Hoekstra, A.Y. and Hung, P.Q. (2002) Virtual water trade. A quantification of virtual water flows between nations in relation to international crop trade. Value of Water Research Report No. 11, p. 166.

Hoekstra, A.Y., Chapagain, A.K., Aldaya, M.M. and Mekonnen, M.M. (2011) *The Water Footprint Assessment Manual: Setting the Global Standard.* London: Earthscan.

Hoekstra, A.Y., Mekonnen, M.M., Chapagain, A.K., Mathews, R.E. and Richter, B.D. (2012) Global monthly water scarcity: Blue water footprints versus blue water availability. *PLoS One* 7 (2), e32688.

Hof, A. and Schmitt, T. (2011) Urban and tourist land use patterns and water consumption: Evidence from Mallorca, Balearic Islands. *Land Use Policy* 28 (4), 792–804.

Horner, R.R. (2007) Investigation of the feasibility and benefits of low-impact site design practices ('LID') for Ventura County. Report prepared for the Natural Resources Defense Council and submitted to the Los Angeles Regional Water Quality Control Board, Los Angeles, CA.

Howe, K.R. (2007) The last frontier. In K.R. Howe (ed.) *Vaka Moana: Voyages of the Ancestors* (pp. 16–21). Honolulu: University of Hawaii Press.

Hu, C. and He, M.X. (2008) Origin and offshore extent of floating algae in Olympic sailing area. *Eos, Transactions, American Geophysical Union* 89 (33), 302–303.

Hudson, S. and Hudson, L. (2010) *Golf Tourism*. Oxford: Foodfellow Publishers.

Iacovides, I. (2011) Water resources in Cyprus: Endowments and water management practices. In P. Koundouri (ed.) *Water Resources Allocation: Policy and Socioeconomic Issues in Cyprus* (pp. 11–21). Dortrecht: Springer Netherlands.

IATA (International Air Transport Association) (2013) *Alternative Fuels*. See www.iata.org/whatwedo/environment/Pages/alternative-fuels.aspx.

IEA (International Energy Agency) (2012) *World Energy Outlook 2012*. Paris: OECD/IEA. See www.iea.org/newsroomandevents/speeches/weo_launch.pdf.

IFEN (2000) *Tourisme, environnement, territoires: les indicateurs*. Orléans: IFEN.

IPCC (Intergovernmental Panel on Climate Change) (2007) Summary for policymakers. In *Climate Change 2013: Impacts, Adaptation and Vulnerability. Contribution of Working Group 2 to the Fourth Assessment Report of the Intergovernmental Panel on Climate Change*. See www.ipcc.ch/publications_and_data/ar4/wg2/en/spm.html.

IPCC (Intergovernmental Panel on Climate Change) (2013) Summary for policymakers. In *Climate Change 2013: The Physical Science Basis. Contribution of Working Group I to the Fifth Assessment Report of the Intergovernmental Panel on Climate Change*. See www.ipcc.ch/report/ar5/wg1/#.Upyi_aUrTHg.

IPCC (Intergovernmental Panel on Climate Change) (2014a) Chapter 3 – Freshwater systems. In *Climate Change 2014: Impacts, Adaptation and Vulnerability. Contribution of Working Group 2 to the Fifth Assessment Report of the Intergovernmental Panel on Climate Change*. See http://ipcc-wg2.gov/AR5/images/uploads/WGIIAR5-Chap3_FGDall.pdf (accessed 15 October 2014).

IPCC (Intergovernmental Panel on Climate Change) (2014b) Summary for policymakers. In *Climate Change 2014: Impacts, Adaptation and Vulnerability. Contribution of Working Group 2 to the Fifth Assessment Report of the Intergovernmental Panel on Climate Change*. See http://ipcc-wg2.gov/AR5/images/uploads/WG2AR5_SPM_FINAL.pdf (accessed 15 October 2014).

IRENA (International Renewable Energy Agency) (2012) Water desalination using renewable energy. IRENA and IEA- ETSAP (International Energy Agency Energy Technology Systems Analysis Programme) Technology Brief I12. Abu Dhabi: IRENA.

Johnson, D. (2002) Environmentally sustainable cruise tourism: A reality check. *Marine Policy* 26, 261–270.

Jones, B., Scott, D. and Gössling, S. (2006) Lakes and streams. In S. Gössling and C.M. Hall (eds) *Tourism and Global Environmental Change. Ecological, Social, Economic and Political Interrelationships* (pp. 76–94). Abingdon: Routledge.

JPMorgan (2008) *Watching Water: A Guide to Evaluating Corporate Risks in a Thirsty World*. Washington, DC: World Resources Institute. See http://pdf.wri.org/jpmorgan_watching_water.pdf (accessed 15 October 2014).

Kavanagh, L.J. (2002) Water Management and Sustainability at Queensland Tourist Resorts. Gold Coast: CRC for Sustainable Tourism.

Kent, M., Newnham, R. and Essex, S. (2002) Tourism and sustainable water supply in Mallorca: A geographical analysis. *Applied Geography* 22 (4), 351–374.

Korkosz, A., Ptaszynska, A., Hanel, A., Niewiadomski, M. and Hupka, J. (2012) Cullet as filter medium for swimming pool water treatment. *Physicochemical Problems of Mineral Processing* 48 (1), 295–301.

Kotler, P., Roberto, N. and Lee, N. (2002) *Social Marketing: Improving the Quality of Life* (2nd edn). Thousand Oaks, CA: Sage.

Koundouri, P. and Birol, E. (2011) Introduction. In P. Koundouri (ed.) *Water Resources Allocation: Policy and Socioeconomic Issues in Cyprus* (pp. 1–9). Dordrecht: Springer.

Kuoni (2013) Kuoni water management manual for hotels. See http://www.kuoni.com/docs/kuoni_wmp_manual_0.pdf (accessed 20 November 2013).

Kuss, F.R., Graefe, A.R. and Vaske, J.J. (1990) *Visitor Impact Management. A Review of Research, Vol. 1.* Washington, DC: National Parks and Conservation Association.

Lamei, A. (2009) *A Technical Economic Model for Integrated Water Resources Management in Tourism Dependent Arid Coastal Regions; The Case of Sharm El Sheikh, Egypt.* AK Leiden: CRC Press/Balkema.

Lamei, A., Tilmant, A., van der Zaag, P. and Imam, E. (2009) Dynamic programming of capacity expansion for reverse osmosis desalination plant: Sharm El Sheikh, Egypt. *Water Science and Technology: Water Supply* 9, 233–246.

Langumier, A. and Ricou, C. (1995) *Le fonctionnement estival des services d'eau dans les communes du littoral normand. Analyse de l'impact des populations et activités saisonnières.* Paris: Agence de l'eau Seine Normandie.

Lazarova, V., Hills, S. and Birks, R. (2003) Using recycled water for non-potable, urban uses: A review with particular reference to toilet flushing. *Water Science and Technology: Water Supply* 3 (4), 69–77.

Lehr, V.A. (1995) Hot water for lodging properties. In D. Stipanuk and S. Robson (eds) *Water Resources for Lodging Operations* (pp. 69–80). East Lansing, MI: Educational Institute of the American Hotel and Motel Association.

Lenzen, M., Moran, D., Bhaduri, A., Kanemoto, K., Bekchanov, M., Geschke, A. and Foran, B. (2013) International trade of scarce water. *Ecological Economics* 94, 78–85.

Lipchin, C., Pallant, E., Saranga, D. and Amster, A. (eds) (2007) *Integrated Water Resources Management and Security in the Middle East.* Dordrecht: Springer.

Liu, D., Keesing, J.K., Xing, Q. and Shi, P. (2009) World's largest macroalgal bloom caused by expansion of seaweed aquaculture in China. *Marine Pollution Bulletin* 58 (6), 888–895.

Lloyd's (2010) *Global Water Scarcity: Risks and Challenges for Business.* London: Lloyd's. See http://awsassets.panda.org/downloads/lloyds_global_water_scarcity.pdf (accessed 15 October 2014).

Lo, J.Y., Chan, W.W. and Wong, K. (2011) A comparison of cold-water thawing options in Chinese restaurants. *Cornell Hospitality Quarterly* 52 (1), 64–72.

Loehr, L.C., Beegle-Krause, C.J., George, K., McGee, C.D., Mearns, A.J. and Atkinson, M.J. (2006) The significance of dilution in evaluating possible impacts of wastewater discharges from large cruise ships. *Marine Pollution Bulletin* 52, 681–688.

Low, M.-S. (2005) Material flow analysis of concrete in the United States. MSc in Building Technology thesis, Massachusetts Institute of Technology, Cambridge, MA.

MAF (Ministry of Agriculture and Forestry) (2011) *The Dairying and Clean Streams Accord: Snapshot of Progress 2010/2011.* See www.mpi.govt.nz/news-resources/publications.

aspx?title=Dairying%20and%20Clean%20Streams%20Accord:%20Snapshot%20 of%20Progress.

Mangion, E. (2013) Tourism impact on water consumption in Malta. *Bank of Valetta Review* 47, 61–85.

McKenzie-Mohr, D. (2011) *Fostering Sustainable Behavior: An Introduction to Community-based Social Marketing.* Gabriola Island: New Society Publishers.

Medeazza, G.M. (2004) Water desalination as a long-term sustainable solution to alleviate global freshwater scarcity? A north-south approach. *Desalination* 169, 287–301.

Mekonnen, M.M. and Hoekstra, A.Y. (2011a) National water footprint accounts: The green, blue and grey water footprint of production and consumption. Value of Water Research Report No.50. Delft: UNESCO-IHE Institute for Water Education. See www.waterfootprint.org/Reports/Report50-NationalWaterFootprints-Vol1.pdf.

Mekonnen, M.M. and Hoekstra, A.Y. (2011b) The green, blue and grey water footprint of crops and derived crop products. *Hydrology and Earth System Sciences* 15 (5), 1577–1600.

Mekonnen, M.M. and Hoekstra, A.Y. (2012) A global assessment of the water footprint of farm animal products. *Ecosystems* 15 (3), 401–415.

Merritt, R., Truss, A. and Hopwood, T. (2011) Social marketing can help achieve sustainable behaviour change. Guardian Professional Network. *guardian.co.uk*, 17 March. See www.guardian.co.uk/sustainable-business/blog/ social-marketing-behaviour-change.

Meyer, A. and Chaffee, C. (1997) Life-cycle analysis for design of the Sydney Olympic Stadium. *Renewable Energy* 10, 169–172.

MFE (Ministry for the Environment) (2007) *Environment New Zealand 2007.* Wellington: NZ Ministry for the Environment. See www.mfe.govt.nz/publications/ser/enz07-dec07/environment-nz07-dec07.pdf.

MFE (Ministry for the Environment) (2013) *Water Quality Trends at National River Water Quality Network Sites for 1989–2007.* Wellington: NZ Ministry for the Environment. See www.mfe.govt.nz/publications/water/water-quality-trends-1989-2007/index.html.

Michel, D. and Pandya, A. (2009) *Troubled Waters: Climate Change, Hydropolitics and Transboundary Resources.* Washington, DC: Henry L. Stimson Center. See www. stimson.org/images/uploads/research-pdfs/Troubled_Waters-Complete.pdf.

Monaghan, R.M., Wilcock, R.J., Smith, L.C., Tikkisetty, B., Thorrold, B.S. and Costall, D. (2007) Linkages between land management activities and water quality in an intensively farmed catchment in southern New Zealand. *Agriculture, Ecosystems and Environment* 118 (1), 211–222.

Mouchtouri, V.A., Bartlett, C.L., Diskin, A. and Hadjichristodoulou, C. (2012) Water safety plan on cruise ships: A promising tool to prevent waterborne diseases. *Science of the Total Environment* 429, 199–205.

Nilsson, J.H. and Gössling, S. (2013) Tourist responses to extreme environmental events: The case of Baltic Sea algal blooms. *Tourism Planning and Development* 10 (1), 32–44.

OECD (Organization for Economic Cooperation and Development) (2012a) *Environmental Outlook to 2050: The Consequences of Inaction.* Paris: OECD. See http://dx.doi. org/10.1787/9789264122246-en (accessed 15 October 2014).

OECD (Organization for Economic Cooperation and Development) (2012b) *Environmental Outlook to 2050: Key Findings on Water.* Paris: OECD. See www.oecd.org/env/indicators-modelling-outlooks/49844953.pdf.

OECD (Organization for Economic Cooperation and Development) (2013) Effective policies for growth. In-progress Report No. CFE/TOU(2013)10.24, September. Paris: OECD.

OECD and UNEP (2011) *Sustainable Tourism Development and Climate Change: Issues and Policies*. Paris: OECD.

O'Neill and Siegelbaum and The RICE Group (2002) *Hotel Water Conservation. A Seattle Demonstration*. Seattle, WA: Seattle Public Utilities.

PADI (Professional Association of Diving Instructors) (2014) *Worldwide Corporate Statistics 2014*. Rancho Santa Margarita, CA: PADI. See www.padi.com/scuba-diving/about-padi/statistics/.

Page, S.J., Essex, S. and Causevic, S. (2014) Tourist attitudes towards water use in the developing world: A comparative analysis. *Tourism Management Perspectives* 10, 57–67.

Parry, M., Arnell, N., Berry, P., *et al.* (2009a) *Assessing the Costs of Adaptation to Climate Change: A Review of the UNFCCC and Other Recent Estimates*. London: International Institute for Environment and Development and Grantham Institute for Climate Change.

Parry, M., Lowe, J. and Hanson, C. (2009b) Overshoot, adapt and recover. *Nature* 485, 1102–1103.

PCE (Parliamentary Commissioner for the Environment) (2001) *Managing Change in Paradise: Sustainable Development in Peri-urban Areas*. Wellington: PCE. See www.pce.parliament.nz/assets/Uploads/Reports/pdf/Paradise_full.pdf.

PCE (Parliamentary Commissioner for the Environment) (2012) *Water Quality in New Zealand: Understanding the Science*. Wellington: PCE. See www.pce.parliament.nz/publications/all-publications/water-quality-in-new-zealand-understanding-the-science/.

Peeters, P. (2013) Developing a long-term global tourism transport model using a behavioural approach: Implications for sustainable tourism policy making. *Journal of Sustainable Tourism* 21 (7), 1049–1069.

Peister, C. and Scott, D. (2014) *Water Use in Ontario's Golf Industry*. Waterloo: Interdisciplinary Centre on Climate Change.

Peters, G.P., Andrew, R.M., Boden, T., Canadell, J.G., Ciais, P., Quere, C.L. and Wilson, C. (2013) The challenge to keep global warming below 28°C. *Nature Climate Change* 3 (1), 4–6.

Polansky, L., Bergstein, J., Potent, J. and Ramos, C. (2008) A quantitative assessment of the environmental resource impacts of the hospitality sector (lodging facilities) in US EPA Region 2. 2008 EPA NNEMS Fellowship Paper, Stanford University, Stanford, CA.

Pombo, A., Brecada, A. and Aragón, A.V. (2008) Desalinization and wastewater reuse as technological alternatives in an arid, tourism booming region of Mexico. *Frontera Norte* 20 (39), 191–216.

Portmann, F., Doll, P., Eisner, S. and Florke, M. (2013) Impact of climate change on renewable groundwater resources: Assessing the benefits of avoided greenhouse gas emissions using selected CMIP5 climate projections. *Environmental Research Letters* 8 (2), 024023.

Postel, S.L., Daily, G.C. and Ehrlich, P.R. (1996) Human appropriation of renewable fresh water. *Science* 271 (5250), 785.

Prideaux, B. and Cooper, M. (eds) (2009) *River Tourism*. Wallingford: CABI.

Prudhomme, C., Giuntoli, I., Robinson, E.L., *et al.* (2013) Hydrological droughts in the 21st century: Hotspots and uncertainties from a global multi-model ensemble experiment. *Proceedings of the National Academy of Sciences* 111 (9), 3262–3267.

Pryor, S.C., Scavia, D., Downer, C., Gaden, M., Iverson, L., Nordstrom, R., Patz, J. and Robertson, G.P. (2014) Mid-west. climate change impacts in the United States. In J.M. Melillo, T.C. Richmond and G.W. Yohe (eds) *The Third National Climate*

Assessment, US Global Change Research Program (pp. 418–440). See http://nca2014.globalchange.gov/report/regions/midwest (accessed 15 October 2014).

Qur'an (2014) *Verse (21:30)* (English translation). See http://corpus.quran.com/translation.jsp?chapter=21andverse=30 (accessed 15 October 2014).

Rahmstorf, S. (2010) A new view on sea level rise. *Nature Reports Climate Change*, 6 April. See www.nature.com/climate/2010/1004/full/climate.2010.29.html.

Redlin, M.H. and deRoos, J.A. (1995) Water consumption in the lodging industry. In D. Stipanuk and S. Robson (eds) *Water Resources for Lodging Operations* (pp. 17–42). East Lansing, MI: Educational Institute of the American Hotel and Motel Association.

Richardson, K. and Lewis, L. (2014) Human dynamics of climate change. Met Office Technical Report. London: HM Government.

Rico-Amoros, A.M., Olcina-Cantos, J. and Sauri, D. (2009) Tourist land use patterns and water demand: Evidence from the western Mediterranean. *Land Use Policy* 26 (2), 493–501.

Rico-Amoros, A.M., Sauri, D., Olcina-Cantos, J. and Vera-Rebollo, J.F. (2013) Beyond megaprojects? Water alternatives for mass tourism in coastal Mediterranean Spain. *Water Resources Management* 27 (2), 553–565.

Ridoutt, B.G. and Pfister, S. (2010a) A revised approach to water footprinting to make transparent the impacts of consumption and production on global freshwater scarcity. *Global Environmental Change* 20 (1), 113–120.

Ridoutt, B.G. and Pfister, S. (2010b) Reducing humanity's water footprint. *Environmental Science and Technology* 44 (16), 6019–6021.

Rosselló-Batle, B., Moià, A., Cladera, A. and Martínez, V. (2010) Energy use, CO_2 emissions and waste throughout the life cycle of a sample of hotels in the Balearic Islands. *Energy and Buildings* 42 (4), 547–558.

Rübbelke, D. and Vögele, S. (2011) Impacts of climate change on European critical infrastructures: The case of the power sector. *Environmental Science and Policy* 14 (1), 53–63.

Sadhwani, J.J. and Veza, J.M. (2008) Desalination and energy consumption in Canary Islands. *Desalination* 221, 143–150.

Saito, O. (2013) Resource use and waste generation by the tourism industry on the big island of Hawaii. *Journal of Industrial Ecology* 17 (4), 578–589.

Sanders, K.T. and Webber, M.E. (2012) Evaluating the energy intensity of water in the United States. *Environmental Research Letters* 7: 034033.

Schahn, J. (1993) Die Rolle von Entschuldigungen und Rechtfertigungen für umweltschadigendes Verhalten. In J. Schahn and T. Giesinger (eds) *Psychologie für den Umweltschutz* (pp. 51–61). Weinheim: Beltz.

Schernewski, G., Neumann, T., Podsetchine, V. and Siegel, H. (2001) Spatial impact of the Oder river plume on water quality along the south-western Baltic coast. *International Journal of Hygiene and Environmental Health* 204 (2), 143–155.

Schewe, J., Heinke, J., Gerten, D., *et al.* (2014) Multimodel assessment of water scarcity under climate change. *Proceedings of the National Academy of Sciences* 111 (9), 3245–3250.

Schlosser, C.A., Strzepek, K., Xiang, G., *et al.* (2014) *The Future of Global Water Stress: An Integrated Assessment*. Cambridge, MA: Joint Program on the Science and Policy of Global Change, Massachusetts Institute of Technology.

Schwarz, H.E., Emel, J., Dickens, W.J., Rogers, P. and Thompson, J. (1990) Water quality and flows. In B.L. Turner II, W.C. Clarck, R.W. Kates, J.F. Richards, J.T. Mathews and W.B. Meyer (eds) *The Earth as Transformed by Human Action: Global and Regional*

Changes in the Biosphere over the Past 300 Years (pp. 253–270). Cambridge: Cambridge University Press.

Scott, D. and Jones, B. (2007) A regional comparison of the implications of climate change of the golf industry in Canada. *Canadian Geographer* 51 (2), 219–232.

Scott, D., McBoyle, G. and Mills, B. (2003) Climate change and the skiing industry in southern Ontario (Canada): Exploring the importance of snowmaking as a technical adaptation. *Climate Research* 23, 171–181.

Scott, D., Peeters, P. and Gössling, S. (2010) Can tourism deliver its aspirational greenhouse gas emission reduction targets? *Journal of Sustainable Tourism* 18, 393–408.

Scott, D., Gössling, S. and Hall, C.M. (2012a) International tourism and climate change. *Wiley Interdisciplinary Reviews – Climate Change* 3 (3), 213–232.

Scott, D., Gössling, S. and Hall, C.M. (2012b) *Climate Change and Tourism: Impacts, Adaptation and Mitigation.* Abingdon: Routledge.

Scoullos, M.J. (2003) Impact of anthropogenic activities in the coastal region of the Mediterranean Sea. *International Conference on the Sustainable Development of the Mediterranean and Black Sea Environment, May, Thessaloniki.*

Sebake, T.N. and Gibberd, J.T. (2008) Assessing the sustainability performance of the 2010 FIFA World Cup stadia using the sustainable building assessment tool (SBAT) for stadia. In *5th Post Graduate Conference on Construction Industry Development, Bloemfontein, South Africa, 16–18 March.* See http://researchspace.csir.co.za/dspace/handle/10204/3238 (accessed 15 October 2014).

Sedlak, D. (2014) *Water 4.0: The Past, Present, and Future of the World's Most Vital Resource.* New Haven, CT: Yale University Press.

Shaalan, I.M. (2005) Sustainable tourism development in the Red Sea of Egypt: Threats and opportunities. *Journal of Cleaner Production* 13, 83–87.

Shah, M.M. (2013) *New Method for Calculating Evaporation from Occupied Swimming Pools.* Cleveland, OH: HPAC Engineering. See http://hpac.com/humidity-control/new-method-calculating-evaporation-occupied-swimming-pools (accessed 15 October 2014).

Shang, J., Basil, D.Z. and Wymer, W. (2010) Using social marketing to enhance hotel resuse programs. *Journal of Business Research* 63 (2), 166–172.

Shiklomanov, I.A. (1993) World fresh water resources. In P.H. Gleick (ed.) *Water in Crisis: A Guide to the World's Fresh Water Resources* (pp. 13–24). New York: Oxford University Press.

Shlozberg, R., Doring, R. and Spiro, P. (2014) *Low Water Blues: An Economic Impact Assessment of Future Low Water Levels in the Great Lakes and St. Lawrence River.* Toronto: Council of the Great Lakes Region.

Skiresort.info (2013) *Ski Resorts Worldwide.* Skiresort.inifo app. See www.skiresort.info/ski-resorts/.

Sleeman, R. (2009) *Akaroa Tourism Carrying Capacity.* Lincoln, New Zealand: Faculty of Environment, Society and Design, Lincoln University. See http://researcharchive.lincoln.ac.nz/dspace/bitstream/10182/1154/1/LEaP_rr_10.pdf (accessed 15 October 2014).

Smith, M., Hargroves, K., Desha, C. and Stasinopoulos, P. (2009a) *Water Transformed – Australia: Sustainable Water Solutions for Climate Change Adaptation.* Australia: The Natural Edge Project (TNEP).

Smith, P., Martino, D., Cai, Z., *et al.* (2009b) Agriculture. In B. Metz, O.R. Davidson, P.R. Bosch, R. Dave and L.A. Meyer (eds) *Climate Change 2007: Mitigation. Contribution of Working Group III to the Fourth Assessment Report of the Intergovernmental Panel on Climate Change.* Cambridge and New York: Cambridge University Press.

Speidel, D.H. and Agnew, A.F. (1982) *The Natural Geochemistry of Our Environment*. Boulder, CO: Westview Press.

Srinivasan, V., Lambin, E.F., Gorelick, S.M., Thompson, B.H. and Rozelle, S. (2012) The nature and causes of the global water crisis: Syndromes from a meta-analysis of coupled human-water studies. *Water Resources Research* 48 (10).

Staub, C. and Climent, J.C. (2012) *Preparing for Water Scarcity: Raising Business Awareness on Water Issues*. London: Ernst & Young. See www.ey.com/Publication/vwLUAssets/Water_Point_of_view_paper_for_design/$FILE/Water_Point_of_view_paper_for_design.pdf.

Stoll-Kleemann, S., O'Riordan, T. and Jaeger, C.C. (2001) The psychology of denial concerning climate mitigation measures: Evidence from Swiss focus groups. *Global Environmental Change* 11, 107–117.

Stipanuk, D.M. and Robson, S. (eds) (1995) *Water Resources for Lodging Operations*. East Lansing, MI: Educational Institute of the American Hotel and Motel Association.

Steg, L. and Vlek, C. (2009) Encouraging pro-environmental behaviour: An integrative review and research agenda. *Journal of Environmental Psychology* 29, 309–317.

Styles, D., Schoenberger, H. and Galvez-Martos, J.L. (2015) Water management in the European hospitality sector: Best practice, performance benchmarks and improvement potential. *Tourism Management* 46, 187–202.

Thaler, R.H. and Sunstein, C.R. (2008) *Nudge: Improving Decisions About Health, Wealth and Happiness*. London: Yale University Press.

Thompson, D. (2002) *Tools for Environmental Management: A Practical Introduction and Guide*. Gabriola, BC: New Society Publishers.

Thompson, S. (2008) Assessing water resource management in a small island lifestyle community. Unpublished Masters of Resource Management (Planning) research project. School of Resource and Environmental Management, Simon Fraser University.

Throssell, C.S., Lyman, G.T., Johnson, M.E., Stacey, G.A. and Brown, C.D. (2009) Golf course environmental profile measures water use, source, cost, quality, and management and conservation strategies. *Applied Turfgrass Science*; doi:10.1094/ATS-2009- 0129-01-RS.

Tomascik, T. and Sander, F. (1986) Effects of eutrophication on reefbuilding corals. II. Structure of scleractinian coral communities on fringing reefs, Barbados, West Indies. *Marine Biology* 94, 53–75.

Tortella, B.D. and Tirado, D. (2011) Hotel water consumption at a seasonal mass tourist destination. The case of the island of Mallorca. *Journal of Environmental Management* 92 (10), 2568–2579.

Tourism Concern (2011) *Tourism: A Thirsty Business*. London: Tourism Concern. See www.tourismconcern.org.uk.

Tourism Concern (2012) *Water Equity in Tourism: A Human Right, a Global Responsibility*. London: Tourism Concern. See http://www.ircwash.org/resources/water-equity-tourism-human-right-global-responsibility (accessed 15 October 2014).

Truong, V.D. and Hall, C.M. (2013) Social marketing and tourism: What is the evidence? *Social Marketing Quarterly* 19 (2), 110–135.

UN (United Nations) (2013) *World Population Prospects: The 2012 Revision*. New York: United Nations. See http://esa.un.org/wpp/ (accessed 15 October 2014).

UNDESA (United Nations Department of Economic and Social Affairs) (2012) *World Urbanization Prospects, the 2011 Revision: Highlights*. New York: United Nations. See www.un.org/en/development/desa/publications/world-urbanization-prospects-the-2011-revision.html.

UNDP (United Nations Development Programme) (2006) *Human Development Report 2006. Beyond Scarcity: Power, Poverty and the Global Water Crisis.* New York: United Nations. See http://hdr.undp.org/sites/default/files/reports/267/hdr06-complete.pdf (accessed 15 October 2014).

UNEP (United Nations Environment Programme) (2011) *Towards a Green Economy: Pathways to Sustainable Development and Poverty Eradication.* Geneva and Nairobi: UNEP.

UNEP (United Nations Environment Programme) (2001) *White Paper: Coastal Zone Management in the Mediterranean.* Split: Mediterranean Action Plan Priority Actions Programme (MAP/PAP). See www.pap-thecoastcentre.org/pdfs/ICAM%20in%20 Mediterranean%20-%20White%20Paper.pdf.

UNEP–UNWTO (United Nations World Tourism Organisation) (2012) *Tourism in the Green Economy – Background Report.* Madrid: UNWTO. See www.unep.org/ greeneconomy/Portals/88/documents/ger/ger_final_dec_2011/Tourism%20in%20 the%20green_economy%20unwto_unep.pdf.

UNESCO (2009) *United Nations World Water Development Report 3. Water in a Changing World.* Paris: UNESCO. See www.unesco.org/new/en/natural-sciences/environment/ water/wwap/wwdr/wwdr3-2009/.

UNESCO (2012) *World Water Assessment Programme. Vol. 1: Managing Water Under Uncertainty and Risk.* Paris: UNESCO. See www.unesco.org/new/en/natural-sciences/ environment/water/wwap/.

UN Water (2006) *Coping with Water Scarcity: A Strategic Issue and Priority for System-wide Action.* New York: United Nations. See www.unwater.org/worldwaterday/campaign-materials/documents-and-information-resources/en/.

UN Water (2010) *Climate Change Adaptation: The Pivotal Role of Water.* New York: United Nations. See www.unwater.org/worldwaterday/campaign-materials/documents-and-information-resources/en/.

UN Water (2014) *Water and Energy. The United Nations World Water Development Report 2014.* New York: United Nations. See http://unesdoc.unesco.org/images/0022/002257/ 225741E.pdf (accessed 15 October 2014).

UNWTO (United Nations World Tourism Organization) (2004) *Indicators of Sustainable Development for Tourism Destinations. A Guidebook.* Madrid: UNWTO.

UNWTO (United Nations World Tourism Organization) (2007) *Handbook on Tourism Market Segmentation – Maximising Marketing Effectiveness.* Madrid: World Tourism Organization and European Travel Commission.

UNWTO (United Nations World Tourism Organization) (2010) *UNWTO Tourism Highlights* (2010 edn). Madrid: World Tourism Organization.

UNWTO (United Nations World Tourism Organization) (2012) *UNWTO Tourism Highlights* (2012 edn). Madrid: World Tourism Organization.

UNWTO (United Nations World Tourism Organization) (2013a) *Message by UNWTO Secretary-General Taleb Rifai.* Madrid: World Tourism Organization. See http://wtd. unwto.org/en/content/unwtosg (accessed 15 October 2014).

UNWTO (United Nations World Tourism Organization) (2013b) *UNWTO Tourism Highlights* (2013 edn). Madrid: World Tourism Organization. See http://mkt.unwto.org/en/publi-cation/unwto-tourism-highlights-2013-edition (accessed 15 October 2014).

UNWTO (United Nations World Tourism Organization) (2013c) *Background Paper on Tourism and Water.* Madrid: World Tourism Organization. See http://wtd.unwto.org/ en/WTD13backgroundpaper (accessed 15 October 2014).

UNWTO (United Nations World Tourism Organization) (2014) *UNWTO Tourism Highlights* (2014 edn). Madrid: World Tourism Organization. See http://dtxtq4w60xqpw.

cloudfront.net/sites/all/files/pdf/unwto_highlights14_en.pdf (accessed 15 October 2014).

UNWTO, UNEP and WMO (UN World Tourism Organization, UN Environment Programme and World Meteorological Organization (2008) *Climate Change and Tourism: Responding to Global Challenges*. Paris and Madrid: UNWTO and UNEP.

US Army Corps of Engineers (2008) Great Lakes recreational boating. In response to Public Law 106-53, Water Resources Development Act of 1999, section 455(c), John Glenn Great Lakes Basin Program, Great Lakes recreational boating. Main Report – final. Detroit: US Army Corps of Engineers. See www.lre.usace.army.mil/Portals/69/docs/PPPM/PlanningandStudies/JohnGlenn/boating.pdf (accessed 15 October 2014).

US Department of Energy (2012) *Consumptive Water Use in the Production of Ethanol and Petroleum Gasoline* (2011 update). Lemont, IL: Argonne National Laboratory. See http://greet.es.anl.gov/publication-consumptive-water (accessed 15 October 2014).

US Environmental Protection Agency (1995) Ecological impacts from climate change: An economic analysis of freshwater recreational fishing. Report No. 220-R-95-004. Washington, DC: US Environmental Protection Agency.

US Environmental Protection Agency (2000) *Cruise Ship White Paper*. Washington, DC: EPA.

US Securities and Exchange Commission (2010) Commission guidance regarding disclosure related to climate change; Final rule (17 CFR Parts 211, 231 and 241). *Federal Register* 75 (25). See www.sec.gov/rules/interp/2010/33-9106fr.pdf (accessed 15 October 2014).

van der Linden, S. (2014) Towards a new model for communicating climate change. In S.A. Cohen, J.E.S. Higham, P. Peeters and S. Gössling (eds) *Understanding and Governing Sustainable Tourism Mobility: Psychological and Behavioural Approaches* (pp. 243–275). London: Routledge.

van der Meulen, F. and Salman, A.H.P.M. (1996) Management of Mediterranean coastal dunes. *Ocean and Coastal Management* 30 (2–3), 177–195.

van Oss, H.G. and Padovani, A.C. (2003) Cement manufacture and the environment. Part II: Environmental challenges and opportunities. *Journal of Industrial Ecology* 7 (1), 93–126.

Vanham, D., Hoekstra, A.Y. and Bidoglio, G. (2013a) Potential water saving through changes in European diets. *Environment International* 61, 45–56.

Vanham, D., Mekonnen, M.M. and Hoekstra, A.Y. (2013b) The water footprint of the EU for different diets. *Ecological Indicators* 32, 1–8.

Veloia-IFPRI (2012) *Finding the Blue Path for a Sustainable Economy*. Chicago, IL and Washington, DC: Veloia Water and International Food Policy Research Institute. See www.veoliawaterna.com/north-america-water/ressources/documents/1/19979,IFPRI-White-Paper.pdf (accessed 15 October 2014).

Vörösmarty, C.J., Green, P., Salisbury, J. and Lammers, R.B. (2000) Global water resources: Vulnerability from climate change and population growth. *Science* 289, 284–288.

Wang, X.H., Li, L., Bao, X. and Zhao, L.D. (2009) Economic cost of an algae bloom cleanup in China's 2008 Olympic sailing venue. *Eos, Transactions, American Geophysical Union* 90 (28), 238–239.

Water Disclosure Project (2013) *Moving Beyond Business as Usual: A Need for a Step Change in Water Risk Management. Carbon Disclosure Project*. Global Water Report 2013. London: Carbon Disclosure Project. See https://www.cdp.net/CDPResults/CDP-Global-Water-Report-2013.pdf (accessed 15 October 2014).

Water Footprint Network (2013) *Water Footprints*. AE Enschede: Water Footprint Network. See www.waterfootprint.org.

WBCSD (World Business Council on Sustainable Development) (2009) *Water, Energy and Climate Change: A Contribution from the Business Community.* Geneva: WBCSD. See www.c2es.org/docUploads/WaterEnergyandClimateChange.pdf (accessed 15 October 2014).

WBCSD (World Business Council on Sustainable Development) (2014) *Water.* Geneva: WBCSD's Water Task Force. See www.wbcsd.org/work-program/sector-projects/water.aspx (accessed 15 October 2014).

WEF (World Economic Forum) (2014) *Global Agenda Council on Water.* Geneva: World Economic Forum. See www.weforum.org/reports/global-agenda-council-water-security-2012-2014 (accessed 15 October 2014).

WHO (World Health Organization) (2009) *Guidelines for Safe Recreational Water Environments. Vol. 2. Swimming Pools and Similar Environments.* Geneva: WHO. See http://apps.who.int/iris/bitstream/10665/43336/1/9241546808_eng.pdf?ua=1 (accessed 15 October 2014).

WHO (World Health Organization) (2011) *How Much Water is Needed in Emergencies. Technical Notes on Drinking-water, Sanitation and Hygiene in Emergencies.* Geneva: WHO. See www.who.int/water_sanitation_health/publications/2011/tn9_how_much_water_en.pdf (accessed 15 October 2014).

Wolbier, J. (2004) Matters of scale – planet golf. *Worldwatch Magazine* 17.

World Bank (2012) *Turn Down the Heat: Why a 4°C Warmer World Must Be Avoided.* Washington, DC: World Bank. See www.worldbank.org/en/news/feature/2012/11/18/Climate-change-report-warns-dramatically-warmer-world-this-century (accessed 15 October 2014).

World Bank (2014) *World Water Partnership Strategic Action Plan.* Washington, DC: World Bank. See http://water.worldbank.org/node/84262 (accessed 15 October 2014).

Worldwatch Institute (2004) *Rising Impacts of Water Use.* Washington, DC: Worldwatch Institute. See www.worldwatch.org/topics/consumption/sow/trendsfacts/2004/03/03/ (accessed 15 October 2014).

World Water Council (2014) *Water Crisis.* Marseille: World Water Council. See www.worldwatercouncil.org/library/archives/water-crisis/(accessed 15 October 2014).

WWAP (World Water Assessment Programme) (2012) *The United Nations World Water Development Report 4: Managing Water Under Uncertainty and Risk.* Paris: UNESCO.

WWF (World Wide Fund for Nature) (2004) *Freshwater and Tourism in the Mediterranean.* Rome: WWF Mediterranean Programme. See www.panda.org/downloads/europe/medpotourismreportfinal_ofnc.pdf (accessed 15 October 2014).

WWF (World Wide Fund for Nature) (2014) *The Imported Risk. Germany's Water Risks in Times of Globalisation.* Berlin: WWF Germany. See www.wwf.de/fileadmin/fm-wwf/Publikationen-PDF/WWF_Study_Waterrisk_Germany.PDF (accessed 15 October 2014).

Yang, H., Reichert, P., Abbaspour, K.C. and Zehnder, A.J.B. (2003) A water resources threshold and its implications for food security. *Environmental Science and Technology* 37 (14), 3048–3054.

Yang, H., Wang, L. and Zehnder, A.J.B. (2007) Water scarcity and food trade in the southern and eastern Mediterranean countries. *Food Policy* 32 (5–6), 585–605.

Zaizen M., Urakawa T., Matsumoto Y. and Takai H. (2000) The collection of rainwater from dome stadiums in Japan. *Urban Water* 1, 355–359.

Zapata, M.J., Hall, C.M., Lindo, P. and Vanderschaeghe, M. (2011) Can community-based tourism contribute to development and poverty alleviation? Lessons from Nicaragua. *Current Issues in Tourism* 14 (8), 725–749.

Index